Magical Moments
of Change

MAGICAL MOMENTS of CHANGE

How Psychotherapy Turns Kids Around

LENORE TERR

W.W. NORTON & COMPANY

New York · London

For information about permission to reproduce
selections from this book, write to
Permissions, W. W. Norton & Company, Inc.,
500 Fifth Avenue, New York, NY 10110

For information about special discounts for bulk purchases,
please contact W. W. Norton Special Sales at
specialsales@wwnorton.com or 800-233-4830.

Composition and book design by Charlotte Staub
Manufacturing by Quebecor World Fairfield Graphics
Production Manager: Leeann Graham

Library of Congress Cataloging-in-Publication Data

Terr, Lenore, 1936–
    Magical moments of change: how psychotherapy turns kids around /
Lenore Terr. —1st ed.
        p. ; cm.
    Includes bibliographical references and index.
    ISBN 978-0-393-70530-0 (hardcover)
    1. Child psychotherapy.   I. Title. [DNLM: 1. Child.   2. Psychotherapy—
methods.   3. Mental Disorders—therapy.   4. Professional-Patients
Relations. WS 350.2 T232m 2008]
RJ504.T47   2008
618.92'8914—dc22   2007016745
ISBN 13: 978-0-393-70530-0

W. W. Norton & Company, Inc., 500 Fifth Avenue,
New York, N.Y. 10110
www.wwnorton.com
W. W. Norton & Company Ltd., Castle House, 75/76 Wells St.,
London W1T 3QT

1 3 5 7 9 0 8 6 4 2

FOR FOUR GREAT SPIRITS

SELMA FRAIBERG and STUART FINCH,
who taught me child psychiatry,

FLORENCE MARSH,
who taught me to write,

and LEON EPSTEIN,
my California colleague and friend.

CONTENTS

PART THREE: "Getting" the Child

PART FOUR: Reacting in a Timely, Pungent Fashion

Magical Moments
of Change

Celebrating Large and Small Moments of Change

"How many psychiatrists does it take to change a light bulb?
Only one. But the light bulb has to *want* to change."

— Anonymous

Yesterday, I spotted an elderly woman wearing a flag. Ordinarily I'd think, "How odd!" But yesterday was special. It was the weekend of July 4th and I was wandering through a small-town antique fair in Healdsburg, north of San Francisco. The woman didn't look strange at all, sporting her carefully sewn remnants of an old Old Glory. In fact, we smiled slightly at one another, knowingly. I have found that on this particular midsummer holiday, most Americans experience a meeting of the minds, regardless of where they stand politically, religiously, and culturally. Our eyes greet one another. We let people in. No matter how angry or disappointed we may have felt last week about our country, on this particular holiday—year after year—we celebrate a national moment of change.

What does it take for this transformation to happen? First of all, the occasion is marked by high drama: parades, family picnics, good smells, good music, fireworks. Second, there's the atmosphere: the best weather of summer and the brightest of color combinations—red, white, and blue. Third, there's the history: how Americans much like us—Adams, Jefferson, Washington, Madison—"did their thing." Fourth, there's the fun: We play all day long. I bought an old blue and white quilt at the fair and loved bargaining and then figuring out where it might go in my still-to-be-built writing studio up the hill. Best of all, there's a mutual, tacit understanding among Americans on this day. We know that the baseball statistics on Independence Day may very well predict who will play in the World Series in October. We silently think about issues like "freedom" and metaphors like "melting pots." Whether the nation is standing high in the world's favor—or entirely in hot water—we're all standing together. The togetherness is a positive turnaround. Unfortunately, that sense of togetherness passes in a day or two—that is, until early next July.

Over the past few years, my professional life as a child and adolescent psychiatrist has been revolving around much smaller but longer-lasting moments of positive change. These are the times when young people in psychotherapy exhibit dramatic, meaningful turnarounds. Angry as they may have been, conflicted as they may have felt, frightened, even terrified, something passes from a child to me—or from me to the child—within the space of minutes, or sometimes even in an instant. And this "something" impels the child to begin looking at himself differently. It impels entirely new behaviors. In fact, the child is indeed changed for the better.

From my perspective, a key moment may occur as a child and I venture together through some sort of child-initiated test. Or when a preschooler's toy does something atrocious to my toy, requiring a quick-witted response on my part (or my toy's part). An adolescent might challenge me to just dare to treat him. What am I to do? Almost without thinking I ordinarily say or do something apt. Later, and only rarely—by watching the patient—can I grasp what really happened during our tiny instance of crisis or of mutual understanding. It has represented a moment of change, a turning point in the child's young life.

I have also become aware of another kind of therapeutic moment with children that is more evident in retrospect than at the time it occurs. Occasionally, I belatedly realize that a very difficult youngster has dramatically turned around in psychotherapy. Perhaps she suddenly plunged into treatment after resisting for a while. Perhaps she reframed a better self-image. Sometimes I recognize a sudden rapid rate of improvement in a traumatized kid, one who had just been slogging along before. What led to such a complete turnabout? Was it related to therapy? There have been times—not many, just a few—when I found my answer. In these cases, as in the cases where a young person's treatment has come to a crisis or to an instance of mutual understanding, the solution lay in something I had said or done, the office atmosphere I created, a gesture, a new way we played together, an inside joke between us. Interestingly enough, I sometimes also caught wind of how long the change had come to last—years later, a parent, or even the child, now all grown up, might say something.

A case I had been working on since 1991 began to fit into my general interest in childhood change. That year, a 29-month-old toddler was brought to me—growling, spitting, sniffing sex organs, hissing, hitting—from 7 hours driving distance in the Central Valley of California. Before Cammie turned 13 months old, her 3-week-old sister, Bethany, had been murdered at home by being shaken and bitten all over her tiny body. Her father, Nick, and mother, Bonnie, were the prime suspects because the bite marks on the dead infant were adult and of both genders. Eventually, however, only Cammie's father went to prison, convicted by a jury of killing the baby "without malice." Cammie, too, had been bitten all over. She had also been shaken, and a local ER team found her to have been sexually abused as well. But no criminal charges were ever filed on her behalf. She was placed in an unusually good foster home, run by Sandra and Tom Brooks. Despite more than a year of their warm and loving care, however, barely a dent had been made in Cammie's nakedly sexual and aggressive behavior.

When I first met Cammie, she was more animal-like than human. She barely could speak. She attacked strangers, adults and children alike. She was the closest thing to a "wild child" (a youngster supposedly raised in the woods by beasts) I had seen in years. She had been tested by two well-qualified psychologists and diagnosed by each as "mentally retarded." My assignment was to work with Cammie for an hour once a month (the foster parents couldn't bring her more frequently due to their lack of proximity to San Francisco), and to do the best I could.

Cammie is now 17. "Feral" children historically have not done well in therapy.[1] For instance, Victor, the famous "wild boy of Aveyron" from the late 18th century, looked promising at first, receiving almost daily visits in Paris from the French pioneer of psychiatry, Jean Marc Gaspard Itard. Victor's early progress, in fact, was celebrated in Francois Truffaut's film *Wild Child* (1970), which showed the boy's emergence from the woods, where he was supposedly raised all alone, to the mental hospital where Itard tried to re-raise him, human style.[2] Ultimately, however, Victor's treatment proved unsuccessful. He remained in an animal-like state and could not be restored to society. "Genie," a 20th-century, neglected, mistreated, "wild" teenager of Los Angeles (and the subject of both Susan Curtiss's 1977 monograph on "psycholinguistic" treatment and of Russ Rymer's 1993 book on how inadvertently destructive interprofessional competition can be[3]), wound up in long-term care in a California mental institution. Cammie, my "wild" toddler, came to fare much better. In my 15 years of therapy with her (and counting), we faced eight, or perhaps nine, turning points similar to the ones I was beginning to notice as one-time events in a few of my other shorter-term psychotherapy patients. Cammie's moments of change would educate me further about what worked—and, for that matter, what didn't—in more ordinary young people's psychological treatments.

In early 2004, Saul Harrison, one of the child-psychotherapy teachers from my training years at the University of Michigan, died. What could we do to celebrate Saul's life? He had always taught us to attend to the realities of the psychiatrist-patient relationship, no matter how painful or embarrassing it might be for the doctor. Could a number of us put together a group of striking child psychotherapeutic turnarounds from which we could learn? By looking beyond just a single psychiatrist's practice, we could increase our chances of understanding what happens during these relatively rare "moments" of therapy-induced change. I sent a nondirective letter to twenty colleagues from Michigan and UCLA (where Saul had taught later in his life). Six "moments" came back by return mail (and I had a seventh in my own files). Yes, these brief and true tales were helpful in understanding what—in child psychotherapy—inspires massive positive turnarounds. In fact, Saul's lifelong point that the realities of the doctor-patient relationship had the power to create transformations in kids was evident in each of the seven cases we published in his honor.[4]

There must be more to dramatic instances of childhood change than "real" moments with therapists, however. I asked my peers— once again—to send me their cases. Over the past 3 years, 34 psychiatrists (including myself) have written up 48 vignettes (including six of my own) in answer to the question: "Have you ever seen a moment of dramatic change in a child or adolescent during psychotherapy? Describe it and explain its meaning in 500 words." Not everyone I corresponded with was known primarily as a psychotherapist. Some of them were young, others old. Some had cultural backgrounds very different from the typical "American middle class" homes most of us child psychiatrists come from. Yet, when the cases arrived from this wide array of colleagues the analysis of childhood change began to fall into well-delineated patterns. These categories represented what psychiatrists working in all sorts of settings—offices, hospitals, juvenile institutions—think dramatically works with kids. We published a total of four peer-reviewed articles based on our new findings.[5] I then found myself considering putting them all together. With a book, the process of childhood change would become clearer and, in a way, more compact. One doctor's perspective on what had caused a momentous turnabout could be put side by side with other doctors' perspectives. We practitioners could learn from each others' change moments with children, whether the turnabouts happened during evaluations, brief therapies, family therapies, or more standard individual psychotherapies. Other professionals working with kids in medical, social, or educational settings might benefit from a collection of such cases, too. And parents struggling with difficult children might find a collection like this, and its explanations, useful as well.

I decided to use my 15-year treatment of Cammie as a framework for the book.[6] While pointing out her turning points as she longitudinally moved from wildness to civilization, from unconsciousness to awareness, I would bring in related but smaller cases that could be considered for comparison. I would use the 48 vignettes I had in hand as illustrations of topics including how the psychiatrist employs aspects of his or her personality, the atmosphere he or she creates, his or her understanding of the child, and what is said between doctor and patient to influence dramatic childhood change. The way a good psychotherapist works with kids would be the book's main emphasis.

Although I didn't know it at the time I began this book, a small number of adult psychoanalysts had also developed an interest in this very same subject. In 2000, Ethel Person, a New York analyst, published a chapter titled "Change Moments in Therapy" (in Joseph Sandler's *Changing Ideas in a Changing World,* London, Karnac Books[7]), which talked about how mature individuals suddenly change. Although Dr. Person's question was similar to ours—what propels a person into a momentous positive turnaround?—her chapter, which included just a couple of clinical examples and the overriding dramatic example of the fictional "Nora" in Ibsen's *A Doll's House*, didn't purport to find any answers. Although Dr. Person said she could not characterize what makes these change moments happen, she did say that she hoped others would.

At the same time, a group of Boston psychoanalysts, led by the infant researcher and adult analyst Daniel Stern, had been trying, through a series of regularly scheduled meetings, to understand the moments of change they observed in their adult psychotherapy patients. Dr. Stern eventually published a book (*The Present Moment in Psychotherapy and Everyday Life*, New York, Norton, 2004[8]) based on his own, and his group's, conclusions. Their impression was that an instant of subliminal human understanding, similar to the understanding a parent and baby experience when their eyes meet, accounts for moments of psychotherapeutic change.

Neither of these psychoanalytic writers specifically delineated what therapeutic techniques led to the dramatic turnabouts they observed in adults. Neither spoke to the issue of childhood. But when our group of 34 child/adolescent psychiatrists collected our vignettes describing momentous changes in young patients, our conjoint effort made it more possible to arrive at specific, though certainly not final, conclusions about technique. We hope that others eventually will follow our trail and teach us even more about how therapy works with kids.

And we also hope that eventually adult and child psychotherapeutic techniques will find a wider expanse of common ground.

All of the main vignettes in this book are about children or adolescents, and all of the young people we describe experienced a moment of change, according to what their doctor observed. The names of these young people have been changed to protect their identity, and certain identifying features have also been changed. Their permission or their parents' permission to use their stories were obtained whenever possible. In a few situations, however, the case was old and the family had either moved away or could not be located. In these situations, we even more deeply disguised the identifying details. In fact, in a few we felt it best to change one or two details that had already been disguised differently in other professional writings about the same patient. Two contributors to the book, who told their stories to me outside of vignette form, asked that their names be changed as well, because their tales, though true, felt a little too personally revealing for them to feel comfortable seeing them in print. No "composite" cases or massive changes to age, race, diagnosis, or stage of development were used in this collection. The stories remain entirely true to what happened between doctor and patient.

Any nonmedical therapist will note that my choice of words—*psychiatrist, doctor, patient, office*—almost automatically identifies me as writing from a medical perspective. I rarely use *counselor, therapist, playroom, client*. Please accept my explanation for this as being a reflection of the way I think and not any sort of elimination or omission of the nonmedical therapeutic fields. The reader will also find the same sort of wording in the 48 vignettes that appear in this book, because all of the contributors are practitioners of child/adolescent psychiatry. We encourage you to interpose your own words to our stories according to what you do in your own practice.

This is a book about the art and science of psychotherapy, as expressed through many true tales of dramatic childhood change. Its focus is individual psychotherapy, acknowledging the Freudian roots of the treatment, while adding, where applicable, some of the newer aspects of the field (cognitive-behavioral approaches, trauma therapy, family therapy, parent counseling, art and play techniques).

Whatever has a bearing on massive turnarounds in childhood is explored. Our approach is eclectic, and we emphasize humor, play, storytelling, and metaphor, the special languages of childhood.

All sorts of disorders are covered in this book. The reader will find a range from mild adjustment and developmental problems to severe juvenile delinquency and schizophrenia. The reader may find, however, more cases of post-traumatic stress disorder than one would ordinarily expect in a collection like this. This is due to the fact that many traumatized children come to me because of my research reputation in the field, and because many of the professionals who took me up on my invitation to write vignettes happened to work with trauma in their research and practices. All ages of childhood, from infancy through college, appear among our vignettes. Both genders are represented. A wide cultural, economic, and ethnic mix of children is evident. Some of our child patients were also being treated with medications, and their pharmacotherapy is explained.

The thesis of *Magical Moments of Change* is that new insights into the therapeutic process come from understanding when, why, and how children in psychotherapy dramatically change. Because the question "Why and how does child psychotherapy work?" underlies everything the reader will encounter, the true stories are largely told from the doctor's point of view. What the doctor says, does, and thinks is clearly expressed. What the child says and how the child acts is also clearly expressed. However, what the child thinks and feels inside is only implied. It is the therapist's subjectivity, not the child's, that stands at the core of the book.

We thus are looking at highly effective child psychotherapeutic styles and techniques. I show them in three ways: through relating "moments" from at least six of my own cases, through conveying and comparing "moments" from 33 of my distinguished colleagues' cases, and through watching my "wild child" patient, little Cammie, develop her eight "moments" over a period of 15 years. These "moments" are rare. But by pooling them together, or by looking at how they develop over a long period of time in a single individual, we will be able to achieve further understanding of the process of change in child and adolescent psychotherapy.

With this in mind, I sit here today writing these words at a rustic, 19th-century dining room table on the Fourth of July, America's day of change. I've touched base with my extended family by phone, and with some lifelong friends whose daughter just gave birth to a fine little boy. The antique quilt is soaking in detergent, hopefully to get rid of its old stains. Everything looks positive today—upbeat and optimistic. And that's what *Magical Moments of Change* is all about. How do you form something positive from a hard-to-fashion hunk of clay? How do you convert an ugly duckling into a pretty little duck? Much as I've studied hideous childhood traumas for all of my adult professional life, I've decided to look for a while at their opposite—childhood "epiphanies." I will begin this book as I end it—with sincere hope and a glass half full.

Part One

USING the PROFESSIONAL PERSONA

"One man in his time plays many parts."
— Shakespeare, from *Hamlet*, act II

CHAPTER ONE

An Idealized Parent, or Even a Lesser God

She was a little over 2 years old and a little under 2 feet tall, yet she daunted me. There was something about her that crossed the gap between surprise and shock. This toddler was almost an animal, in fact. She ran rather than walked. Nimble to an extreme, she moved in bursts—into unexpected places, and onto unexpected objects. When I wasn't looking, she enucleated the glass eye of a tiny stoneware cat. How she did it, I still do not know. I immediately painted in a black eye for the roughly constructed feline. It couldn't have cost more than a dollar, but I placed the cat back on my desk. All this was for her benefit. "I can fix things," I implied. On her face, a grim look of determination precluded any chance of a smile. Her eyebrows, well-defined for a baby's, worked themselves straight across her brow without the hint of an arch. Dressed all in pink, there wasn't another pink thing about her.

Her skin was brown. Her hair was black and Chinese-shiny. Her gleaming white teeth were used to grimace, and to bite the skin of her arms into large purple dots. The skin on both legs was all scratched up. Tiny fingers had been busy, I supposed. Her eyes were black as midnight, but more opaque than any night sky I'd seen. Her nose was upturned but the nostrils flared. What was this? She was sniffing a number of the inanimate objects in my office—the desk, chairs, loveseat, carpet, toys. In fact, she was doing something else when she thought I wasn't looking—she was shaking herself. The whole room shook. The rhythm started slow and got faster. Like sex!

It wasn't that Cammie scared me physically. I was fully able to pick her up, if I needed to. I could take away anything I found in her grasp—not that I wanted to. I could hold her still if necessary. No, it wasn't anything physical that felt daunting to me. It was something else.

She picked up a baby doll I had taken out of my toy cabinet, which was too high for her to reach. Flinging the baby down, she growled, "Die, baby," in a loud basso hiss. A horrifying sound. "Baby die," she hissed again. She climbed a chair by the child's desk that sits along a wall. There, she found two wooly sheep, given to me by the president of a shearling coat company when I spoke to his young-executives' association. "Die sheep," she intoned in that unnatural voice. "Sheep die."

How does a little voice get so low? Who helped propel such ordinarily sweet sounds into the basement? I placed a tiny doll family onto the floor—a boy, girl, mother, and father, fully dressed. Picking up the miniscule mother, she screamed in her shocking bass-baritone tones, "Got boobies." She almost spat the words. "Trow away," she hissed once again. Then she flung the mommy doll to the opposite wall. She stared at a wooden green-and-red striped Zuni snake I had bought years ago in New Mexico. "Huut [hurt] guhs [girls]," she whispered in that impossible voice. Then she looked up at Mr. Nutcracker, high on one of my bookshelves, and cringed and screamed, "He bite!" A string bass, played badly, could not have competed with the piercingly basso quality of this youngster's sounds.

What was giving me pause—okay, daunting me—was Cammie's voice. She was a primitive child, all right, and had only primitive things to say. But it was her voice that was well beyond primitive. It was animalistic, in fact. In this way—and as I later learned, in a few other ways as well—young Miss Cammie more resembled a jungle beast than a human being. Indeed, if I ever treated her psychiatrically, this poor child would have a long, long way to go.

What was being presented to me here was a "wild child," similar to the "feral" children reported for more than 200 years in the psychiatric literature. Most of the classic papers on children like this assume that they were raised by bears, wolves, even a gazelle. The Romulus and Remus myth tells us that the twin founders of ancient Rome were brought up by a she-wolf.[9] There have been a couple of contemporary psychiatric reinterpretations of what created the so-called feral children, however. Chicago child psychiatrist Bruno Bettelheim[10] and, separately, British autism specialist Uta Frith[11] saw the childhood spectrum of autism-related disorders as the true culprit. An autistic child would grow up not speaking, not listening, not attending to the social cues, or even to the explicit directions of others. Out of frustration, the child's parents, rural and certainly not understanding what was learned more than 100 years later (that the child was suffering from a serious, genetically caused mental disorder), would abandon the youngster in a nearby forest. Somehow the child would survive, be discovered by others, and then be explained—often, to the world—as an animal-raised individual. This explanation, similar to the Romulus and Remus myth, would give a mysterious, fairytalelike quality to a reality that nobody wanted to face. The autism model did not fit young Cammie, however. She showed definite signs of social awareness. She used language appropriately.

A second recent model for the feral children, one evident in the story of "Genie," the mistreated and terribly neglected early teen of Los Angeles, fit my wild little patient better. In this second reinterpretation of the "wild child" myth, a youngster becomes so seriously neglected by guardians or family that he or she can learn only minimal language. This kind of youngster trusts no one. When the child emerges into society, he or she is amazingly backward. Michael Rutter, a distinguished English psychiatrist, observed this phenomenon in children in neglectful Romanian orphanages.[12] I had seen the same phenomenon only once before Cammie, when the workers from a social agency brought me a 7-year-old girl whose psychotic mother had tied her into a crib all of her young life. Not only was Lila unusually small, but she also hardly could talk. She hardly could walk. In fact, she scrambled about on all fours—like a disabled animal. Unfortunately, I was allowed to see Lila only once for evaluation, not treatment. Lila had been hobbled by her upbringing, not her genetics. A century before, she, too, might have been considered a "wild child," although there had been no woods or forests in her background.

Cammie's foster parents, Sandra and Tom Brooks, had been trying to attend to their "wild" charge for over a year. They'd exerted everything they had in the way of emotional support. They were well-trained and experienced, too. Sandra had been educated as a social worker, although she never practiced. Together, she and Tom, a lawyer, had tended to over 50 foster kids, until they decided to "retire." Then they got Cammie (after two county workers had begged them to take the child[13]). But poor Cammie had made little progress. Because she was so tenuously attached, she could, for instance, easily come into my office alone and never look back for Sandra. In other words, she hadn't developed the normal "separation anxiety" you see in a well-loved, well-raised infant. She barely talked, other than those horrible basso screams. And when she chose to speak, she picked three subjects: death ("die, baby"), sex ("got boobies"), and terror ("huut guhs" and "he bite").

Realizing that they had barely touched Cammie's emotional and mental problems, Sandra and Tom had sought a number of professional consultations before coming to me. Two prognostications regarding serious mental retardation came first. Then, Stanford Pediatrics confirmed Cammie's early sexual abuse with an external genital examination. But the pediatricians were even more concerned about that voice of hers. "She growls!" they reported, as if it were a revelation. It appeared that other professionals, beside me, felt a bit daunted as well.

Cammie could hardly be taken anywhere. Fearlessly, she approached adult strangers, sniffing and grabbing at their genitals, breasts, buttocks. There were two exceptions. She fled from Hispanic-American men and screamed and hid whenever she spotted an extremely obese woman (as these people resembled her birth parents). As for children, Cammie lunged at anything small. She bit. She hit. She spit. And she vomited at will. Then, there was the worst of it—that growl! What were we to do?

In considering how to set up a treatment program for a person, no matter how young, you have to deliver the diagnosis first. My diagnosis of Cammie was "post-traumatic stress disorder" (PTSD). Her "wildness" was caused by psychic trauma. She was not experiencing the effects of severe neglect, autism, or a long experience with animals in the woods. She had been traumatized by being bitten by her father (and probably by her mother, too). She had been physically exposed to adult sex, though we didn't know exactly what she had seen and what had been done to her. She'd been shaken, probably to sexually stimulate her (she was almost addicted to shaking herself to some sort of "climax" whenever adults seemed not to be looking). She had witnessed harm to—and even, perhaps, the death of—animals ("sheep die"). She had witnessed the last moments of her infant sister, Bethany ("die baby"). She suffered from a number of the symptoms of trauma[14]—repetitions of sexual and aggressive behaviors, terror of those she considered harmful (Hispanic men, obese women), occasional distancings from life (trancelike lapses, according to her foster parents), a permanent sort of despair (with no joy at play or in anticipating the future), and a dangerous tendency to reenactment (doing aggressive and sexual acts similar to those originally done to her). In fact, during the months I was beginning her treatment, Cammie threw down a small poodle her family had recently brought home and injured his back so severely that he was paralyzed for an entire afternoon. (To protect him, Sandra and Tom gave him back to his original owners.)

Cammie's PTSD was severe enough to make her into a "wild child." This had been accomplished in only 13 months. Cammie was so unnaturally developed, as a matter of fact, that even UCLA's excellent child psychologists considered her retarded. I wasn't so sure about that dire prediction, however. Cammie had shown me one thing that retarded kids don't exhibit—she was the proud owner of an enormous imagination. At 2 years and 5 months of age, she could pick up a doll and play, grim as it was, with "death," "sex," and "injury." She knew how to use symbols—a Zuni snake, two sheep, a big-toothed wooden nutcracker—and then respond to them in play. Not only that, but physically Cammie was agile, nimble, and adept, whereas many retarded kids are not. If I could fix Cammie's trauma, perhaps I could fix her "retardation," too. In fact, perhaps I could help fix the whole child.

In the first year that Sandra and Tom Brooks held temporary custody of Cammie, Nick had gone off to prison. He had "beaten" the murder "rap" for Bethany, being convicted of killing his baby without malice (a form of "manslaughter"). Meanwhile, however, Bonnie, who remained free, was devoting considerable energy toward getting Cammie back. First, someone tried to kidnap the toddler. Cammie screamed out one night—an unusual scream, even from her—and Sandra and Tom rushed into her bedroom to the sounds of their burglar alarm and the sight of a baby in extreme distress. They found a bent screen lying on the ground and Cammie's window half open. The sheriffs were summoned but no one was caught. Then Bonnie sought out a local counselor for "psychotherapy." The counselor became convinced that Bonnie would be just fine as a mother. With Bonnie's petition for reunification, and the counselor's stellar recommendations, the court granted Bonnie once-monthly chaperoned visits.

The maternal visits had been carried out a few times by the time I met Cammie. The Brooks family asked me to help them to get the visits stopped. Bonnie had very likely been a perpetrator against Cammie, and every time the child saw her mother now, she regressed. Before visits—and especially afterward—Cammie acted "wilder." During the visits (Sandra and a local child psychologist were "chaperones"), Cammie sniffed Bonnie and registered physical disgust. There was no affection either way. Bonnie talked baby talk to the toddler. Cammie growled at her mom, who didn't register surprise at this. Bonnie told a number of people, in fact, with no apparent concern in her voice or demeanor, "That's just how Nick used to talk to Cammie." She chattered on to social workers and a police investigator that "Nick was a devil worshipper" and that he "wanted Cammie to sound like a devil-child," as if this baby was something out of *The Exorcist*.[15]

At Cammie's foster parents' request, I wrote the court. I suggested that Bonnie's reunification program with her natural daughter be put on hold. This poor child did not have to be in contact, even for an occasional chaperoned visit, with the person who had hurt her so badly. Here was a child who could only say of a "mother" doll in my office, "Got boobies" and "Trow away." Not only had Bonnie neglected her, but she also had exposed her to her baby sister's unnatural death, to adult sex, to biting, to shaking, to a man's growly speech. How could the California reunification program apply here?

The judge temporarily stopped Bonnie's visitations. Now we had to figure out the rest of Cammie's program. I suggested to Sandra and Tom that they immediately get Cammie into speech therapy. It had to be pleasant, nonaggressive. But that voice had to be changed. I told Sandra, too, about a storytelling technique she might try with Cammie. (I'll describe it a bit later.) And then I asked Sandra what she wanted to do about psychotherapy.

"Would you be willing to see Cammie once a month?"

"Sure." (I wasn't certain what I could accomplish on this schedule, but I was willing to try.)

"Only for an hour?"

"Okay." I thought for a second, and then I added a codicil. "I'd have to be in charge," I said. "Over all the other doctors—all therapists." We had to construct a central plan for Cammie, I realized. I didn't want to fracture her treatment with decision-making entirely beyond my control.

When I began seeing Cammie in 1991, I was not aware of the Los Angeles "wild child" Genie, who came into prominence 2 years later with Russ Rymer's journalistic analysis of her terribly sad situation. Rymer called his book *Genie: A Scientific Tragedy*.[16] His main point was that the various helping disciplines—psychiatry, psychology, education, linguistics, the foster-care system—had all battled over Genie. In so doing, they had spoiled any chance of her sustaining the improvements she initially made. Because everybody wanted ultimate control, nobody eventually was able to set up a reasonable program—without challenge. With an on-again, off-again plan, Genie was the main person to suffer.

My insistence on exerting ultimate "control" from the very beginning of Cammie's case had to do with my own early experiences in hospitals, medical schools, and the courts. I had learned that physically abused children were tossed around enough in a neglectful or competitive system to sometimes be considered "rebrutalized." (My first psychiatric research, in fact, was on that very subject.)[17] I also knew how fiercely a surgeon, pediatrician, another psychiatrist, or educator could fight to take over the reins of a case. It sometimes represented a true commitment, a serious research interest. But at other times it could be ascribed to more shadowy motives, like power, one-upmanship, envy, and ambition.

I initially had no idea whether my demand for team leadership—and Sandra's concurrence—would ease our way. As it turned out, however, we have consistently stuck to our gentleman's agreement, most of the time letting the various surgeons, nurses, educators, therapists, tutors, pediatricians, and dietitians "do their thing" without interference. Whenever I have had to intervene, however, there was a tacit understanding that I served as "team leader." It is evident that Sandra has always cleared the way. My attitude about my own function clears the way, too. Our agreement has consistently cleared Cammie's way. And that, of course, was primarily important.

Safeguarding a child's best interests is important enough, in fact, that I must pause to apply this principle to the nonmedical professions. When you, as a counselor or social worker, know that you will be needed to run a complicated case for the next few years, it is crucial that you hold the reins. Will a surgeon listen? Will a school headmaster or a judge? You must feel in charge. That's half the battle right there. You can give a "title" to what you are doing—like "I'm team coordinator on this case" or "I'm the one who's been the child's main treater over the past year" or "I'm little John Doe's professional advocate." To clear the way, you must go to the family or guardians first to make sure that they're with you. If the family backs you and makes sure that the other professionals on the case know who you are and what you mean to the child, you will probably be able to keep your large-scale plan operational. Yes, you may lose a few situations to internecine warfare. But in general, your child patient (or client) will not fall through the interprofessional cracks.

And so we started our once-monthly psychotherapy sessions for Cammie. From the start, I knew exactly how I wanted to act. I didn't even have to think about it. I would use my fun side, my humorous side, my silly being, my song-and-dance persona. No matter what happened, including her taking the eye out of my toy cat, I would never let her see me in a bad mood, in pain, helpless. Daunted or not, I wouldn't allow Cammie to sense it. She'd been exposed to enough "bad karma" for a lifetime. She'd experienced more terror and fright than most people have ever had to endure. With me, she'd be exposed only to my lightness and humor. I would use my personality as a "tool." Cammie would experience psychotherapy sunny-side-up. For her, I'd be Danny Kaye—or, perhaps, the "God of Fun," whose fat little statue you can still see in the desert at ancient Sakkara.

A number of gifted child/adolescent psychotherapists are "born" actors. One, I hear, worked his way through medical school as a stand-up comic. Another memorized almost every joke he heard and then delivered it with hilarious exaggeration. Psychiatry, however, is not the only nondramatic profession that relies heavily on acting skills. Politicians act much of the time, as do the TV reporters who cover them. Salesmen overact, to be sure, but their talent for putting on a good show is obvious. Secret agents' very lives depend upon their naturalistic acting skills. Librarians read stories to children with charm and vocal elaboration. How many times do the police go through their "good cop/bad cop" routines? Old as the drama may be, it works.

One of the main items a child psychotherapist acts with is his or her own "persona."[18] In fact, if the therapist is also a physician, the acting patterns have been ingrained from the very beginning of medical school. Medical training stresses the maintenance of objectivity,[19] of primary interest in the patient (not oneself or one's reactions to the patient), and of remaining calm and unmoved while, perhaps, feeling nauseated, amused, disgusted, frightened, or about to cry or faint. In other words, the doctor's comportment may be miles off from his or her inner world. Yet he or she chooses this comportment on the patient's behalf.

Added to this medical training are the three additional historical origins of psychiatry[20]—each of which adds to the drama of choosing a persona that will aid the young patient. The first is the medicine man, witch doctor, or (today's) "healer." This antecedent to our field has always required a firm belief in oneself and a willingness to use oneself as a "tool" on the patient's or community's behalf. A second antecedent is the Church. This sécond origin of psychiatry requires a respect for ceremony, color, atmosphere, and spiritual and philosophical thinking in helping to effect a cure. The third antecedent is Sigmund Freud. Freud prescribed a certain type of persona that is commonly seen today, both in reality and in parody.

Freud taught his followers (and, by the 1940s and '50s, most of American psychiatry) to consistently maintain a quiet, objective, unshowy, relatively sober, and thoughtful demeanor with the patient. The doctor asks benign questions and offers little opinion. His or her personal life cannot be revealed. What he or she says should be limited to a few brief comments, or "interpretations," put only in terms of the patient. This planned-for inscrutability, unreadability yet benign friendliness was meant by Freud and his followers to inspire a special type of "displacement" (a defense mechanism wherein the patient moves personal conflicts from their origins to a current object). When the displacement is from someone important in the patient's early life to the psychoanalyst or psychiatrist, this mechanism receives the special name "transference." Transference is gradually interpreted to the patient. This helps the patient to achieve a more mature outlook toward others—one that is no longer based upon early reactions to parents.

Behaving in a way that inspires transference requires purposeful, dramatic manipulation of the psychotherapeutic persona. Many of us are naturally outgoing, impulsive, eager to talk, colorful. Yet we were told by mid-20th-century writers on dynamic psychotherapy, such as Colby, Tarachow, and Wolberg,[21] to carefully maintain the same non-intrusive, quiet persona that Freud had prescribed in the early 1900s. We were, thus, trained as Freudian "actors," and we have trained others to act this way, too.

What of Freud himself? Did he behave in his real life the way a traditional psychoanalyst is supposed to act? No. With patients, he used himself as a "tool" to create the appearance of the model psychoanalyst. Outside the psychotherapy office, however, Freud generated terrible fights with those "in" and "out" of his camp.[22] Some say he conducted a passionate love affair with his wife's sister,[23] yet with patients, he was passively distant. Toward the end of his life, he suffered horrible mouth and neck pain from cancer. But he went on advising, teaching, and treating individuals in the mode of the model psychoanalyst. Dr. Freud, in other words, was a great actor. "The psychoanalyst" was his most compelling dramatic creation.

So in almost impulsively deciding how to act with Cammie, I was following the lead of Sigmund Freud—in figuring that I had an "act" to put on. But I was not participating in the particular "play" that Freud had written. That would have required me to be unphased, steady, quiet, objective—the passive interpreter of human behaviors. And this "scene," I figured, would get me nowhere with a child who was more animal than human. I had to represent a strong contrast to Cammie's sadistic, neglectful, violent, and frightening birth parents. So I chose the "god of fun."

When psychodynamic psychotherapy—the shorter, more direct, sit-up, once-or-twice-a-week little brother of psychoanalysis—was invented, its practitioners adopted the psychoanalytic persona. This became a standard for mid-century psychologists, social workers, counselors, nurses, and educators as well. Children and adolescents, however, often read these Freudian roles as unnatural and unreal. What if a child patient swam at the same community pool as the child psychiatrist? What if an adolescent viewed his child psychologist on TV? What if a kid looked up his "shrink" on the Internet? Could a psychiatrist still maintain the same quiet, distant anonymity?

Ordinarily, children and adolescents cannot relate easily to a psychotherapist playing out the Freudian ideal. But there are exceptions. Freud was a genius, and his psychoanalytic persona occasionally works gloriously in child/adolescent psychotherapy—if the time, the setting, and the child is right. If it's the correct role to play for a particular kid, one might even see a striking "moment" of change.

Two of the 48 pooled "moments" in children's psychotherapy I collected from my colleagues' cases and my own case files occurred when the doctor consciously picked an extraordinarily benign, steady, calm way of being with a child. The two doctors inserted their chosen role, the "psychoanalytic persona," into a situation where everyone else around the youngster was acting extremely upset. In the first case vignette I present, a boy's divorcing parents were so antagonistic to one another that they were barely bothering to raise him. In the second of these cases, the people who loved a sick little girl were so grief-stricken because of her incurable leukemia that they could hardly speak to her without weeping. The two physicians, who tell their tales here, briefly considered the youngsters' situation by listening to the history as produced by one or both parents. Then each doctor, almost automatically, put forward his best "psychoanalytic persona." In the doctors' view—and from what the two children said—a psychoanalytic approach was "just what the doctor ordered." Ultimately, the Freudian role, as played by these therapists, encouraged a "magical moment of change."

Monkey in the Middle

CONTRIBUTED BY VICTOR FORNARI, MD

Scott was 6½ years old when his mother contacted me for a consultation. She was concerned that her son was locked in the never-ending battle between her and her ex-husband. Scott often looked worried. He cried over the smallest things. And he seemed more fearful than his peers. An only child, he was 12 months old when his parents separated, and 5 when the divorce finally came through. Scott's mom, a virologist, described her ex-husband as a "resistant bacteria." Scott's dad, a hedge fund manager, believed that physicians do "harm to people" and that psychiatrists do "the most harm." He described his ex-wife as a "nut who relies on what the shrinks tell her." Scott lived with his mother and visited his father on alternate weekends and one weekday evening. Each parent made Scott keenly aware of how negatively they viewed the other. They had already put Scott through three court-ordered psychological evaluations.

When I first met the little boy, I was struck by how remarkably mature and sensible he acted. I remained relatively passive, yet interested, as he began his interview with accurate descriptions of how each of his parents behaved. Then, quickly, he shifted to me and wondered out loud how different life would be "if you had been my father." He remarked that neither of his parents was sensible. "I could come here to see you every day, and that would not change what happens at home!" He asked me why I was so reasonable as compared with his parents. "How does this happen—some adults can be so unreasonable?" I wondered out loud how it was that a young man of 6 could figure that out. He replied that through my few questions he was able to understand that I "made sense."

I believed that Scott was a normal child beset by very abnormal circumstances. He knew how to negotiate his way through adult conflict, trying to let each parent know how hard he had to work to please the other. But with me, he felt he could relax. He was constantly worried at home about disappointing a parent. "You are like a Monkey-in-the-Middle," I remarked to him, with some resignation. He nodded solemnly and asked if he could come back to visit me again.

MEANING OF THE MOMENT

From the very beginning, Scott wanted to enter into therapy with me. Why? He was "normal." He wished, however, to be candid with someone serene, steady, and understanding. His warring parents had forced him to seek as much calm as he could find. "I could come here every week for the rest of my life," he confided that very first day. What he really needed, we both realized, was someone who could help him navigate the uncharted waters of an ordinary voyage through childhood. I would help him, I promised. And I did—although he did most of the hard work himself.

I Can Walk!

CONTRIBUTED BY RONALD M. BENSON, MD

Darlene was 6½ years old when she was referred to me. She came because she had totally stopped walking. Her pediatrician determined that there was no physical cause of this "paralysis." However, Darlene suffered from a type of leukemia for which there currently was no cure.[24] Her young, sad-looking mother brought Darlene in a wheelchair into my office. I then made sure she was comfortable in a child-sized chair, and I pushed her wheelchair into an adjoining room. Darlene was very pretty, with curly blond hair and blue eyes. However, she was pale and wan-looking, and she didn't talk or smile back when I smiled and said hello. When I asked her if she'd like to play and talk, she nodded in a passive manner. She looked around but made no effort to play with any of my toys.

As we began to talk, Darlene gave one-word desultory responses to my questions. She did not initiate any conversation until I asked her if she could walk. "I am able to," she said. I asked her why, then, was she in a wheelchair. Darlene looked at me fully for the first time and said, "I'm sick." I asked her to tell me about being sick. She said she didn't know. I asked if she was a little sick or a lot sick. She told me she was a lot sick. She didn't know any more about it, however, because when she asked her mother, Mommy became too sad and would cry. She didn't like to ask her father, either, because he cried, too. She didn't even like to ask her pediatrician because he also got sad. I told her I was very sorry she was sick. I asked if she'd like to talk to me about it. She studied my face. She wanted to see if I could take it. I showed her nothing—just friendly interest.

She then launched into paragraphs. She said she thought she was very, very sick and would never get better. She wasn't afraid, because she knew she would be going to heaven. Even if she had to leave Mommy and Daddy for a while, she'd meet them again when they came to heaven. Darlene made it very apparent that she knew she was dying and there was little to no hope. I told her I'd try to work with Mommy and Daddy and her doctor in order to help her with her feelings. She smiled and said she'd like that.

Our time was up and I started to push Darlene's wheelchair back into my office so she could get in. The little girl, however, did not wait. She stood up and ran from my playroom to the waiting room and hugged her mother. She could walk!

MEANING OF THE MOMENT

This story illustrates the value of neutral listening within a therapeutic relationship,[25] *even when the relationship is very brief. Because I was neutral and objective, Darlene felt safe enough with me to reveal her knowledge of her fate and her fear of her parents' and doctor's grief. She made her revelation to me because she felt I could accept her feelings without emotionally reacting too much. Sometimes even the most loving of feelings can be experienced as a burden to a frightened child.*

I never saw Darlene again, but I learned from her doctor that she continued to walk until near the end. She did well emotionally through the entire ordeal.

The thoughtful professional or trainee might wonder if Victor Fornari's young casualty of an enraged divorce was sick enough, changed enough, to be considered "disordered" at all. Yet this relatively unsick boy, Scott, represents many of the children we see in offices from White Plains, New York, to Carmel, California. He, like a number of adults in psychoanalysis, needed a strong therapeutic contrast to the people who were raising him. He responded with enthusiasm to a steady point of view that was polite and not overly friendly. Dr. Fornari immediately offered the young man a quiet place to talk. And the talk would be just about him. From this moment on, young Scott could emotionally develop almost on his own. As long as someone else, an adult, really listened to him, his anxiety could resolve. The boy's turning point came so early—on his first day of evaluation—that it might appear unmagical indeed. But to the boy and to Victor Fornari, the moment felt special. Scott had a virtual parent now, a third person helping, more objectively, to raise him. His anxious oversensitivity resolved. The "psychoanalytic persona" had worked its magic on this boy. But rather than functioning to inspire transference, it offered instead a total and very real contrast to what young Scott lived with every day.

As for the miraculous "cure" of paralysis that Ron Benson effected with his "psychoanalytic persona," he, too, presented himself in sharp contrast to a child's distraught parents, even though it must have taken tremendous self-control to act the way he did. The poor mother and father were so devastated they could hardly listen to what their little daughter had to say. In choosing the Freudian role—one very natural to Dr. Benson, who is a classically trained analyst—the doctor found a perfect contrasting persona to enact for his desperately sick little patient. For the little girl and Dr. Benson, their first meeting represented a moment of revelation and change. The doctor asked a few questions, participated objectively in a difficult conversation, and greatly relieved a dying child of her suffering. His help was invaluable. For the few months she had left, he turned her completely around.

Both of these cases illustrate how the classic "psychoanalytic persona" can work stunningly. But contemporary child/adolescent psychiatry does not usually emphasize or teach this kind of persona. In many instances, in fact, our training puts a premium on being "real" with kids. In more seriously disturbed children, an even more proactive, positive, approach than "real" is considered desirable (and is sometimes taught). Here, psychotherapists make the conscious decision to "act encouraging." The idea of being "consistently accepting" is a similar kind of take on the doctor's persona as the Freudian "act." Certainly, positiveness and accepting behaviors won't work when a therapist feels very angry at a child. But it is rare, when a case is new, that "countertransference" (the doctor's unreasonable, personally based responses to a patient) interferes in assuming a certain psychotherapeutic role. At the time of evaluation, the doctor perceives what the child will psychologically need and then acts in that fashion. This usually keeps the case moving along and may actually prevent negative transference and countertransference from arising.

The reader must understand, however, that not every case requires a decision from the therapist about how to act. Usually the doctor is simply "himself" or "herself." The "real" doctor can be highly effective. But there are certain cases where some drama helps.

The idea of manipulating one's own persona on behalf of a child sounds strange, and even a little concerning. But consider a further exaggeration of this idea—manipulating an entire institution's personality on behalf of the children in it. An institutional "persona" may have a great deal to offer kids in the way of change. Children in special schools, group foster homes, and juvenile delinquency facilities are there because they suffer severe emotional problems, for which major corrections need to be found. Many of these disorders have

genetic and biochemical origins, but a number of environmental interventions (and medications count as one of these) are usually needed
to help the young person adjust. With regard to the most severe of
childhood mental conditions, we're not necessarily talking about a
"cure" or "winning a war." Instead, we're talking about achieving more
normal mental functioning, so that the young person can exist, eventually on his own, in an ordinary community and in an ordinary home.

So institutions, too, develop "personalities." These "ways of being"
are taught to the staff, and the whole place eventually comes to achieve
a certain feel. The vignette I present next has to do with a particularly
positive persona that Saul Wasserman, the medical director of a San
Jose, California, institution for severely maladjusted latency-age kids
and subteens, pursued with his staff. Because Saul was aware of how
neglected so many of his young charges had been in their homes of
origin, he wished to counter this with a consistently positive approach.
Rather than taking privileges away, he desired an atmosphere of
giving. In order to help train his staff and to keep them well-trained,
Dr. Wasserman often demonstrated, with the institutionalized kids,
the persona he wanted his staff to assume. On one of these occasions,
Saul's preplanned "institutional persona" created a dramatic moment
of change in a young girl named Susie.

Security Is in the Freezer

CONTRIBUTED BY SAUL WASSERMAN, MD

*On the inpatient unit, we saw many children who had been
seriously mistreated. As a policy, we decided to revise our
treatment strategies toward the positive in order to correct for
old negative life experience. As a part of that process, we liked
to serve meals family style. One day, the kitchen sent up a 5-
gallon tub of ice cream for dessert. While most of the children
patiently waited in line, 10-year-old Susie aggressively pushed
her way to the front, disrupting everyone. I took her aside and
we talked. I asked her if she had ice cream in her home, and
she said, matter-of-factly, that all they ever had in the refriger-
ator was beer. I took her down the hall to the unit kitchen where
we had a big freezer, and surprised her with the statement that*

she could have all the ice cream she wanted. Naturally, Susie took a giant bowl and ate every bit. We did this for several days, and I noticed that her self-served portions were getting smaller. Finally, one day while she was playing with friends, I offered to take her down to the freezer for her ice cream and she smiled and said, "That's okay, I know it's there if I want it."

MEANING OF THE MOMENT

In my view, the most basic function a parent serves for a child is feeding the child. Although one might tend to generalize the term nurturance *to include a wide variety of ways in which a parent cares for a child, for me, feeding remains at the core of maternal love. The infant rapidly learns to associate the process of being fed with the feeder. The primal relationship that soon develops becomes the prototype of all positive human relationships.*

For children who have been abused and neglected, with a very damaged pattern of relationships and a worldview that reflects the harsh treatment they have received, the sense of deprivation, of "not having gotten enough," can be very strong. The urgency of the needs and the anger over "not getting" can easily lead the child into problematic behavior. Part of the therapist's task is to instill within the child some hope that the child's needs can be fulfilled by adults, and that the child has enough worth for the adult to want to do this (I wrote about this idea with Alvin Rosenfeld in 1990[26]). This sense, that we are worthy and have a reasonable possibility of getting our needs fulfilled, is a significant part of the development of inner security. Security is not something that can be learned by talking about it. It must be experienced by the youngster in the concrete and specific way in which a child views the world. Thus, my first and last trips to the freezer with Susie became moments I clearly remember today. She did reasonably well in our program and ultimately went to live in a therapeutic foster home.

In this inspirational and moving story, one human being (and the institution he directed) helped a girl change—and stay changed—by rewarding her ravenous hunger, responding to it positively. Susie was pushy and greedy because no one had gratified her in her original home. Rather than respond negatively to her greed (one of the "seven deadly sins," after all), Dr. Wasserman and his childcare institution acted counterintuitively. They carefully precalculated their positive "act," and then they surprised her with it. Susie almost immediately gave positive feedback to them. Within days, she offered them a peek at a new person, a child who could now get along within society at large.

In looking at Sigmund Freud and Saul Wasserman, we see very conscious professional decisions about how to act—even teaching and training others about how to act—with emotionally disordered young people. Is it possible for parents, too, to adopt certain kinds of personae to deal with difficult offspring? Parents are often on the spot at home. And they are also passionately and meaningfully engaged with their children. This makes "acting a part" potentially dangerous because kids can easily detect falsehoods, especially those close at hand. Inconsistency, in fact, is almost immediately detectable by smart children. If, on the other hand, parents agree in advance that a certain youngster has to be treated more positively, or that they need to demonstrate more overt love to a certain kid, or that they need to back off and not fight so hard with a specific child, they might be able to help the youngster a great deal. As parent counselors, we professionals might discuss with a mother, father, grandparent, or guardian the option of calculating a new way to act. If caretakers agree on a new plan of action, then helping them to establish and then maintain this new choice is an excellent function for us indeed.

I remember an angry father, Dr. Brandon Willets, a successful cosmetic dentist, whom I had to counsel for over a year about how to remain patient, calm, and relatively passive with his 10-year-old son, Richard, who had been sexually abused by a Pacific Heights neighbor. I was primarily treating the tall, skinny, dark-haired boy. But his dad had to be taught to play a part, to adopt a new persona. What Dr. Willets really wanted to do was to rail at everyone involved in his son's abuse, including his youngster. He was almost choking on his own anger. What bad luck poor Richard had run into! What the boy really needed was a calm sense of acceptance from his dad. It was gratifying to me to watch the change that occurred over a long period of time as Dr. Willets calmed down and Richard worked out his trauma. Richard, who had worried privately to me that he might eventually become "gay," began seeing himself as an ordinary young fellow who had been attacked for no reason other than neighborly convenience. Dr. Willets gradually moved into his new "part," now warmly accepting his son without rage or blame. The two became better friends than they had ever been before. In fact, one of the boy's unconscious reasons for lending himself originally to his neighbor's repeated abuses was that he had felt avoidant and frightened of his dad; their improved relationship made this reason no longer operational.

The following case involves another angry patient, who was institutionalized at a correctional facility that employs the unusually optimistic child/adolescent psychiatrist Bill Sack. Bill has always been an extraordinarily nice, pleasant person. So he didn't have to "act" a "nice" part for the assaultive, combative delinquent he was assigned to treat. All the same, Dr. Sack consciously decided to exaggerate his already stellar personal attribute. He would be doubly nice. He decided from the very beginning that every time he would see this troubled boy, he would find something about the young man to praise. That wasn't so easy. The juvenile institution where the boy was confined was constantly discovering behaviors that required serious punishment. It took a long time for Bill Sack to work his therapeutic miracle, but his steadiness of purpose and his doubly positive persona eventually won out.

Waiting for the Words to Flow

CONTRIBUTED BY WILLIAM H. SACK, MD

Tim was a 16-year-old convicted sexual offender who had been committed the year before I met him to the Oregon juvenile correctional institution where I work. I saw him every few weeks for medication management and behavioral assessment. Tim had failed several outpatient treatment programs before being incarcerated; and at the 1-year mark, he was also seen as a treatment failure by our facility. He hated the cottage staff and avoided his peers. Periodically, he would have horrible blowups, blacking someone's eye or kicking somebody down. He'd then have to be sent to a secure facility to "cool off." In our 15-minute get-togethers, Tim presented as a surly, alienated young man with a huge chip on his shoulder. He would answer my inquiries with a condescending rebuff or a sneer. Around the hard edges, however, there was a loneliness to Tim that gave me hope.

I had always been taught to proactively "go for the affect" in working with a behavioral problem. One needed to know what feeling was generating the patient's unacceptable actions. But here, my instincts told me not to probe. Tim might fight me! Instead, I focused, time after time, on positive things.[27] In asking about his daily routines—for instance, his sleep, his medications, his visits with his family—I consistently tried to find something good[28] for which I could give him institutional "points" or personal kudos. I was waiting for his words to flow. It took a year.

One afternoon, after he shoved an attendant aside and had to go to the secure unit, Tim came to his session looking furious. I waited, throwing off a few phrases about the weather, the time of year, the flora and fauna outside. Suddenly and seemingly out of the blue came a torrent of tears, rage, and choked-out words. Tim hated all men and couldn't trust them. "Men abuse you!" he blurted out. Then came a graphic description of how, as a young kid, he was repeatedly sexually abused by his grandfather. My inner response was one of relief. I now knew why Tim was so enraged. I also knew why he had been driven to commit a sexual crime. I immediately endorsed the legitimacy of Tim's anger and the importance of his sharing it with me—and my pleasure that he hadn't acted on his feelings with me but instead had expressed them out loud.

Tim's verbal catharsis, late as it was, brought about a significant change in his life. He began to make progress in his sexual-offender treatment group, and his peer relationships turned positive. No more trips to the secure facility! As I write, Tim will be leaving our institution soon.

MEANING OF THE MOMENT

This therapeutic turning point taught me to revise the old dictum of "going for the affect." At times, it is better to "wait for the emotions to arrive." It also reminded me that therapeutic moments can happen even if one isn't doing formal office-based psychotherapy. It reinforced the idea of heeding your own instincts. And it encouraged me to keep on accentuating the positive.

Both Susie and Tim required an unfailingly positive approach because they had been neglected and betrayed by the adult relatives and guardians who had raised them. In a less severely disordered way, my 10-year-old patient, Richard Willets, needed calm, positive make-up time with his angry father. These three cases required "acting." But they needed an acting style different from the "psychoanalytic" or "psychodynamic" one. Rather than always being pleasantly distant and nondirective, today's child therapist chooses a certain way to behave (or to ask parents to behave) with a certain child, based on that particular child's needs. The therapist doesn't usually develop an entirely new style of acting, but rather accentuates personality traits that are already operational. This therapeutic way of being often functions in sharp contrast to what the child knew at home.

Drs. Wasserman and Sack were not given much information about their patients' backgrounds, but, recognizing the neglect and abuse so rife in these kinds of cases, they chose positiveness as their way of representing a likely contrast. They chose correctly. In advising Richard Willets's father how to "act," I chose calmness instead of positiveness. I could sense this man's almost uncontrollable rage. (In fact, for several months I gave him divalproex sodium [Depakote] to stabilize his mood and damp his anger.) Richard sensed the irritation behind his father's round, smiling face and had avoided it by staying away. By learning to act cool, Dr. Willets gradually came to represent a contrast to his son's perceptions of the old, original "dad." In Richard's case, however, there was no distinct "moment" of change. He just showed me the more commonly observed slow movement that a child makes toward normalcy.

What impelled the wild, 2-year-old Cammie to move quickly to my 19th-century Austrian tea set, I'll never know. But shortly after starting her long journeys to San Francisco for monthly visits with me, the pink-clad toddler picked up the beautifully decorated, child-sized china cup, delicately and gingerly holding it in her little brown hand. "C'mon, let's play tea," I said. Moving a couple of tables from beside the couch, I said on impulse, "Who do you want to invite?"

She didn't know what I meant.

"Well, teas are fun when you can have other people come, too." I put out the Babar teapot I bought at a French shop just down the street from my office. She carefully placed the Austrian plates all around the tables.

She looked about the office. There were just us two.

"Mr. Nutcracker?" I asked. "Snake? The sheep? We could invite them," my voice trailed off.

Her black eyes went dense and those straight eyebrows knit. She then jumped up and gestured toward the toy cabinet, which I opened for her.

"Guhs," she grunted in that horrible voice of hers. "Big guhs."

I pulled out two beautiful Madame Alexander dolls and she seated them on the couch. We drank our pretend tea and ate the most delicious of imaginary cookies. Satisfied with our very first tea party, we ended the hour by cleaning up. But it was just the beginning. Cammie and I had launched a series of tea parties that would last for 2 years. She had been able to sit still for almost a half-hour. She had used delicacy and restraint in handling the child-sized china. She touched two dolls with respect and courtesy. Just in that one psychiatric hour, Cammie was already showing me (through play) that she could be taught "civilization."

I immediately realized that within tea parties, I could act as a kind of "goddess of civilization." I could teach Cammie the rules of society inside of our play. So I persisted in asking her to add to our guest list.

"Let's have more people come," I suggested after a couple of parties with just the "guhs." "The baby?" I asked.

"Die!" she growled. "No."

"The dogs?"

"Okay." She took out some tiny china dogs and put them on the table.

"Cats?"

"No!" She looked frightened. *What happened to a cat in her first 13 months of life?* I asked myself.

Within our teas, I could talk easily to Cammie about how people are supposed to act. I could also easily talk to her about who is safe to come to a tea. I was pretty certain that we could ensure safety for all our guests. But how could we absolutely make sure? We worked it all out together. "Maybe we should teach Mr. Nutcracker how to behave," I suggested after a while. "And Snake, too." I told Cammie about the police. We talked of jails and prisons. I was telling her all about society. And from my newly determined, godlike position as the interpreter of civilization, she believed me.

She wouldn't touch Mr. Nutcracker or Snake, so I did it instead. She hissed her instructions to the two perpetrators. "Not bite," she urged Mr. Nutcracker. She shook her finger at him. But it took many, many admonitions before he was allowed to attend a tea. The same went for Snake. "Not huut," she instructed him. She had to repeat her instructions for a number of months. We were fully prepared to kick Mr. Nutcracker and Snake out of the party if they misbehaved. We were even prepared to put them in jail. But Cammie never let that happen.

The hardest, most difficult invitation to procure for our tea parties was the one for Baby, a big, beautiful infant doll in diapers and a bathrobe. The mere mention of Baby invoked terror in Cammie. "Baby die! Die baby!" "We have to love Baby and treat her gently," I told Cammie. "We have to feed her baby food and just a few drops of tea." Babies are fragile. But they don't usually die unless people fail to take care of them. We'd learn how!

We talked and talked about Baby. Cammie wasn't afraid *of* her; she was afraid *for* her. Eventually the "big guhs," my Madame Alexander dolls, put the baby between them and helped watch her and keep her safe.

In the 2 years that the "wild" toddler took tea with me, she made a remarkable turnaround. Out in public, she began to hold her foster mother's or father's hand and no longer lunged at others. She became quieter at the shopping malls and fast-food restaurants. The hitting, spitting, vomiting, grabbing, and sniffing still existed—but they were more muted and saved for home.

To move into human society, Cammie used and incorporated the two godlike figures I personified at our teas: The "god of fun" insured that our tea parties were true "parties," even though they lived only in our imaginations. The "goddess of civilization" helped Cammie transform herself from a feral toddler into a preschooler who was at least considering joining humankind. She could handle the big, distant groups at the malls better than she could manage the little, close associations at home. But she had made a remarkable turn for the better.

My decision to act in certain ways had begun to pay off. I could tell that Cammie was enjoying her chance to come to San Francisco. And I could tell she was enjoying her time with me. She left my office happier than she came. She smiled a little. Every so often, she laughed. And once in a while, she could even make a joke herself. Retarded? I could hardly believe any longer that it was possible.

As a matter of fact, in 2 years of taking tea with me, Cammie didn't mar a doll, didn't dirty a thing, and never broke a dish. The only item that got hurt was Snake, who broke in half when she banged him hard against a wooden table while passionately admonishing him against injuring "guhs." I immediately glued him together as Cammie watched, restoring him to his former self.

Cammie was learning—things, like broken "guhs," can be fixed!

CHAPTER TWO

A Teacher, Trainer, or Coach

Across from my house in San Francisco is the Presidio, a great cypress-filled park that used to be a Spanish, and then an American, army post. When my husband, Ab, and I take our after-work walks in the Presidio, I tend to notice what children of all ages are doing when they're just "doin' stuff." I recently saw something that amazed me. It was a 4-year-old blonde who was "footling" (not "handling") a soccer ball as a professional would. The petite player was a natural. Though a coach was working with about twelve other under-fives, he didn't have to teach this particular little girl. She'd watch, and then she'd do, spectacularly!

Large numbers of kids—the vast, vast majority—learn this very same way. They just pick things up. They don't have to be taught. They may not be geniuses at soccer the way the little blonde at the Presidio was, but they watch, they listen, they catch on, they do.

In fact, many kids hate to be officially "taught." There is something about teaching that reminds little people of harping, or of preaching (when they're older), or of admonishing. "Explaining" is different. That's okay. "Discussing" is fine. And "helping," when necessary, is appreciated. "Playing" is an altogether different category, and if an adult really wants to play, the child, unless warned off, will usually go for it. Play can teach a lot.

When you think about it, much normal development proceeds by watching older children and adults, noticing peers, and then taking advantage of the inbuilt genetic and anatomic facilities that are ready to be put into operation. You don't have to teach a child how to walk or talk—you just say "Come here," or "Get the cookie," or "Who's that over there?" or "Look who just came home!"

In child and adolescent psychiatry, however, as in all the allied mental health professions, we become quickly aware of the huge numbers of young people who simply don't "get it" by watching and doing. There are several reasons for this, and although I won't be able to name them all, I'll mention a few. First, some kids are afraid to take the next step, usually for a very personal reason that others don't suspect. Second, many kids have genetic, anatomical, or medical mountains to climb when they face certain new goals that are required for further development. There are hundreds of thousands of smart youngsters, for instance, who have serious enough visual-motor or attention problems that they struggle with reading and writing skills that come almost naturally to "reading ready" children. Third, there is a whole category of children who don't know how to take social cues from other human beings (autism, Asperger's, and related disorders), so they cannot learn in the same fashion as the vast majority. Fourth, there are children, who, because of poverty, severe neglect, or personal tragedies in their families of origin, are so preoccupied with mastering the search for food, putting a (drunk) mommy to bed, or watching out for dad when he has that "look" in his eye to be able to bother with the mastery of the more mundane skills. All of these youngsters can't be taught in the simple, ordinary way. Many times they need us to help teach them. There are no "naturals" like my little Presidio blonde here.

So rather than setting out to "uncover" a child's problems, the psychological professional is often in a better position to function as a teacher or coach than as an investigator, magician, or—heaven help us—a "shrink." I suppose that if Cammie, my miniscule growler, had lived in a town miles away from any speech therapist, I would have had to find a way to train her voice myself—or better yet, to send her to a vocal coach in San Francisco. But we were lucky, and Cammie's voice, in hardly noticeable increments, was beginning to sound more normal due to her twice-a-week "play date" with a very nice "lady" close to home. I wish I knew exactly what that speech therapist did, but it probably was far more involved than the simple move of watching and then doing.

When I was training as a child/adolescent psychiatrist in Ann Arbor, one of the most promising young faculty members there, Jack McDermott, was actually "training" somebody other than our residency group. Dr. McDermott was up against the problem—in an older child—of how to train the boy to properly defecate. Did this boy want to be taught? No, of course not. Did he want to understand? Maybe. Jack's blow-by-blow story—hilarious, especially when it's read aloud—shows all of us how coaching, in and of itself, can be powerful enough to turn a child around.

"Bowel Training" Psychotherapy
CONTRIBUTED BY JOHN F. MCDERMOTT, MD

Eight-year-old Leon was referred by his pediatrician for treatment of secondary encopresis. Physical causes had been ruled out, and he had been placed on a high fiber diet and daily mineral oil. Nevertheless, accidents continued to be more frequent than ordinary bowel movements. Because he soiled his pants several times a week, he was teased unmercifully by classmates at school and was nicknamed "Stink Bomb."

Leon presented as a shy, mildly depressed underachiever. In the office he chose to play with family figures. As he fussed with them in the playhouse bathroom, it was relatively easy for me to move in and out of the displacement of his play to talk with him directly about his soiling. Leon was aware of it but unable to control it. When I asked him to describe how he went about going "number two" on the toilet, he replied that he just sat there, thought of nothing, and nothing happened. Evidently there was no effort, no bearing down. I showed amazement, and offered that he had to push if he wanted to make his bowels move. They couldn't do much all by themselves. So I asked him to just pretend to be on the toilet and make believe he was pushing down.

"Uh," he muttered softly.

"I can't hear it, Leon," I said. "You'll have to go 'UUUUUH-HHH, UUUUUHHHH' if you want things to happen."

"I don't want to do that," cried Leon. "Something might break!"

MEANING OF THE MOMENT

Leon's symptom, as well as his anxiety, had both real and symbolic meaning. Just relearning bowel dynamics wouldn't be enough.[29] Leon's passivity covered up his fear of an unknown that he couldn't control. He was afraid something terrible could happen from an assertive effort at moving his bowels. When I asked him to draw a picture of what might happen, he drew one of a boy with all his insides coming out.

Twelve weekly appointments were scheduled, and we spent part of each hour in the clinic restroom, the two of us talking to each other from adjacent stalls. Reassured through our exchange of drawings that his own insides would be okay, Leon began bearing down harder and harder, with louder and louder grunts. Indeed, he insisted that I compete with him to see who could grunt the loudest.

As the weeks passed and he began to achieve some conscious success, he allowed himself to become aware of omnipotent fantasies of "bowel power." The boy who had said he thought about "nothing" on the toilet now delighted in confiding that he could make his BMs go all the way to another city where his estranged father was living. Expression of rage at his father for leaving was followed by more regular bowel movements, and with them, as one might expect, his soiling disappeared. By the end of our brief psychotherapy together, Leon was standing up to his peers at school. The lonely boy who had watched TV at home every afternoon now wanted to join their T-ball play—although he said he could use some lessons from me first!

Can you imagine the smile on young Leon's face as he sat on his toilet listening to his dignified psychiatrist grunt! It was fun for him. This was not a stupid old sermonizer making a point. The boy lost his fear due to the levity and utter frankness of the whole affair. He had been taught, and, in the process, had come to understand himself as much as he had come to understand the act of elimination.

Psychic trauma, the natural psychological response to an event that threatens a child's life, bodily integrity, or connection to those caring for him or her (or threatens those same functions in someone else, as witnessed by the child), requires relearning and retraining. Trauma is, in fact, an example of one-trial learning.[30] What is learned is usually bad for the child. With the enormous emotions attendant to traumatic events, the child cannot help but instantaneously absorb the lessons inherent in the terror. This is how terrorists teach: "Don't go outside," "Don't trust your government," "Don't back certain nations," "Don't ride the train," "Don't walk alone," "Watch out for brown-skinned people carrying liquids or gels."

To correct for terror in a young person, that person must "abreact" (express all the emotions stirred up by the trauma), find "contexts" (fully understand what happened and how the event fits in with others), and discover "corrections" (how to fix such events—what to do personally and what might be done in communities, even if it is a pipedream).[31] In other words, terror lessons, once taught and forever absorbed by a terror victim, must be untaught, and new, better lessons must eventually be accepted and integrated. How does a psychiatrist give these lessons without sounding like a preacher and second-guesser? Often times, by playing. By using art. By story telling. He or she does it the way the greatest of teachers do.

But let me insert my own short example here. The following vignette about a patient of mine is not an example of great teaching. It does show, however, how play exposes what a child needs to learn as well as how the psychiatrist may function as a trainer and coach.

Barricading My Office Door[32]

Betsy was 9 years old when her divorced mother discovered that her roomer, Ed, was "wanted" in another state for armed robbery. Betsy's mother decided the child should stay at Grandma's. Grandma fretted aloud, however, that Ed might try to steal her new car. Early one morning, Grandma's doorbell rang and she spotted Ed outside. "Betsy, call the police!" The child absolutely froze. "Never mind," grumbled Grandma, and she opened the door. Ed entered, ate breakfast, and insisted that they take the new car out and drive Betsy to school. After immersing herself in schoolwork, Betsy returned that afternoon to find policemen and a ransacked house. She was not allowed to enter the kitchen where Grandma had been murdered. Betsy immediately believed she'd be murdered, too. But the police quickly apprehended Ed, who wrecked the new car and then shot himself. The child moved on to another concern. She blamed herself for Grandma's death. She should have called 911, she said.

A social worker brought Betsy to me a week after the murder. The little girl cried bitterly over her loss and her guilt. In her second session, Betsy told me that before opening the door to Ed, Grandma had said to her, "You're no help." Betsy then abruptly switched subjects. "What are those lights on your phone?" I knew that a person's thought associations between diverse topics are often significant. "Would you like to try my phone?" I set it so that Betsy could play. She dialed 911. She explained Grandma's dilemma to her pretend police. After a couple of play-throughs, I told Betsy that a person could dial, leave the line open, and say nothing, and that the police would listen and trace the call. She tried pretending that, too.

I then switched our focus. "You've been trying to protect Grandma, but how could Grandma have protected you?" Betsy looked shocked. The idea of adult responsibility was entirely new to her. I proposed that an adult can bar an apartment door. We shoved a chair against my door. Then we propped a small table under the doorknob. I set my phone so it could receive calls again and buzzed my assistant, Scott Lindstrom, asking him to come into my room. We heard Scott fiddling with the door. He then called me back, and I held the receiver up so that the amazed little girl could listen. "I can't get in!" Scott said.

MEANING OF THE MOMENT

In playing at barricading my door, Betsy and I dramatically brought two of the three elements of trauma psychotherapy together. Betsy had already emoted her sadness and guilt. Now she gained perspective on what adults could do to protect themselves and their children (context). At the same time, she proved herself able to stop a full-grown man from entering my office (correction). Betsy saw me twice a month for 4 more months, during which time she grieved over her grandmother's death and her mother's problems with parenting. Her father, who lived in another state, eventually took Betsy away to grow up under his care.

The idea of my work with Betsy was to instill the sense of being able to protect herself. Hopefully, too, she would gain a sense that adults learn things throughout life about protecting themselves and others. If she and the adults around her didn't panic, Betsy would have a fighting chance. Human beings of any age need to feel that events are, at least somewhat, within their own control. So Betsy's belated knowledge (indeed, much too late to save Grandma) was sufficient to restore her own sense of well-being. In the future, she felt, she could take care of herself.

Much of what I did with Betsy might be considered an individualized form of cognitive-behavioral therapy (CBT).[33] Whereas child psychodynamic psychotherapy traces its roots back to Sigmund and Anna Freud, CBT places its beginnings with Ivan Pavlov, B. F. Skinner, John B. Watson, and Joseph Wolpe.[34] The idea, at least of the "behavioral" part of CBT, is to "condition" a human being into adopting a new, healthier behavior, one that becomes almost unconsciously automatic. The desired behavior is practiced, paired with purposeful relaxation at each phase, often with weekly or biweekly "homework" assignments.

What has been added in more recent times to CBT is the cognitive part of the package. It has been found over the years that if patients understand their disorders and can grasp the illogic behind what they do, they become more cooperative and willing to change their maladaptive behaviors. Large-sized sessions, like Alcoholics Anonymous or for groups of, say, bipolar-disordered patients or depressed people, are set up to include leader-led discussions and then group participation.

Suggestions are offered by group members or the leader in order to modify actions that are common to the group. Finally, the leader makes behavioral "assignments" that are to be coupled with positive thinking. At several stages of the game, mental diversion and self-relaxation techniques are taught and emphasized.

With children, two main models of CBT have been in fashion,[35] and both have been proven to be very useful. One is manualized group CBT and the second is individualized CBT, set up for a certain specific youngster. With a manual, the entire formula of how to proceed with a certain diagnosis on what day and in what order is entirely preset, without tending to the individualities of any particular kid. If it is a "grief group," for instance, then the manual spells out what will be discussed and what exercises will be arranged. Groups for different disorders use different manuals, but the same general principles apply. The idea is to teach a child how to relax, to discuss some of the attitudes universally generated by the particular condition or that actually drive the condition, and then to find ways to practice new behaviors that were not possible before.

Individualized CBT carries the same goals of changing a youngster's attitudes and actions while teaching the child to relax. Feared items are faced and mastered. Individual CBT has the advantage of being tailored to the specific child. Theoretically, if the child trusts the therapist, he or she will share secrets and thus be open to having them appraised, discussed, and exposed as illogical. He or she may also become willing to expose other behaviors that need to be extinguished. The child might also play or do art in such a setting. Of course, individual CBT carries the disadvantage of greater expense and not being able to "cover" as many kids. But it is an effective procedure nonetheless.

The difference between individualized CBT and what Jack McDermott did with young Leon, or what I did with poor Betsy, was that the two of us were both looking for—and ultimately found—the child's underlying fantasies. Because Jack and I are both interested in psychodynamics, we believed it was important to deal with underlying psychological issues in addition to those elements inherent in the diagnosis. Jack's young patient needed to learn to deal with his explosively angry nature and his killing fury at his divorced father. Betsy had to face, and perhaps forgive, the inabilities of the women in her life to protect her (and themselves). Because many of my colleagues and I are fascinated with the unconscious, much of what you will find on these pages is eclectic. It is "Freud spotted with Watson" or "Minuchin spotted with Anna Freud"[36] or even a mix of three or four important influences. At times, child psychotherapy is so mixed, in fact, that it seems almost entirely reinvented on each occasion it is carried out.

When a psychiatrist decides that a child patient needs teaching or coaching, the psychiatrist often chooses not to participate directly in this aspect of the treatment plan. A frightened youngster, for instance, may need judo lessons. Thus, she goes to judo school. In the 1970s, a few department stores used to offer modeling classes for preteen girls. They were terrific for those young girls who felt awkward, didn't understand the rules of etiquette, and needed postural correction. At this stage of life, a girl could accept considerably more teaching from a model than from Mom.

Orchestra practice is a traditionally stellar way to train a child to have community spirit. He or she learns sharing, blending into the background, and coming up front as a momentary star. Orchestra or choir often inspires a lifelong love of music. Of course, team sports are a good way to learn a number of positive attributes, too. Many of the kids I've treated have benefited from having their parents hire a high school athlete to teach and train them individually in ball-handling skills, running, exerting strength, and trying to endure the small pains and fatigue of sport. These extras—these special and corrective educational experiences—are what a psychotherapist dreams up for the specific child. For Cammie, it was early speech therapy. And then I dreamed up another preschool educational experience for her. Sandra and I eventually came to call it "The Sally Stories."

I needed Cammie to understand that terrible situations can be fixed. Toddlers do not automatically know such things. One has to educate them. So for Cammie to perceive that real corrections can be found in life (not just in inked-in cats' eyes and glued-together snakes), I made a teaching assignment, actually a therapeutic assignment, for Sandra. This idea came in part from the Cleveland psychoanalyst

Erna Furman, who wrote about "filial therapy," the treatment of a child through the youngster's parent.[37] It was, in fact, exactly what Sigmund Freud had done by indirectly treating his famous patient "Little Hans" through the 5-year-old boy's father.[38] The way I looked at it, not only would Sandra be a mom to Cammie, but she'd be my fellow therapist, too, and an educational one at that.

One evening when Cammie was still 2, Sandra asked the toddler to give her a girl's name she liked. Cammie answered, "Sally."

"Let's tell a story about Sally," Sandra said. "Once upon a time, there was a girl named Sally. And . . ." Sandra turned over the tale to her foster child.[39]

"Baby die." Cammie told the only story she knew.

"Yes, the baby died," Sandra agreed sadly. "But Sally lived. And she was taken to a nice, new house and a nice, new family."

"Again!" Cammie demanded. She loved Sandra's personally styled tale, never recognizing that it was she who was the protagonist. For a month or so, the nightly tales continued on exactly the same theme. Then Cammie became more flexible. "Sally huut," she said as her addition to Sandra's "Once upon a time, there was a girl named Sally."

Sandra was ready with our pretailored ending to this new plotline about Sally being injured. "Good people took Sally to the hospital," she said. "The doctors helped her, as they help anybody who is hurt— in their offices, or in the hospitals, or in the ER."

"Again! Again!" the toddler requested. Not only was Cammie learning that corrections were possible, but she also was finally learning to trust a kind and loving woman, who, night after night, was finding herself a little more in love with this tiny and very energetic girl.

Sandra, the storyteller, and I, the part-time "goddess of civilization," were working in tandem. Together, we were inserting societal corrections into Cammie's nighttime stories and Cammie's monthly visits to San Francisco. Both of these techniques accounted for Cammie's decision to join human society.

Good child and adolescent psychiatrists use whatever facilities they can find to help teach and train. I wish there were more cooking classes, violin lessons, tennis coaches, group golf instruction for preteens, boating, hiking, rafting—even modeling!—around. But one of the great facilities we do have throughout the United States is our educators, although we often don't take enough advantage of them. I can't tell you how many kids I've treated could have used a teacher—one still actively teaching or who has retired—to help them learn something that has personal importance.

A tutor is a very, very desirable thing. I look at tutoring a little differently from most parents. Most parents, I think, consider tutors to be make-up workers—people who compensate for what a child didn't learn at school. They see it as the school's responsibility to make sure everybody learns the material and retains it afterward. If the child missed learning something, here is where the tutor comes in. And many mothers and fathers resent it. It's an "extra" that they're individually paying for but that should have been provided by the school. Why didn't the school make sure their child "got" the material they were teaching in the first place?

I certainly understand that point of view and appreciate it as a reasonable argument. In my view, however, tutoring should be proactive, not after the fact (of a failure, a problem learning, a defeat). If a child has a "different" learning style, or if he or she needs help buttressing-up emotionally, or if the youngster can't grasp the idea of watching and doing, this particular child may need a long-term relationship with a tutor. The tutoring is used to help the youngster gain confidence. It is also used to encourage a certain kind of mental playfulness. After all, what discoveries were ever made by an uncreative mind?

I look at tutoring in the sense of the "tutoring" done at Oxford and Cambridge. At these prestigious universities, a student is assigned an individual tutor who discusses the lectures, readings, outside-the-college politics, films, music, books, and plays. Everything is integrated. Anything is discussable. Here—with a personal tutor—the student becomes a truly educated citizen of the world, or, at the least, of Great Britain.

Let me give you three brief examples of what I mean. None of the three are miracles of psychotherapy, but in a sense, they are miracles of teaching. The first case is a little girl I met when she was just over

4 years old. Martha was a sad little creature whose grandmother, with whom she had been close, had recently died. Her mom suffered from severe migraine headaches and often spent her days in bed. Martha's little next-door neighbor, who had been a very friendly playmate, was about to move to another town. Martha's father, a busy Silicon Valley executive on his way up the ladder, was totally committed to his little girl but had very, very little time for her. Martha was sad, but she was also smart and funny. Once started, she loved to talk. We saw each other a couple of times, and I quickly recognized that no one had the time (father) or energy (mother) to get her to the city once a week for treatment. "Find her a tutor," I suggested, "to get her super-prepared for kindergarten. Make school really easy for her, so she can develop a number of friendships and use her talents socially. And then try, if you can, to keep the tutor active in her life through at least third grade, so that Martha can learn and retain all her 'basics.' " I kept in touch with Martha's father. He found a retired schoolteacher in their neighborhood. Martha and the schoolteacher became fast friends and discussed the world of happenings together. Not only did the child become a classroom leader, but she also developed a magnetism that attracted people of any age, including her peers. Her father reported much later that the tutor had, in fact, become a key member of their family.

My second example is the case of a bright little boy who had learned to read at age 2 by watching and listening to television ads. What his school didn't realize until they tested him in the third grade was that he had no reading comprehension whatsoever. In other words, he read for the 2-year-old trick of it, for the joy of linguistic de-coding. But he never realized that he might listen to the story a writer was trying to impart to him. This was a boy who needed the very best reading tutor he could get. His parents went to the head of a school that his younger sister was attending. Could she think of anyone to take this young fellow on? Yes, as a matter of fact—she, herself, might consider it as an after-school proposition. The newly acquired tutor produced a miracle of change in the boy's reading patterns—she had to provide him with the easiest of stories, with the highest of interest potential—plus a great deal of chocolate! The 9-year-old boy loved her (and her cat), as he eventually learned to read for content. The job had been accomplished because a specific understanding of a specific child led to a specific educational program set up just for him. This was a use of corrective tutoring in its best sense.

The third example is a personal one. My family knows and loves a little Chinese-American girl whom we see several times a year. When she was 8, I recognized how bright Jessie was and—as a game—I wondered if I could teach her how to abstract. Jean Piaget, the great Swiss child psychologist, wrote that abstraction becomes possible at around age 12.[40] Could this little girl beat the world's authority by 4 years? For the sheer fun of it, I informally gave Jessie proverbs to interpret. She described a chicken hatching, eggs in baskets being counted, houses made of glass—all of the "concrete operations" Piaget had predicted for an 8-year-old child. But I, as tutor, explained, "A proverb is a rule for life. You must think of the chickens silently, and then tell me out loud what counting chickens means about the world of people." We practiced a few times. She loved the game, and understood quickly that she might think silently about the broken glass on ill-built houses, but out loud she must identify a rule for life. When Jessie was 9, the principal of her school called her privately into the main office and tested her. Not knowing what I had done in the way of tutoring, the school saw Jessie as a kind of mental miracle. Jessie is 11 now, and she still asks me what new proverbs I've found for her. Beating Piaget was no game for her, but proverb interpretation still is!

Sometimes a child psychiatrist "tutors" without fully realizing that this is what the young patient is taking from session. When my colleagues' and my first article about child psychotherapy, featuring seven magical moments of change, came out in 2005, I received an email from Los Angeles. It came from one of the revered pioneers of child and adolescent psychiatry, Barbara Fish, who years ago set up treatment plans for some of the most mentally disturbed kids in New York City. She was one of the first of us to use medications on children (always with the utmost care and concern). What I found so fascinating in Barbara's email to me was not her history of mid-century American psychiatry but rather the instantaneous change that she

had witnessed in a private-practice case from much earlier in her career. Following is an edited version of Barbara's email to me. It represents a magical moment that occurred in a situation where, without
even meaning it consciously, the psychiatrist set herself up as teacher,
trainer, and coach.

Dear Lenore,

In reading your article, I suddenly recalled one "moment" of my
own, in the prehistoric days of my early private practice before 1955.
My patient was 8 and had continuing enuresis [wetting herself]. I saw
very few children with such mild problems. During those ancient days
I was apparently the only child psychiatrist in the NY-NJ-CT area who
saw very disturbed and psychotic children in my office and didn't try to
psychoanalyze them. So I mostly ended up treating severely ill children
until I took over Lauretta's [Bender] full-time job at Bellevue. I had
been fully certified to do psychoanalysis by the William Alanson White
Psychoanalytic Institute and had been supervised by Janet Rioch,
Clara Thompson, Ed Tauber, and Frieda Fromm-Reichmann [the doctor in *I Never Promised You a Rose Garden*].

In contrast to analysis, the considerably sicker children we treated
on the Children's Service at Bellevue got better much more quickly and
remained "engaged" with their talking or play therapies just once a
week. Of course, I also worked regularly with the family and the child's
school, and I used a psychologist, social worker, and remedial teachers
to help the child's environment. I also simultaneously tried in sequence, and carefully titrated, the doses of what few medications we
then had available, from the mildest (the amphetamines [today's
Adderall, for instance] and diphenhydramine [Benadryl] to chlorpro-
mazine [Thorazine] when it first came out).

But back to my "moment." I remember seeing this little 8-year-old
enuretic girl sitting in the "grown-up" chair at that very first office. She
was quite verbal, and I "wondered" aloud with her about lots of reasons
someone might still wet the bed when they were already pretty grown
up. I said "sometimes someone feels like" this or that, giving her common examples (I can't recall all the specifics at this distance). We discussed each one carefully. At the end of the hour we got up and I
opened the door to the tiny waiting room where her parents were sitting. I was prepared to make a follow-up appointment for the little girl
and a subsequent one with her parents, whom I had already interviewed to get their version of her history.

But my patient jumped the gun. She rushed to them saying, "I like that lady. And I'm all better now!" And it turned out, as they reported later, she was. The enuresis vanished without a trace. It seems to me that she had simply responded in kind to being treated seriously, "like a grownup," and decided she was. That was the only "instant" cure I ever accomplished.

Warm regards,
Barbara

Barbara Fish's story shows how unspoken teaching is sometimes more potent than active, conscious education. The implied lessons were: "You can sit in a big chair," "You are big yourself," "I will treat you as if you were big," "In fact, I believe you *are* a big girl."

All of these implications led up to the most important and specific question of all—still entirely implied from the doctor's behavior. "Why should a big girl wet herself?"

"Of course not," reasoned the child. "I won't wet anymore." This moment between an experienced doctor and an inexperienced child represents a spectacular episode of "one-trial learning." It is no wonder that after so many years, the moment still is a very distinct memory for a grand lady of psychiatry.

With fascination, we watch young people learn. But we must also keep in mind that there are several different styles of learning. There are many, many lessons to be learned. Some are entirely unconscious. A number become cues toward behavioral modification. Others change attitudes or prompt revelations about civilization itself. During these educational pursuits, whether they be with a tutor or with a therapist, children may experience stunning moments of change.

CHAPTER THREE

An Investigator

In classic psychoanalysis, the analyst occasionally slips into the role of "investigating detective." Patiently waiting day after day, week after week, for revelations from the analysand's past and for ghosts of early relationships in the analysand's transference, the analyst inspects and then interprets small bits at a time. Watching the analysand on the couch for assent to the doctor's interpretations, and carefully observing changes afterward in the patient's behaviors or attitudes, the analyst decides and redecides whether the suppositions he or she originally made were correct. The important clues come from following the patient's trail of "associations." Like the best of bloodhounds, the analyst sniffs out what thought comes before or after which thought, which follows from what. This trail tells the analyst how a particular adult thinks. Other important keys to the patient's inner being are his dreams and talk around them (associations, again), jokes, slips of the tongue, a casual remark (especially at the beginning or end of an hour), comments about the analyst, a behavior that fits into a larger pattern of behaviors, and, just the opposite, a behavior that doesn't fit in at all. In psychoanalysis, as in its younger sibling, psychodynamic psychotherapy, there is no opportunity for a crime scene investigation (a "CSI"). All evidence is circumstantial.

Although most analysts do not tend to think of themselves as detectives, a number of playwrights, novelists, and filmmakers have enjoyed thinking about psychoanalysis this way. In Tennessee Williams's *Suddenly Last Summer*, made by Joseph Mankiewicz into a 1959 film, the secrets of the supposedly psychotic Elizabeth Taylor character are uncovered by a neurosurgeon, played by Montgomery Clift. Letting his scalpel go in favor of a purely psychiatric investigation, Clift's "investigator" successfully brings an ugly family mystery to light. In 1945, Alfred Hitchcock made the film *Spellbound*, another vivid example of this kind of "psychomystery." Here, Ingrid Bergman, playing the part of a psychoanalyst in a mental institution (a self-canceling phrase these days), uncovers the fact that her new boss, played by Gregory Peck, has assumed the name and life of an eminent psychiatrist he didn't even know. The female analyst, along with her friend and analytic colleague, a much older man, combine their skills to discover what inner mystery is impelling her boss's weird behavior. They solve it, of course, but not before the female analyst romantically entangles herself with her boss, who is also her patient by now. (Boundaries are indeed elastic in Hitchcock's vision of psychiatry.)

When a child/adolescent psychiatrist sets out to solve the mysteries of a child's mind—as opposed to an adult's—he or she depends far less upon transference and trails of thought. These phenomena certainly need to be kept in mind, however. Once in a while, a child behaves in a way that indicates a strong transference reaction (in fact, in the vignette contributed by Dr. Nancy Winters, transference helps to solve the case). But transference is not usually prevalent with children who are still deeply involved inside their families of origin. And children's thought associations are harder to follow than those of adults because kids may drop only one or two deeply personal comments in an entire hour. (How do we follow their journey from "a" to "b" when the two are 25 minutes apart?)

So we rely on a number of other indicators of a child's inner mystery besides associations and transference. Children's play—their drawings, imaginings, songs, poems, jokes, manipulations of toys, manipulations of our office furniture—and what they say about it (their associations to their play)—give us our most important clues.[41] I almost always write down what kids say about their art. "Tell me a story about it," I request when they finish a drawing. I write the tale down, telling them to go slowly if they're talking too fast. Then we look at the picture together and I read the story back. I keep their artwork in the chart, and I often pull the pictures out later to look at them as a series. Together, we tell the tales once again. There they are—the themes and the variations! What a child's art and play tell us may express a tragedy or a scene of abject horror. But a child's drawing may also unravel a deeply internal mystery, such as a phobia, an obsession, or a worry. The mystery may be as intriguing, in fact, as a 1940s or 50s movie melodrama.

In order to do a good assessment of a child or adolescent, any mental health professional must temporarily take on the role of investigator. In the sessions one has alone with the child (or with an onlooker, like a parent), one asks openly and directly about the child's problem. What does he or she think about the problem? But one needs to make sure to observe some play, artwork, music, or poetry, too. Asking a child for "three wishes" is also often helpful in understanding the youngster. (I especially listen to the second wish. The first is usually something immediate and concrete, like "lunch after this appointment." The third may be sincere but very general, like "world peace.") Asking about the best and worst things that ever happened in the child's life is also particularly useful. A child's favorite books and movies, school, peers, daily routines, divorce routines, activities, loves, hates, ideas about the personal future—all of this is helpful to know. The "investigator" begins putting these together with what is also being observed in the kid's attitudes, affects, and actions.

The "investigator" must also assess a number of external factors. After taking a history from the parents and meeting with the child, standard gumshoe work during the assessment phase might include understanding the child's siblings, phoning the child's teachers, going to school for a conference (with parental permission, of course), getting neurological or psychological testing, fully evaluating the child's physical health, interviewing nannies, finding out about pets, peers, fetishes, fears, and so on. I've spoken with more than one minister, nun, priest, and rabbi about my child patients, in fact. The more we learn—early—the more intelligent planning we can put into a young person's quick and complete recovery.

Evaluation is probably the main sphere where the psychological "investigator" enters the child's or adolescent's world.[42] In fact, assessment is considered so important today that, beginning in the late 1980s, a number of technical types of investigation were pushed within the various sectors of mental health. Hypnosis, Amytal interviews, EMDR (eye movement desentization and reprocessing interviewing), MRIs and PET scans (magnetic resonance or positron emission tomography imaging), sleep studies, and EEGs (electroencephalograms) have all been done to investigate kids. Much of this technical stuff is set up for research. And some is also clinically warranted for particular child patients. Useful as these techniques may be, however, problems can arise when they become the psychiatrist's "shtick." Now, the child or adolescent is being used to further the psychiatrist's agenda. This isn't research per se. It's an indulgence in the doctor's pet technique. And it can create fears in already frightened kids or, even worse, dependencies in already dependent young people. Thus, although there are times when one of these special techniques is indicated in an investigation, in most cases careful observation, history-taking from parents, and direct "talk and play" evaluation of the child gives us all we need.

And what *do* we need? Enough to determine a "diagnosis" (i.e., the synthesis of history, observation, and tests, leading to the indication of a certain medical condition that is treated in a prescribed way). Every bit as important, too, we need enough data to determine a "formulation" (the working psychological explanation for a patient's feelings, behaviors, and thinking).[43] Ideally, both formulation and diagnosis go hand in hand, especially in child and adolescent psychiatry. In a sense, they represent the "art" and "science" of medicine and mental health. Sometimes we put more emphasis on the diagnosis, and sometimes the formulation takes ascendancy. But coming out of an assessment, a child or adolescent patient should have been given both. With both in hand, we set out to treat the young person.

After the original assessment, child therapists don't always feel the need to investigate. They are treating the child, and, rightly, they build a kind of wall between evaluation and treatment.[44] After all, if you treat while you're evaluating, you may easily lose crucial background information. And if you investigate while treating, the youngster may sense that you are unsure of yourself, or ambivalent, or "wimpy." But if you tell a child or adolescent what you're doing—"I'm still trying to learn more about you, so we can work as effectively as we can together"—the youngster may eagerly join you in the detective work inherent to ongoing treatment.[45] Almost every child, in fact, loves a mystery. The mystery is even better when it has to do with the self.

As therapists today, we're not just investigating a child or adolescent's fantasies, beliefs, unconscious conflicts, hidden motivations, and defenses. We're also looking for genetic patterns, biochemical makeup, and other physical conditions. And beyond all that, we're also searching for the "real." What real events have molded this child—this family? Sometimes these questions come up long after the treatment has started. Yes, the "investigator" must go back to work. Yes, it's okay to call Grandma with a question. It's okay to ask a babysitter to come in. Old, real episodes can carry enormous meaning and clout. And finding out about them may well make an important difference in the treatment of a child.

There are times when a psychiatrist continues his or her "investigator" persona well into a child or adolescent's treatment. Great moments sometimes happen when this kind of ongoing investigation strikes gold. There are no fancy brain scans, drug-interviews, hypnoses, or EMDR finger waggings in the following two vignettes. Instead, you will read about two very imaginative doctors who indulged in two imaginative methods of investigation during their treatments. Both psychiatric "investigators" engineered on-the-spot moments of change in their little charges. Their techniques were simple, clever, and spontaneous.

Mr. Krueger, Mr. Craven, and James

CONTRIBUTED BY JERRY W. DODSON, MD

One day, a sleepless 8½-year-old boy came to see me in rural Texas. James had recently moved from rural Oklahoma and suddenly began having nightmares about Freddy Krueger, the murderous character in the movie Nightmare on Elm Street. *In the dreams, the monster murdered James's parents and then came around to kill him. James had first seen* Nightmare on Elm Street *while overnighting with young cousins. In the weeks that followed, he bugged his parents into letting him view two additional sequels. All of this took place a couple of months before the family moved.*

On evaluation, the dark-haired, olive-skinned young fellow checked out negative for deep-seated neurotic conflicts and past personal traumas. He denied problems with his new home or school. What seemed to be bothering him was the simple fact of having been exposed to an extremely scary film. I wondered if a cognitive-behavioral process called "corrective redreaming"[46] would help, so I suggested that James plan ahead an escape from Freddy, including, perhaps, putting me into the dream. Then he should relax and allow himself to go to sleep. James returned to his second session with the announcement that Freddy had chopped me up but good!

In the interval before the next session, I decided to view the movie myself. I also researched the writer, Wes Craven. Finally— James still wasn't sleeping—I decided to write Mr. Craven. With the parents' permission, I briefly described young James's predicament and commented that people writing horror fiction sometimes have experienced childhood traumas of their own. Was that true for Wes? Could he offer James and me any insight?

Much to my surprise I received a long letter in return. Mr. Craven said he had been exposed to scary fights between his parents when he was 3 years old. When Wes was 4, his alcoholic father left the family and died the following year. This prompted a lifelong series of horrible dreams. "Almost everything I have written has come from my nightmares," Wes said. His fear of his father, as a matter of fact, became personified by a character he dreamed up at 8 or 9, "Freddy Krueger." Freddy was "always there in some dark corner. When I [later] created Freddy [for the movies], that was my template." After I received Mr. Craven's letter, I sent my heartfelt thanks by return mail,

called in James (and his parents), and read it aloud. As I read,
James almost visibly puffed to the size of a comfortable boy.

MEANING OF THE MOMENT

James's nightmares were initially triggered by the stress of a
move. Yet they expressed no grief about leaving Oklahoma, nor
any fear of starting over in Texas. The terror, in fact, largely be-
longed to someone else. It was a case of "trauma by conta-
gion."[47] In order to follow the source of James's trauma back to
its origins, I used the perhaps unusual psychotherapeutic tool
of doing some playful "research." Writing the letter to Wes
Craven was fun for me—and his answer made it an almost mo-
mentous occasion, sad and frightening though it was on sev-
eral levels. I could now show my little patient that at a slightly
scary time in his life, he had encountered a terribly scary time
in somebody else's life. On the few later occasions that James's
nightmares returned, his parents cut the cycle short by again
reading to him from Mr. Craven's letter.

Jerry Dodson had thought a bit about James's terrible insomnia,
watched the movie that caused it, and then, almost on impulse, addressed his playful "research" inquiry to Wes Craven. Amazingly, and
happily for the boy, Mr. Craven wrote back. And lo and behold! The
boy and man both had sleepless nights in common. Mr. Craven's bad
nights as a child, however, came from real, true fears of a drunken, violent father. James's bad nights came instead from Mr. Craven's
fictional concoction, an invented character who symbolized Wes's dad
after he died. A traumatic fright, the detective-psychiatrist learned,
had been transmitted by contagion from the traumatized writer to the
untraumatized film viewer. The little film viewer was very ready to be
frightened, in fact, because he was in the process of moving from one
state to another. The mystery thus unraveled. When the truth of all
the various realities came out, the boy instantly recovered.

With enough psychotherapeutic time, Jerry Dodson might have
been able to expose James's use of the defense displacement in ways
other than the dramatic means he chose. But instead of working day

by day, week by week, the way most of us do with a hard-to-treat phobia, Dr. Dodson conceived of a way to bypass all that by presenting Mr. Craven—as a child—to James. James could size himself up, fear by fear, reality by reality, against the young Wes Craven. Who was more scared? Wes. Who had a harder life? Wes. What a wonderfully good deed Mr. Craven did by writing that letter. And what a wonderfully imaginative piece of detective work Dr. Jerry Dodson did. In fact, the Craven letter was so magical in and of itself that it solved the few sleep problems that James encountered later.

In the following case, a more usual office-based series of weekly interviews had been taking place between Dr. Nancy Winters of Portland, Oregon, and a young girl who had suffered for years with life-threatening feeding disturbances. Dr. Winters brought the child, Lucy, far enough back to normalcy that she could dispense with her feeding tubes. But then young Lucy got stuck. What clues did Lucy offer as to the source of her worries? In the fashion one ordinarily sees with kids—a few intense comments and a lot of play—Lucy conveyed her problem in "code" to her doctor. When the "investigator" put the clues together, she confronted young Lucy with them. Was the child shocked at hearing her unconscious announced out loud? Read on to see.

Foodstuffs and Boy Stuff

CONTRIBUTED BY NANCY C. WINTERS, MD

Lucy had a longstanding feeding disorder, requiring a gastrostomy tube from the time she was 4. She entered psychotherapy with me when she was discovered, at 7, compulsively weighing herself. She wanted to be thin, she said. Lucy began her treatment by repeatedly putting me in jail during our play. She also liked to pretend that good food turned bad, and vice versa. Later, she demonstrated that she had unconsciously merged eating and sexual issues by having a doll get married, eat a meal, become pregnant, and exercise to "lose her pregnancy fat." She confided a secret (it turned out to be imaginary) that her dad took her to soccer games that her mom didn't know about.

Around this time, her mother mentioned that Lucy wanted to see a "boy" therapist.

As we worked together, Lucy gradually became able to get off her tube feedings. Almost counterbalancing this improvement, however, her play became compulsively ritualized. She repeatedly set up an "educational" scenario for me, the "student," and expected me to give her the "right answer." When I encouraged her to use her imagination, she became even more rigidly entrenched.

One day, Lucy purposely kept my office door open. "You'd like to be in charge, wouldn't you?" I said with an encouraging smile. The next time I saw her, Lucy immediately began drawing imaginative, colorful pictures. As she drew, I mused aloud. "Sometimes you wish for a boy therapist, don't you? Maybe you think that a man could help you be freer in your play." After a pause, I suggested that Lucy try some of the "boy" stuff in my toy chest. She looked surprised. But she pulled out a bag of wooden blocks and began to build "the tallest building ever." I said, "I notice that when you feel in charge you are colorful, lively, and fun. . . ." She enthusiastically interjected, "and imaginative!" During the rest of the session Lucy engaged me in jubilant music-making.

MEANING OF THE MOMENT

Lucy had struggled for years with conflicts around eating. Whose body and whose eating was it anyway—hers or her mother's? The conflict had grown as Lucy developed. It was clear from the way that she put me in jail and then released me early in her therapy that Lucy's feeding conflicts had become "fat" with implications around control (for more about food and control, see Anna Freud's 1965 "developmental line," which concerns eating).[48] Gender and the Oedipus complex soon entered into the equation, as well. When, over two sessions, I confronted Lucy with her wishes for power, for a "boy therapist" and for "boy" toys, I showed her that I was not bound by gender expectations around power and control, nor should she be. A little girl's attempts to achieve pleasure, autonomy, and creativity should not be tied in any way to masculinity or femininity—nor, in fact, to eating or to family romances. When Lucy added that she was "imaginative," she immediately began to show me through her play that she now knew exactly how to proceed—in life and in play.

What impressed Nancy Winters, the "investigator," were two verbal clues from the child and two ways of playing that young Lucy strongly favored. The doctor put the little girl's fantasy, stated as fact, about attending soccer games in secret with her dad (a kind of child-minded adultery) side-by-side with her request for a boy therapist. Did Lucy want to fall in love? No, it seemed to be something else. Then the doctor took into account the mode of playing that had been occurring in her office—endless games of teaching school and one game of managing the doctor's office door. Control was obviously important to this little girl. But she had to keep practicing it—she didn't really feel fully empowered, did she? It looked to Dr. Winters as if Lucy resented her psychiatrist for being a woman. Did Lucy feel that women were inferior to men? Would little Lucy ever be able to run things? Be powerful enough?

One beauty of working with kids is how deftly they take to condensations. Dr. Winters condensed a world of inferences about gender differences, power politics, creativity, and love into five remarks, spread over two sessions. In this case, the transference was very important. Nancy Winters dealt with it directly. But the reader will also notice that Nancy didn't link her transference interpretation back to Lucy's parents. She left the idea just between herself and the patient—and there it stayed. The child did not have to follow every single link to its source. She "got" the whole picture when confronted with it by her doctor. And then she changed.

I personally have always liked the psychodetective model, despite the fact that a number of my peers say they don't care for it at all. In thinking about my little wild patient, Cammie, I was intrigued by exactly what Nick and Bonnie and their large family (including Bonnie's folks, her younger sister, and another older sister who lived nearby with her kids) did. What happened in secret during those first 13 months of Cammie's life?

From the beginning we knew, almost for certain, that Cammie had witnessed part or all of her baby sister's death. The police had found a dead infant in a large house in which Cammie was running around. We also knew she had been bitten by adults. We inferred that she had been severely shaken, from her own shaking behaviors and her hyperactivity (shaken baby syndrome). We also assumed she'd been spoken to in a Satanic fashion by Nick (according to Bonnie's informal comments to Sandra and others, as well as her more formalized statements to the court in her attempt to blame everything on Nick and regain Cammie's custody). We knew (from an external exam done on Cammie within hours of coming to Sandra and Tom's) that she'd been sexually misused. Exactly what was done to her, however, remained a mystery.

In fact, we didn't know almost as much as we knew. What had happened to a cat? What had happened to sheep? Why did Cammie hurt animals? Why did she vomit? Why did she spit? Why, indeed, did she live when her younger sister Bethany died?

Then there were the future "whats." What kind of physical problems would turn up as Cammie became older? What kinds of school problems would she have? What could we expect in the future if she were left alone with small children? What genetics did she inherit from such terrifying people?

By the time she was 3½ years old, Cammie began offering her own clues to that horrible year that had started her life. Her first drawings at home were entirely trauma-related. She drew herself ("me with breasts") with no mammaries but rather with stuff that looked like pubic hair on her chin and between her legs. In black, she drew two nude adult women with breasts and stick legs angled far apart. One had bright red splotches near her genitals. "Not talk bout dat," she warned Sandra off the subject. During this same early period of artwork, she drew a male "biting monster." He had about twice as many teeth as anyone would expect. Mouth gaping open, teeth sharpened to points, he was one of the most frightening pieces of preschool imagination I have ever seen.

Then a new kind of clue emerged. Four-year-old Cammie was caught in the Brooks's kitchen, looking like a zombie and cutting into her bare shins by using a large spoon with holes in it. "Not huut!" she immediately defended herself to Sandra. Cammie's foster mom was shocked by the child's dissociative self-mutilation.

"I'll show you what hurts!" Sandra pinched Cammie's arm as hard as she could.

Later, Sandra confessed to me how guilty she felt about her response. But Cammie did not self-mutilate again.

The investigator in me has never observed a better parent than Sandra Brooks (except, maybe, my own parents—and here, I'm definitely prejudiced). We had all decided 2 years earlier not to talk to Cammie about the facts of her first year of life. Before I met them, Tom and Sandra had made the same decision. Like her drawings, Cammie's self-mutilation trick came in when she was old enough to be capable of doing it. Would we ever learn any new facts, other than inferences, from Cammie's behaviors? I guessed not. But as you will see later in this chapter, I turned out to be wrong.

Just as psychotherapists must act as investigators during assessment and treatment of their patients, parents, too, should monitor what's going on at home, at school, and with their children's peers. They don't have to be "nosy," but they do need to know and understand their children. After all, they're raising them, aren't they?

This could be the subject of a whole book, but for the sake of brevity, let's take a quick look at a few short examples. In buying a computer for a kid—and the child really, really wants a particular laptop—a parent might say, "I'm going to have to check the computer once in a while." That might mean a random look at what the youngster is watching, writing on "MySpace," or playing. That's reasonable. Or, if a teenager made a lot of money over the summer, a parent would have every right to understand how the youngster plans to spend it (or already has spent it)—yes, the kid's bankbook can be checked and yes, the new clothes can be modeled. I use the word "understand" here, not "control." By this, I mean that parents have the right to know what their adolescents are doing, but they don't have the right to run their kids' lives.

Suppose a high school kid has used the family car all day. There's no reason why a parent can't do a "before" and "after" mileage check. Further, bedrooms are not "off limits" to randomly timed parental inspection; garages may need an occasional "once over" as well. Certain items—drugs, weapons, cigarettes—can be declared "forbidden." But the parental right to check up on a child would not extend to invasions of privacy, such as reading diaries and love letters. Parental investigations sometimes must extend outside the home. Other parents hosting "overnights" can and should be phoned, for instance. Kids may act resentful about being inspected, but they are far more resentful about being neglected.

The following vignette illustrates what may happen when the psychotherapist neglects the "investigator" role. It is a case from my own files—a situation in which the investigator in me completely shut off. I don't fully know why this happened. I may have been too certain what was wrong with my teenaged patient, Annaliese, to investigate any further. Part of it may have been that I had already treated Annaliese's younger sister and thought I knew what was occurring in their family. But honestly, I still don't really know what caused this lapse on my part. Suffice it to say that although I have spent my entire career studying childhood trauma, with Annaliese I didn't see the trauma that was right in front of my nose, and I still feel awful about it.

Missed Moment

Annaliese was a sad, awkwardly tall, virtually ignored high school sophomore. She received Bs and Cs at school, participated in no extracurricular activities, came home and did housework and babysitting, and walked the family dog. She had three younger sisters, one of whom I had previously treated. Marlena, the girl's mother, was born in Germany and married and conceived her three children by an American soldier stationed there. Marlena chose to maintain her and her girls' American citizenship, despite the fact that the father of the family went AWOL when Annaliese was just 7. The girls' mother had always worked as an administrative assistant on army bases. She eventually moved to an air force base where she met and married her second husband, Hobie. Soon afterward, they were deployed to northern California.

I attributed both the oldest and youngest sisters' sadness to their sudden, inexplicable paternal loss. I also saw them as suffering from a difficult change in cultures. Working along these lines with 10-year-old Trudi, the second-youngest, led to a brightening of her affect and considerably improved efforts at school. When I declared Trudi "better," Marlena decided to have me treat her oldest daughter, Annaliese. Both mother and stepfather came to see me in conjunction with Annaliese's treatment. I learned that there were some ongoing military problems with Hobie. He'd been late for work, absent a couple of times, and suspected of pilfering (but not caught). The couple, however, seemed relatively devoted and happy. Marlena worked long hours. Hobie prided himself on coming home early to tend to his stepdaughters.

Under my care, Annaliese did not complain, nor did she respond very much. She insisted that was not really suffering from the loss of her father or from cultural adjustment. She looked bored as we talked and often drifted into hazy, daydreamy states. Then one day she announced that she had joined a "born-again" church. Within weeks, Annaliese, a Catholic, was attending fundamentalist Protestant church activities almost every day. She barely had time to come to my office. She told me that religion had "saved" her. Nobody danced, drank, or swore. Skirts were long. Tops were loose. She no longer helped much at home. All her friendships revolved around the church activities. Weekends were totally taken up. Although Annaliese's dismal affect and pessimistic statements did not change, she insisted that she felt better now and no longer needed me. Her parents concurred.

I received a letter from Annaliese 30 years later. "Why didn't you know?" she wrote me. "My stepfather was sexually abusing me!" Not only had Hobie repeatedly abused Annaliese, she wrote, but later—when she was a teenager—he also sexually *abused Trudi. Eventually Hobie and Marlena divorced. Hobie was never prosecuted. I invited Annaliese to my office for a no-pay session. During a Christmas holiday break, she came to visit her mom and to see me. She was still sad, very, very tall, underweight, lonely, and dreamy. Her love affair with Christian fundamentalism had lasted only a couple of years. I strongly suggested psychotherapy and told her several low-cost ways to obtain it near her home (in a distant state). I doubt she ever did.*

MEANING OF THE MOMENT

Annaliese did not tell me, while I was treating her, that she was actively being sexually abused. Her symptoms—dreaminess, sadness, aloneness, average grades, aloofness from peers— might have suggested incest, but I don't think I could have acted on this group of symptoms alone. Hobie's minor antisocial run-ins may have suggested incest, too, but they were not enough to lead me there. Marlena's work, work, work ethic, while ignoring the girls, suggested a family incest dynamic as well. The church, however, should have been the clincher for me. When a child independently throws herself into 7-day-a-week, rule-bound religious activity, the psychotherapist cannot accept this behavior without investigating it a bit. It was too extreme and too different from this particular child's background. This was reactive, defensive, self-protective behavior that I should have recognized as a red flag for trauma.[49] I could not have known exactly what was happening, but I should have asked— and not just one question, but a gentle and tactful probe.

Asking a piercing question about the patient in mid-treatment sometimes represents a gesture from the doctor that the entire case was waiting for. Such was the case with Annaliese. She couldn't tell me about a personal and secret horror like incest. I had to ask.

We rarely realize what we *didn't* do that might have sparked a turning point in a child or adolescent's psychotherapy. Once in a while, and usually long after the fact, children—as adults—inform us of "moments" lost. If we don't ask, we won't know what we need to understand about our patients. If our curiosity arises during psychotherapy, we must inquire. Who knows how many turning points could have come about *if only we had known.*

It surprises me how many times our professional guesses about patients turn out to be right. The guess must be based on the patient's behavior, what the patient says, some external clues to the patient, one's general store of knowledge, what one's specific professional knowledge and experience says, and how all these things (and sometimes others) fit together. It takes two or more people to prove a therapeutic guess. Certainly, there must be you and the patient. But sometimes we also need a third party. And maybe a fourth.

Here's what I mean about arriving at a team solution: Once a woman came to see me during the height of the "false memory debates" of the 1990s. She was concerned about her fully grown, unmarried daughter. The daughter, who lived miles away, was going through a depression and had sought professional counseling for it. In the course of her psychotherapy, the grown girl had arrived at a "new" memory. Her maternal grandfather had committed incest on her when she was 2 or 3 years old, she said. She could see him, standing at the foot of her bed after he had done something horrible to her "private parts." Maybe it was just "once," in fact. She could almost say for certain that the occurrence had been a one-time event.

The daughter's psychotherapist strongly supported her patient's spontaneous memory return. It connected to her current depression and her difficulties making a permanent commitment to a man. What did the patient want to do about it? Was Grandpa still alive? Could he be personally confronted? Would he admit it?

No, Grandpa had died a year or two before. But he *could* be confronted, in a way. He had been a very famous man, and he was still a celebrity in the music world. Therefore, if the young woman went public, the man's reputation could be killed.

The therapist encouraged the idea of granting a media interview. It would be helpful to "out" abusers, even if they were dead. But the psychotherapist also wisely suggested an intermediate step. "Tell Mom." This way the daughter might not alienate her mother, who had been very fond of Grandpa.

So here was the mother in my office. Her daughter had already told her the disturbing tale. But the woman could not believe that her dad had done such a thing. He'd never laid an ill-directed hand on her. He had been gone "3 days out of 4," when her daughter was 2 or 3. Did he have the time? The mother begged her daughter for "a month to think this out." The daughter agreed to give her mother some time.

Could I help? Perhaps by turning up my "investigator" volume, I might gain some understanding of this situation. The mother's and the daughter's stories did not jibe. Something was askew.

"Tell me all about your daughter," I requested. So the woman told me: A nice girl, a bit shy, but always had one or two good friends. Late at dating. Did well in college. Had a nice boyfriend for 2 or 3 years, but it broke up. Good professional life. Now, mildly depressed.

"Did anything bad ever happen to her?"

"No."

"What about her medical history? Did she ever go through an operation, or a dangerous illness, or something like that?"

"She had a 'giggle bladder,' but that was about all."

"What's that?" I wondered, never having heard the expression before.

"She wet herself if she coughed, or laughed, or ran hard down a hill. It turned out to be mechanical. She had a congenital stricture [narrowing] in her urethra."

"Hmm," I wondered. My "investigator" was waking up. "When did you notice this bladder condition and what did you do about it?"

"Well, let's see," she said. "My daughter was 2 when she was potty trained. Yet she kept coming up with damp panties. Our pediatrician sent us to a urologist, who said she needed a 'sounding.' That meant that they had to put a steel instrument into her urethral opening to expand it."

"Was your daughter anesthetized?" I asked.

"No, I don't think so. I wasn't allowed to be in there while the surgeon did the procedure. I guess she was about 3 when it was done. And she never had a problem afterward. But I remember hearing her screaming from the waiting room. I almost jumped from my chair and ran in. It must have been horrible for a minute or two, maybe longer. It was horrible for both of us."

Now, my "investigator" moved in for the kill. This episode sounded completely in sync with the memory that had suddenly come back to the woman's daughter. Could the young woman have confused Grandpa with the urologist? A child's mind is capable of great feats of remembering. But the child's mind is also capable—within those memories—of making significant perceptual mistakes.

"Is the urologist still in practice?" I asked.

"No," gestured the mom.

"Alive?"

"No."

"What did he look like?"

Something instantly lit in the woman's eyes. It took a second more for her to verbally respond.

"He looked just like my father!" she said. "An incredible resemblance!"

This was a "moment." Here was an adult, who wasn't even officially my "patient," and we were having a magical moment together. In a sense, it was a magical moment of detection.

"Go home," I said, "and talk to your daughter."

She did. She phoned me later to say that they had agreed. It had been a misunderstanding. The daughter, indeed, had belatedly re-membered a true event from her childhood. But she had not been able to grasp its purpose. And she had mixed up its perpetrator. The details were wrong. Much of the memory still existed in a preschool state, with the many errors a preschooler would have been expected to make. The daughter now understood her mom's and my solution to her mystery. And she was relieved.

Grandpa's reputation was left intact. It took three of us (and most likely a fourth, the therapist) to save it. The old man is still revered today.

This case makes me wish that every child having a medical or sur-gical procedure could be given a timely explanation beforehand and the chance to have a parent right there in the room! And I wish, too, that there could always be a later debriefing.

The "investigator," so romanticized in the mid-20th century, still lives in psychotherapy today. We must ask the occasional question, or we may never understand our patients. Such, sadly, was the case with young Annaliese—and who knows how many others.

Sometimes what one wonders about a child is unanswerable—largely because the sources to ask are all gone. Then, later, somebody pops up with an answer, despite one's pessimism about ever finding out what really happened. Such was the case with Cammie's dreaded "cats" and "sheep."

I'll jump ahead in Cammie's story, in just this instance, to describe how our discovery happened. Cammie was 8 years old. As I mentioned earlier, her foster mother, Sandra Brooks, was a recognized expert in foster parenting, having cared for over 50 kids prior to Cammie. One day after Sandra had given a talk on the subject, a woman approached the podium and asked her an unusual question. "Are you taking care of the little girl whose baby sister was bitten to death?" When Sandra nodded yes, the woman told her she was a cousin of Bonnie.

She then volunteered some information. "Bonnie's mom and dad were really mean and weird," she said. "I remember they used to slaughter sheep in front of that poor little child." (So "sheep die" really meant "sheep die"!) Bonnie's cousin went on to say that her own parents had been given an earful. "Bonnie's folks used to brag to my mom and dad, saying that they would catch stray cats on their property and then torture and kill them."

Two of Cammie's mysteries were thus solved in this one little conversation. But other mysteries simultaneously opened up. What was a psychotherapist to do when a patient implicitly mirrored the sadistic behaviors she had observed in her original home? And what was a psychotherapist to do with a young person who might have inherited sadistic, murderous genes from both sides of her family?

The work of an "investigator" practicing in the mental health specialties is not particularly clear-cut. Sometimes a pertinent question is produced without much thought. Other times, the investigation is carefully calculated. Clearly our detective work doesn't follow strict police-officer protocol. But an investigation of a young person is always based on our curiosity. In fact, curiosity is one of the best personal attributes we bring to our psychological work. Let's hope we always use it strictly on behalf of the child.

CHAPTER FOUR

A Real Person

Who am I "for real" this morning as I sit writing these words? I'm relatively "plain" today—a late-August Tuesday—not up, not down. The office is running well, although Scott, our assistant, is off on vacation in Arizona, and Jenny, our nurse, is out sick, a rarity. My husband is giving the allergy shots today, but he seems not to mind. Jim, our youngest staff member, is manning the front desk—in fact the whole place—by himself, and he's doing fine.

Physically, I feel okay. I'm scratching a few mosquito bites from our weekend up north, but that's it. Most of the professional people around the country whom I know and like are away right now. In a strange fashion, that feels a little lonely. I can't write or call anyone. But I'm used to this state of affairs every late August, so it's no big deal.

The weather, which always affects me, is foggy today. In fact, I can't even see Angel Island from my 25th-floor window. The light atop Alcatraz is blinking, but the fog is obscuring its tower. The Bay itself is bleak and gray. Ambulance sirens are screaming for unknown reasons around town. All this, however, is routine for this time of year.

Yep, I'm just feeling plain today. No dreams last night. No specific worries right now. My brother is on vacation in Wyoming. My kids sound fine on the phone. My dear cousin, Barbara, is sick—with cancer, in fact—but I have hopes for her recovery.[50] And I'm writing right now, an act that's always fun for me.

I take stock of myself—like this—most days. I don't want my general reality to impinge too greatly on my patients' realities. Today I'm just plain. So there's very little danger that my persona will impose itself on anyone else. But I think about it. Let's see—who is on this afternoon's calendar? There's a pretty full schedule of patients, although I obviously have *this* hour off. There's nobody I'm very worried about. No new patients to evaluate. No toddlers or preschoolers. Already, that takes a load off my mind. Nobody suicidal. Good. Charlise, an obsessive-compulsive teenager, would be coming in today after spending summer school at Andover. Two years ago (before I knew her), Charlise had had a miserable time, at another Eastern boarding school, feeling cut off from everything familiar to her in Northern California. This year, I'd asked her to phone me from Massachusetts if she developed any problems. She hadn't called. I figured that she'd had a good time back East.

So will I "lose my cool" today? No, I'd bet 100% on myself. In fact, I'd make that bet almost any day. But this doesn't mean that my patients will be blocked from glimpses of the real "me." In fact, despite any precautions I may take, patients will catch my tiny moments of self-disclosure, moments of reaction, moments of reality. And sometimes my moments will perfectly coincide with their own revelations and realities.

This morning, for instance, a number of parts of my own real life tacitly lay on the table for discussion with a patient—if needed. I found myself discussing a certain neighborhood with a young, single business woman who is about to move into her first apartment without a roommate. The ethnicity of the neighborhood, the distance from her mother, the safety, the feel of the block she is considering—all this was food for our thought. How did I know enough to keep up my end of the discussion? I live only three blocks away. Does my patient realize this? I'd guess that she does. With my next patient, a depressed woman, I discussed a small luncheon she'd given last Sunday in Palo Alto for her "significant other." Several of my acquaintances were there, it turned out. I've no comments about people I know or don't know, but my patient is aware that one of her guests is an old friend of my husband and mine from our Ann Arbor days. After all, he referred her to me. These types of little realities about me are always present, waiting to be discussed if a patient wants to—or needs to. Most of the time, however, they're just left to lie there.

Last Tuesday—now that's a different story! A couple of times I partially gave myself, my deeper self, away. It happened each time in a little spurt. And both times it happened with a child. One was an obsessive-compulsive girl, Laura,[51] who told me she had just found out who her next year's teacher was to be. Last year, when she was 9, the emerald-eyed oldest child of three had been so perfectionistic that she was unable to use the bathrooms at her school, even when she desperately had to urinate. As a result, she had suffered from repeated bladder infections.

"Who's your new teacher going to be?" I asked. "What's she like?" I hoped that Laura would use the better-than-bland descriptors that we had been working on throughout the summer, saying what she *really* thought and felt.

"Tough," Laura said. Good. "Ugly," she went on. Pithy adjective. A committed one, in fact.

"And what's ugly about her?" I asked, interested in this girl's analysis of women's looks.

Laura didn't answer, so I prompted her. "Her nose? Chin? Hair? Body?"

A second passed. "She's just old," Laura said, shrugging.

"God," I instantly exclaimed in a whisper. That was the "real me," complaining to the Good Lord for making my lifetime go by so quickly.

Laura quickly looked up. I was beginning to smile. She chuckled. Both of us started to laugh. Both of us were bemused by my reality. Laura's comment had reflected upon not one, but two adults—her teacher and me. If the teacher was a "little old," I was "very old." If the teacher was ugly because she was old, I had to be very, very ugly. That was the first really funny thing I ever heard Laura say, and my real self had blurted out "God" before I laughed. My amusement at her late-latency perspective on life strongly outweighed any pain I might feel about the aging process. She could recognize that the two feelings, mirth and sadness, did not rigidly have to be balanced in anybody of any age. This was something that Laura, the ambivalent perfectionist, needed to see for herself. My very real and unexpected exclamation had prompted a moment of understanding between us. The real, aging (and I don't think ugly) me and the growing (and aging) girl had experienced an instantaneous meeting of the minds.

The second latency-age child I saw last Tuesday was a boy of 12 who was almost fully recovered from an anxiety disorder. He had been treated entirely psychologically because his parents strongly objected to his receiving medication. Young Colin had a sex story to tell me this day. Over the summer, one of the boys in his private-school circle was trying to "teabag" any guy willing to take him up on it. I thought for a moment. For the life of me, I couldn't figure out what "teabagging" was.

The real me interjected, "Colin, what's teabagging?"

The tall, gangly boy turned red. Rusty hair, orange freckles, pink, pink skin. He had become a human sunset. "Do I *have* to tell you?" Colin begged.

"Well I just don't get it. Help me out here." Again I was revealing myself. I was apparently naïve to something that the 12-year-olds in Colin's all-boys school knew better than their decimals or fractions.

"Teabagging," he said, "is when a boy puts his balls in another boy's mouth. Get it?" He went on, "It's like a bag of tea inside a cup."

"That's a new one on me," I said, giving him another glimpse of the real me. Then I said something even more revelatory. "In adult life, teabagging is a kind of minor activity."

Colin laughed out loud. The redness receded. He was obviously relieved to learn that teabagging represented lesser stuff for grown-ups. I could actually feel his gladness, now that I had been frank with him. In fact, he then went on in much greater length about how dreadful it would have been if his sexually obsessed classmate had teabagged him. "What if I slept at his house overnight? What if I woke up with him doing something like that to me?" We worked on some avoidance strategies, like refusing overnights at that particular boy's house. And we discussed some other ways to handle the situation straight away—like an unconditional "no" or a deliberate punch to the

stomach if the boy tried to force him into it. Colin admitted to some
ambivalence—"That guy throws some great parties!" We giggled at
this latest addition. The trade off between party-attending and
teabagging might just not be worth it, we agreed. My willingness to
show pieces of my real self—when called for—had helped us through
what would have been a difficult conversation between any boy and
doctor, any male and female, any younger and older person. My revelations were sudden and delivered in a "blink." We had become better
friends because I had been real and open with young Colin.

On this foggy Tuesday afternoon, it turned out that my 17-year-old
returnee from Andover, Charlise, hadn't wanted to talk much about
her boarding school experience. It had been fun and she'd handled it
fine. Instead, there was a much more pressing issue that Charlise
wanted to discuss. (Bravo! This obsessive-compulsive young lady was
prioritizing which issues and which feelings were really important.)
Charlise and her boyfriend of 3 years had decided—once and for all—
to have sex. They had gotten around to it last weekend.

"How was it?" I asked, knowing that last spring, Charlise and
Freddy had discussed sex a number of times.

"A comedy of errors," she said. "Nothing worked. But I was so glad
we got it over with. And we feel really close now."

I nodded. "Most people find the first time to be awkward, strange,
and a little silly." Was I saying anything about the real me? Yes and no.
But I was being open and straightforward. "And feeling close," I said.
"That's really, really important."

Charlise and I felt close for the moment, too. She smiled. Our eyes
met in warm agreement. "They say," Charlise told me, "that on your
first time a chemical is released inside of you so you'll never forget it."

"I don't know about a chemical," I said. "But you don't forget your
first sexual experience because it's such an important moment in
your life."

That was really me talking. And it was really Charlise too. Her
obsessive-compulsiveness was beginning to give way. Inside, there
was a warm, glowing girl. I felt pleased at the end of my foggy, "plain"
day. Being real usually works better than most other personal strategies. Showing our realities is usually unplanned and spontaneous.

During these moments of revelation, the real doctor, I find, is a potent instrument of change.

Do parents act real with their kids? I sometimes wonder. I can't even count the number of mothers and fathers of preschoolers I've had to correct for speaking of themselves in third person to their children. "Mommy wants you to go upstairs now," she says. "Daddy's home, everybody," he says as he enters the back hall. How about "I," "me," and "you"? It's so much more straightforward. And this way a youngster does not feel condescended to. After all, we're all in the same world, so we might as well speak the same language.

Then, too, there's the business of family secrets. Why should a parent hide an upcoming surgical operation, for instance? The parent will be gone. There may be extra help in the house afterward. What accounts for the gifts of plants and flowers? The child will know that something has happened. And worse yet, the child will realize that the parent has kept it a secret. Most of the time, these episodes are benign—they don't represent cancer or near-fatal heart attacks. The benign episodes help a child recognize that good lives are full of detours and small pitfalls. All this prepares youngsters for their own lives. When the situation is much worse, children do need to know frankly that their parent is seriously ill. Getting ready and facing tough times together is still the best possible course of family action.

Family meals are a great time for each member to speak openly and frankly. Here, kids learn that help is available—not only from parents, but also from siblings. Here, too, they learn to tell a true story about themselves with a beginning, middle, and end. Hopefully everybody will hear suggestions, at times, for handling the politics and pains of everyday life. And here, hopefully, the younger members of the family will learn to cherish and protect what they glean from the openness, frankness, and reality they see and hear in their household.

The "real doctor" is a strange concept—even an almost self-canceling phrase. All of us carry a different "realness" in our personal lives than we take to the office or hospital. At home, we psychiatrists yell at our kids, vehemently discuss contentious issues with spouses, overeat, undereat, make inconsiderate and even selfish decisions, fall asleep at the theater, bang up the family car, miss the movie everybody wanted to see, forget to call our aging parents. You name it—if it's human and flawed, we do it. With our patients, however, we try to rise to the demands of our "best selves."[52] This, too, is the "real" us, but quite a bit better. And we usually don't tell our little patients about the aggravations inherent in getting our banged-up car fixed (unless there's context or a lesson for them in it). The friendships we make with our young patients are strictly one-way streets. All avenues lead to them.

In considering the doctor's persona, I've presented in the first three chapters of this book a number of examples of how the psychiatrist calculates in advance to act a certain way with a certain young person (being "positive," for instance, or always taking a "fun" approach). However, the majority of therapists, I would say, calculate simply to behave as their "better selves." Kids feel comfortable most of the time with "real" people. Real behavior holds up the best on a day-by-day basis. Then, when needed, a therapeutic switch to "teacher" or "investigator" works in seamlessly.

I've also shown at the beginning of this chapter how the real "me" turns up, even when I'm not thinking about it, in tiny, tiny doses. These little glimpses of our own grown-up realities are available to our young patients whenever they want to take them up with us.

But not all "real" moments are so tiny. Unsubtle, revelatory gestures and statements from highly qualified psychiatrists can have an enormous effect, as well. How do these highly dramatic moments of "reality" happen? What feelings from the doctor do they reveal? What do they elicit in the young patient? A sudden glimpse of something from deep inside the doctor may shake a child or adolescent out of a long-standing period of inertia. Depending upon the timing, the prior relationship, the young person's problems, and the immediate issues, an unexpected revelation may inspire an unexpected change. Yes, the young person may leave therapy. And yes, he or she may come back later, too (as did Dr. Peter Blos's patient, whom you soon shall meet). But other times the patient may join the doctor and immediately produce revelations of his or her own (as did Dr. Aubrey

Metcalf's angry teenager). The moment of amplified revelation usually comes in an instant. Within a couple of seconds the entire relationship changes.

For example, long ago, Selma Kramer, a highly respected child psychoanalyst from Philadelphia, told our residency group at Michigan about a special moment she had shared with a patient (I can't remember what this particular child's problem was). Selma used to see her young patients at her home after school. Upstairs, Dr. Kramer's children helped themselves to an after-school snack and were supposed to do their homework. One day, the Kramer children slipped out of their usual routine and were making a huge ruckus directly above the consultation room. The doctor silently fumed. After several minutes with no let up, she suddenly stood up, walked to the door, and yelled upstairs, "Would you please shut up!" Selma shocked herself. Her kids instantly became quiet. But the patient began to talk. "I liked that," the little analysand said. "You're a real mom. That was good!" And the patient immediately developed a better and more effective therapeutic tie to Dr. Kramer. Seeing the analyst's reality had completely changed the dynamics of the doctor-patient relationship.

Here's another example: A distinguished southern California psychiatrist, who shall remain nameless at his request, was trying for 2 years to establish a relationship with a young woman who suffered from depression and severe personality problems. The tall, athletic girl had been living with her aunt in a separate city from her parents because she was unable to get along with her two brothers and one sister, and because she was being groomed at a school near her aunt's home for women's basketball. Although her grades and basketball play were exemplary, coaches and teachers alike were concerned about her anger, stubbornness, bursts of suicidality, and fears of growing into adulthood. Her parents kept her on a short monetary leash, keeping track of almost every expense. Complaining about money, in fact, had become this girl's main subject of conversation with her doctor. One day she came to his office, complaining as usual, but then saying at midpoint that it was her 17th birthday. On impulse, the psychiatrist pulled five crisp twenty-dollar bills from his wallet. "For you," he said. "Why?" "A birthday present," he said.

After that unexpected, counterintuitive, and impulsive demonstration of the doctor's affection (about which he still feels embarrassed) the patient and psychiatrist entered an entirely new phase of treatment.[53] She confided. He helped. By the time she graduated the next year, the blond girl had turned around so dramatically that she went off on a full athletic scholarship to a well-known university with a well-known women's basketball team. She anticipated no further psychotherapy.

These two dramatic gestures differ from each other in several respects. Dr. Kramer became angry at people other than her analytic patient and then suddenly demonstrated her fury right in front of the patient. The doctor of the basketball player felt a surge of loving parenthood toward an angry teenager, and on impulse, he gave her the biggest, most surprising birthday present she had ever received. However, the *similarities* between the two acts are particularly striking. Both gestures were quick and unthinking. Both therapists had been very well trained, and they taught psychotherapy as well, so their intuitive behaviors were well grounded in knowledge and experience. Each doctor made what he or she believed was an embarrassing self-revelation to a patient. But each was able to wait for the patient's reaction and to use it to cement the relationship. The surprise and unexpectedness of the doctors' emotional expressions jarred the patients. In fact, each was jarred into a full commitment to the doctor and the therapy.

The intuitive emotional gestures psychiatrists make often indicate love, liking, warm affection, or parental concern (call it "Eros," if you want to). But they also may indicate rage, despair, a sense of failure, frustration, or fury (call it "Thanatos," if you'd like). These expressions, of course, represent the two basic drives (survival of the species and survival of the individual) that make the world go round. But with children—and in our responses to them—these drives are not expressed as pure sex or pure aggression. Instead, our feelings come out as "fondness," or "irritation," or both. I have not collected any vignettes expressing the pure drives unmodified. In fact, none of the moments sent to me—or the cases in my files—tell that kind of tale. You will find the doctors' gestures to be big, real, and undisguised. But the feelings they express are still subtle and entirely appropriate to the worlds of childhood and adolescence. No "boundaries" are crossed. No "boundaries" are even approached, for that matter.

The "real" gesture expressed in the following vignette comes from Peter Blos, Jr., of Ann Arbor. Peter was confronted with a very difficult situation in which an adolescent patient's mother had bribed her son with a sports car. Peter and his patient had been planning a certain course of action for some time. But the offer of the Corvette made their plan instantly obsolete. Peter, in utter frustration, said something "off the cuff." It was a real statement of the doctor's real feelings. His patient, although he left Peter shortly afterward, showed that he had listened carefully to Dr. Blos. The doctor's statement precipitated gradual movement toward action and away from inertia.

The Red Corvette

CONTRIBUTED BY PETER BLOS, JR., MD

George, the only child of highly intelligent, successful parents, was referred late in his sophomore year because of poor high school achievement, lack of friends, and general unhappiness. His parents were terribly distressed about their son's inability to use his intellect; their efforts to be supportive and exhort George to action had consistently failed. They believed that George lacked willpower. They could not see that George was suffering. The mother stated openly that George's failure reflected poorly on her as a parent; the father told me he found his son confusing.

Twice-weekly psychotherapy proved difficult for George. He had little to say and was convinced that I should tell him what to do. His sense of his own ineptitude and helplessness manifested in his transference to me. In turn, it stimulated in me the urge to rescue him. I tried not to, however. He often arrived late to sessions or fell asleep. These "helpless" actions were humiliating to George, and later he would sheepishly apologize. Despite such impediments, our work together gradually created some improvement in his academic work, and George began to experience a stronger sense of self.

Early in his senior year George decided to postpone college, get a job, and continue his psychotherapy with me. Although we recognized that this would upset his parents, we were totally unprepared for what came next. In January, George's mother suddenly offered to buy him a red Corvette if he would go on directly to college. Struggling to contain my sense of dismay at being surprised and outmaneuvered by George's family, I managed to comment, "I can't beat that!" In the ensuing sessions we explored the seductive power of the red Corvette. I told George that I was genuinely sorry about his change in plans, although I could certainly appreciate his wanting the car. We used the remaining sessions to bring his treatment to a close.

Two years later George telephoned. He had enjoyed the Corvette, gone to college, and promptly flunked out. He was now working days and attending night school. He wished to return to treatment with me. When I asked him how he would pay for his psychotherapy, his reply was swift and brief. "I'll sell my Corvette."

MEANING OF THE MOMENT

Two years elapsed between "our defeat" and George's triumphant return to treatment. This second time around, we worked on George's ambivalent ties to his mother and his disappointment with his father's passivity. The central point to George's turnaround was the very ordinariness of my "I can't beat that" statement. I couldn't compete with a Corvette. I neither was, nor needed to be, an omniscient figure in this young man's life.[54] My statement helped George to begin to experience himself and his family in a more individuated, peaceful, and successful way. When I last heard from him, George had finished college and had gone on to graduate training in a field of his choice. He never revealed—and I never asked—what car, if any, he drove.

Dr. Blos's pivotal comment, "I can't beat that," certainly came straight from the doctor's heart. In fact, Peter's statement carries much in common with Robert Burns's poetic idea: "The best laid plans o' mice and men / Gang aft a-gley." Of course, it was frustrating for Peter, as it would have been for any of us, to see a patient entirely unready for college being impelled by his family to go forward anyway. The statement the doctor made carried all of that concern for the boy, alongside his simultaneous irritation at the boy's mother for failing to understand her son's true needs. Interestingly, Peter's statement lasted far longer in the young man's mind than the car lasted in the young man's garage. It was a wonderful victory for life's intangibles.

Whereas Dr. Blos's comment to his high school senior patient was mixed—conveying both fondness and frustration—the next two vignettes, from Aubrey Metcalf and Maria Pease, are more one-sidedly aggressive. Despite this obvious aggressiveness, however, the patients immediately caught on to their doctors' concern for them. The therapists' timing was just right. In fact, I think that both young patients were "lying in wait" for these moments to come. Their doctors' frustrations were entirely warranted. Once expressed, the kids "got it" and immediately vowed to begin their long, tough journeys toward health.

Eating Humble Pie

CONTRIBUTED BY AUBREY W. METCALF, MD

When one works with adolescents one must be prepared for silence, refusal to admit even pressing needs, contradiction, and outright verbal abuse. Such behaviors are so wearing that they eventually may provoke a response from the psychiatrist that ends the treatment. This was nearly the case with John, the sullen, 14-year-old only child of an elderly pathologist and his attractive second wife. John had been forced to see me because of the upset he was causing at home and at school. He was a master of all exercises in negativity. His grades were poor but his intelligence was high. His insults flowed to friend and foe alike. He seemed to function from a mountaintop, looking down on his fellow humans as mere peons. This clinical picture suggested to me several types of serious disorders, including antisocial personality. But I remained completely in the dark about the reasons John behaved this way.

The boy's persistence in derogatory and disdainful exchanges came close to provoking me, in my exasperation, to counter with something I knew would be fatal to our work together. He maintained his characteristic bravado for weeks, while I exhausted all my techniques of engagement and doggedly restrained my retaliatory impulses. Finally he asked me a straight question that called for a straight response: "Why do I have to come here?" He listened to my answer and then contemptuously said, "You think you know all the answers, don't you?" I swallowed yet another devastating riposte. Thinking back to my own personal analysis, I spontaneously blurted out, "No, I don't have all the answers. But I do know something about my own deficiencies." Something unexpectedly was released in John. He said, "Well I know mine! I'm just a lump of shit."

MEANING OF THE MOMENT

My uncalculated but self-reflective response to John's question suddenly pried his low estimation of himself out from under his defiant defenses. He instantaneously saw that his negativity was brittle and only partially effective. John merely seemed *to have a personality disorder. Inside, he hated himself—and he* knew *it, now that he could hear himself say it aloud. I came to learn much later the origin of John's conflict. His father doted on this child and, in fact, unconsciously identified with his braggadocio. Dad had unwittingly encouraged John's behavior.[55] John's mother had been extremely, but unconsciously, critical of her husband's weaknesses, inadvertently punishing him by refusing to help him deal with the boy. The parents, though loving, had not been able to act authoritatively because of their own unconscious conflicts.*

From what he said to me during our dramatic moment, I could see that, far from being amoral, John was actually hypermoral. The boy's recognition of his internal situation changed the entire course of his treatment.

A Moment of Despair

CONTRIBUTED BY MARIA PEASE, MD

Brett was an almost 11-year-old boy who was quick to feel humiliated and rejected. He was far too aggressive. He attended a private school that was on the verge of expelling him. Still sucking his thumb in public, he recently had been found lying in a fetal position in a school closet. He twice ran away from class, and his school attendance was spotty. When angry, Brett had begun to say he was suicidal. Therapy had been recommended a year earlier, but the boy refused. His mother experienced great difficulty in setting limits; his father relied on shaming and physical punishment.

During his first session, Brett bolted as he approached my office door. The next time, we met in the waiting room for only a few minutes. Once inside my office, he kicked at my dollhouse. "Get me out of here," he pleaded with his mother, who had stayed with him in my room. "You are stupid!" he screamed at me. I respected Brett's unwillingness to engage with me, but I needed to assess his suicidality. I discussed this dilemma directly with him, and he gave me the few necessary, but short, answers. The next several months were mainly silent, punctuated by bursts of Brett's fury. Once he pitched his heavy, wheeled backpack down my long stairwell. More than once, he ran out. He kicked at me on the sidewalk when I found him.

Our turning point came after Brett announced at school, "Guns don't kill people. I do!" This potentially serious threat necessitated an emergency session. He was dragged in by his parents and kicked a hole in a wall along the way. He crawled under my office couch and began kicking and pushing it upwards with all his might. I was afraid I was losing any opportunity to build an alliance with this wildly angry boy. With desperation in my voice, I said, "Maybe we should try medication. Maybe what we are doing here isn't enough to help." "No," he screamed. "No medicine! I'll talk to you." He shrugged the couch off his back, stood up, and looked directly into my eyes. "I will give you five questions," he said with the ghost of a smile. And suddenly, he began to engage me in a game of wits.

MEANING OF THE MOMENT

As I desperately thought aloud about medicating him, Brett experienced this idea and my accompanying affect as a crucial moment between us. Did he see my gesture as a threat? I have wondered about it since, but I don't believe so. At the time, I felt as if I was giving up on being able to help Brett with psychotherapy—yet I didn't really want to give up. I was painfully ambivalent about what to do. I still wanted to help him. I think it was my intense emotional investment in Brett that finally got through to him. From that moment on, Brett chose to have a genuine relationship with me. He could get hurt in the process of healing, but he was now willing to take the chance. Two years after he began to work with me in earnest, Brett was elected the student body vice president of his school.

As these vignettes show, being real with a child (despite traditional admonitions to preserve psychiatric anonymity in order to prompt transference) is an excellent way to promote youthful change. The stories from Drs. Blos, Metcalf, and Pease stress the fact that sometimes a psychiatrist is impelled to say something negative about himself or herself. Drs. Metcalf's and Pease's cases also demonstrate that when the physician admits to a flaw or frustration, the young patient may suddenly abandon his "good guy/bad guy" approach to treatment. Interestingly, both Maria's and Aubrey's admissions of fallibility were made in a flash. This shows that instantaneous gestures—when made by a well-trained, experienced professional—often lead in a helpful direction.

This issue of the spontaneous, unplanned, almost instantaneous psychiatric gesture requires exploration at this point, though it will come up at other times as we move along. The *Washington Post* psychology writer, Malcolm Gladwell, published a very successful book in 2005, called *Blink*.[56] In it, he extolled the frequent brilliance behind the immediate impulse and the educated guess. Aiming ultimately at its usefulness for life—and for the business professions in particular—Gladwell made the point that in many situations, spontaneity outweighs deliberation.

When I translate Gladwell's ideas into the practice of child and adolescent psychiatry, I find that in doing psychotherapy, what Gladwell says is "right on." Many times, the instinctive gesture is the best gesture. In my own office, my carefully wrought strategies often wash out, though I continue to set them up so I know where my patient and I are going. (There's an old proverb on this subject: "If you want to make God laugh, tell him your plans.") But the plans also blend into the instantaneous moves I make in play and the spontaneous things I say to my young patients. Conscious deliberation is not lost. It just becomes more spontaneously put.

There's a danger, however, in taking spontaneity too far. Trainees in the mental health fields need to deliberate far more than they need to react. The whole idea is to take in an excellent training program, to be supervised by the best people you can find, and to read, read, read. Then, too, the idea is to accrue as much experience as you can get—see every kind of patient, or client, or normal kid, you can find. Much that you obtain during your years of training will be retained consciously. And even more will become unconscious, only to be dredged back up to consciousness with considerable effort or a striking reminder. But when the time is right—especially when a patient's unconscious ticks off something in your own unconscious—the patient will provoke a spontaneous gesture from you. These gestures may very well turn out to be indications of your own reality. They will also reflect what you know now and have learned before. But they will also surprisingly mesh with your patient's reality. The two of you will share the moment in what Mr. Gladwell would call a "blink."

The "real me," not "me the doctor," engaged in a "blink" with my wild little toddler, Cammie, when we first met. In fact, it ended up prompting Cammie's initial turnabout with me. It happened on the first day Cammie came to me. She was 2 years, 5 months old when she arrived for her appointment, eyes darting about, hands in motion, feet itching for somewhere to hop, pounce, run. We were alone. I had been warned ahead of time that she'd probably grab at my breasts or dive for my genitals. I waited for the attack. But I glanced down, while waiting, at Cammie's blue registration form. I wanted to calculate her exact age in months, not years.

Lo and behold! Her birthdate was March 27th. That's *my* birthday! I didn't even pause to think. "Know what?" I said. "We've got the same birthday!"

All motion stopped. It lasted at least a second. I could tell that this little whirling dervish knew exactly what a birthday was. Five months ago, back in the unpredictable month of March, Sandra and Tom Brooks must have made a wonderful fuss over Cammie. She had experienced her one and only birthday party in total safety. And she had enjoyed it.

Our eyes met for an instant. Was that the flicker of a smile? If so, it left as quickly as it came. But we had come to a meeting of the minds. Cammie liked her birthday. I liked and enjoyed the very same day. If you follow the logic of a toddler, that might mean that Cammie decided to like *me*.

My instantaneous revelation of my real self—and Cammie's flicker of a response to it—became a moment of change in her young life. I realized it only in retrospect. I came to see that month after month, time after time, this little youngster never made a move against my body, my privacy, my sensibilities, myself. No spitting. No vomiting. No grabbing. My realness in the first moments I met this child established me in a very special category. It had created a palpable instant of mutual understanding.

In his book *The Present Moment in Psychotherapy and Everyday Life,* Daniel Stern has explained this kind of seconds-long meeting of the minds as similar to the implicit understandings that develop between mothers and infants during feedings or play.[57] Cammie liked me enough—because of our implicit moment together—to change, but only in her behavior toward me. From now on, our relationship would be "human to human," not "beast to human," or even worse, "beast to beast." Because I revealed myself as a person the first time I met her, Cammie decided to be a "person" herself, at least with me.

I could now move my aims forward—helping her through our tea parties and Sandra Brooks's "Sally stories"—to achieving her second turning point, "being human in human society."

When a doctor admits to his or her own nature, or a birthday, or even something he or she owns, like a house or a car, how does the treater know that the time is right and that the patient will or won't respond? Sometimes the impulse to tell comes almost in a vacuum, as in my telling Cammie about the coincidence of our birthdays. Selma Kramer didn't figure out in advance how her analytic patient would respond to a holler into the upstairs reaches of her house. And I doubt that Peter Blos knew just how his patient would respond to an "I can't beat that."

But many, many times our young patients torment, or bug, or nag us into a self-revelation. Look back, for instance, at Aubrey Metcalf's and Maria Pease's experiences. Aubrey was attacked enough verbally by his angry, frustrated teenage patient to finally make that breakthrough self-revelation. Maria was almost physically assaulted by her late-latency patient, who egged her on until she had to let out her feelings.

This kind of bugging and nagging was no less intense in the following case of a tall, skinny boy who was car-obsessed and unabashedly nosy and who wished to know exactly what kind of automobile his psychiatrist, J. Michael Deeney, drove. Some of us might have responded earlier. But the point is that the patient questioned, bugged, and even spied until his doctor finally made a personal revelation. The doctor was reticent about this (and obviously a bit shy). But the patient would not let his doctor retreat. He would *have* to respond. There was no other choice. The patient indicated through his behaviors that the timing would be right, whenever the doctor would make his move. This is typical of many of these situations.

Classy Old Sportscar

CONTRIBUTED BY JOHN M. (MIKE) DEENEY, MD

Tommy was 14 and "sort of lost," his mother reported when she brought him for treatment. His father had earlier separated from the family to pursue a new career. His mother was a busy school-system administrator whose job kept her away from home long hours. Tommy, an only child, had few close friends and spent his time apathetically watching television and "hanging around" home. He didn't do much else—no smoking, drinking, or drugs, no community misbehavior, and not much going to school, either. When he did attend classes, he mostly daydreamed or napped. He was of at least bright average intelligence but described school as "boring." Tommy did enjoy being an authority on World War II–era ships and submarines, however, and he also avidly studied old sportscars. Clinically, he was depressed and vaguely angry but was unable to say much about his feelings.

On his second visit, Tommy spotted a classy older British sportscar in our parking lot and couldn't talk about much else. I am a shy and rather private person. I shrugged and mumbled a bit when he brought up the Jaguar, but in truth, it was mine. Tommy became more and more focused on my sporty "classic" as his weeks of therapy went by. I talked about it with him but did not mention the owner. Then one day, his mother brought him particularly early and he spotted me driving in. Our relationship instantly changed. He wanted to sit in the "Jag," to look under the hood, and, if possible, to go for a ride. I agreed, and we did have a brief ride, much to Tommy's delight. Of course he wanted another ride during his next visit, but I put him off with a "maybe someday" and an explanation that we were trying to do therapy in the office.

In the ensuing weeks, Tommy showed little interest in achieving any "insight." However, he became progressively more willing to talk to me about his life story, his relationship with his parents, and his problems at school. Over time, his school attendance vastly improved, as did the quality of his schoolwork. In silent trade for our vibrant discussions about my car, we talked about peers, teachers, sports, pop culture, and girls. At the school year's end Tommy was able to report that he'd earned much, much better grades. We took a longish ride in my car to celebrate. Afterward, Tommy especially enjoyed the sensation of sitting in the driver's seat as the car cooled off. We said a fond goodbye before he left to spend the summer with relatives. He did not return to treatment, nor did I phone to insist that he come back. I felt that our therapy up to that point had probably turned Tommy around.

MEANING OF THE MOMENT

Years later, I was surprised to encounter Tommy's still busy mother at an East Coast educational meeting with which I have professional connections. She reported that Tommy was doing well, and in fact was a manager in the Boston hotel hosting our festivities. She also wanted to share her opinion that it had not been my psychotherapy that had helped her son . . . it had been my car. She postulated that Tommy liked me and was willing to come regularly for treatment because I "shared" the Jaguar with him. He had improved his school attendance and grades in order to please me. I smiled. For whatever reason, Tommy had proven himself able to permanently utilize his relationship with me for the good.[58] *His dramatic change occurred perhaps because of his borrowed "toy," my car, but more importantly, I think, he changed because through the car, he had gotten to know me. One might consider this a "transference cure." But one might also consider this a cure within a real relationship to a real man who just happened to own a real nice old Jag.*

I can't agree with Tommy's mom in her analysis of the cure that my Oregon colleague, Mike Deeney, was able to effect in her son. She saw it as "Jaguar treatment." I see it as a cure through the reality of knowing and visiting with a good and psychologically knowledgeable man. Not every psychotherapeutic change comes through insight, new awareness, and cognitive reworking. Some comes from the relationship itself. Once Tommy forced Dr. Deeney, who had been well-trained in the psychoanalytic model of psychotherapy, into taking a "real" stance with him, his progress became obvious. It wasn't so much a matter of "Jaguar treatment" as it was a matter of a corrective relationship with a very fine psychiatrist.

The doctor's persona can take a number of forms, and probably does in any prolonged course of psychotherapy. All of these forms of "acting" and of "being" have but one goal in mind: the good health of the child. That old medical saying sticks, doesn't it? "First of all, do no harm." In all the chameleonlike changes in the doctor reported in the first section of this book, I haven't yet read or reread a story about a clinical situation where the doctor's motives included something other than the child's best interests. If the young person remains steadily at the forefront of the therapist's mind, whatever "persona" emerges from the therapist's conscious or unconscious will also meet the child's best interests. Some of these personal transformations, as engineered by the psychiatrist, are entirely deliberate and planned. But when a revelation of oneself bursts out without anticipation or full precalculation, don't despair. It may be that this unplanned moment will turn out to be the ultimate one that leads to an important childhood change.

Just after Cammie turned 4, Tom Brooks hired an investigator to talk to Nick in prison and to ask him to sign off his natural rights to his daughter. Without a pause for reflection, Nick put his name to the papers. As Sandra and Tom actively considered adopting Cammie, without knowing yet whether or not she was retarded, she turned up with a physical problem. She had dribbly urination. This required a "double setup" examination in the operating room of the university hospital where I teach. The gynecologist found extensive vaginal stretching and scarring inside of Cammie, but he did not have to surgically correct the situation. The other surgeon, a pediatric urologist, did need to make some corrections. He found urethral strictures. This particular scarring of the urinary system (and also around the anus) had been caused, he felt certain, by adult attempts to have some sort of sex with Cammie as a 1-year-old child. He surgically opened Cammie's urethra. It was a successful operation.

I phoned the surgeons. Would they please write a letter to the judge who, over the years, had been hearing various issues regarding Bonnie's and Nick's custodial rights? Would they describe what they saw, what they fixed, and how they thought the wounds got there? I knew that the judge would pay particular attention to a communication from the UCSF operating room. What better physical proofs could be offered 3 years after a series of attacks?

The implication here was that these particular injuries could not have occurred in an infant without a second parent participating, permitting, or grossly neglecting the child. The judge immediately saw this. He terminated Bonnie's parental rights, once and for all. Inviting Sandra and Tom Brooks to court that same day, he informed them of his decision and declared the little girl to be officially adopted. She now could be called "Cammie Brooks," and it would mean something.

I once asked Sandra whether she and Tom had been unable to have kids. "Sure we could!" she surprised me. "We just wanted, instead, to give a good life to children whose real parents couldn't or wouldn't do it!" When she was 4, I certainly didn't know if Cammie Brooks was destined for a "good life." But I did know that she had just been adopted into the best family a child could wish for. It was worth a celebration.

So I threw Cammie a real tea party, complete with freshly brewed tea, Mrs. Fields's cookies, the 19th-century Austrian child's china, Sandra Brooks, and my office staff. We joked—Cammie and I—about how there was little to no room that day for dolls. By then, however, every one of my dolls, including Mr. Nutcracker, Baby, and Snake, could qualify for a tea. Cammie had already taught them how to behave, or how to get help for themselves.

At the party, I remember joking, gently of course, about how different Cammie looked from her red-headed mother and blond father. She also looked different from her four adopted, mixed Asian, partly African-American, and Caucasian siblings. But we went on to speak about the Brookses being every bit as much a family—now that Cammie was adopted—as other families who all look the same.

Cammie beamed with happiness. She loved our party. But we had also imposed reality into Cammie's world of fantasy. The very realness of our adoption tea spoiled the playful idea behind her pretend. She never suggested playing "tea" again.

To be absolutely "real" with you, I didn't mind. Cammie had gotten about as much out of "tea" as I thought she could. I also knew she'd find something else to play. "The god of fun," who was in charge of my office, told me so.

Part Two

CREATING the "RIGHT" ATMOSPHERE

"The air nimbly and sweetly recommends itself."
— Shakespeare, from *Macbeth*, act I

CHAPTER FIVE

The Spirit of Fun

Today is Labor Day, but here in central Healdsburg, it doesn't feel like a holiday. There aren't many kids about—they must be back in school in their various hometowns. The big Spanish plaza, with its charming, old gazebo and huge redwoods, stands empty. There are sales at the chic stores around the square, but nothing really looks like it's asking to be bought and taken home. The atmosphere is bound to be better at Big John's, the organic market a mile's drive to the north. There, melons with evocative names like *Canary* and *Pure Heart* mix in perfect color harmony with 7 varieties of peaches, straight, super-shiney zucchinis, and enormous nectarines. The pride of John's, all the locals know, are the tomatoes, most of them from ranches, farms, and organic backyards less than 20 miles away. At least 8 different types, led by the show-off, *Mr. Stripee*, vie for my attention. Actually, it's produce that best conveys the true atmosphere of this all-American holiday—summer's drift into fall, man's work, nature's bounty, the luck of being born to this incredible land.

Atmosphere. That's what we child/adolescent psychiatrists hope to create for the children we treat. Most kids hate to go to their pediatricians, despite the fact that these fine doctors regularly give out sweets (after shots) and have child-friendly offices with small chairs, toys, and even televisions. Most pediatricians are very, very nice people. So why do kids hate going? They get hurt. They get em-barrassed. They are prey to procedures they don't understand, and they get frightened. Their mothers and fathers get talked to, and often they, themselves, don't. The whole affair may invoke a feeling of dread. In fact, I remember, as a kid, despising my Cleveland pediatri-cian so much that I made a conscious decision to avert my eyes from his face. No matter what, I looked away. It just so happened that he had three, maybe four, beautiful prints on his wall—of what I thought were Dutch children. I'd stare at them. I came to love those prints. Years later, as a doctor myself, I walked into a Florida antique shop and found the very same picture. What I had assumed were Dutch children were really Austrians. What I had thought were wooden shoes, weren't. But I remembered the figures and faces of the chil-dren perfectly, and I just *had* to have them over my desk. They're up there right now. I still stare at them, but this time with unmitigated pleasure. Do I avoid bad stuff, even today, by looking at those young Viennese faces? Maybe.

Do children feel scared when they sit in my office, even with that big, beautiful print of the Viennese children over my desk? You bet they do. In fact, I think the idea of a "shrink" or a "worry doctor's" of-fice scares them more than the pediatrician's does. *What happens in this place?* they wonder. *And who is this lady at the big desk?* They don't know if I do magic. They don't know if I read minds. They don't know if I'll take them into another room and undress them, give them a shot, or hurt them in other ways. Many times I have to explain myself—eye to eye—with a child. I don't examine anybody. I don't give medicines or shots. Sometimes I suggest a medicine to parents, though. They'll know about it if I do. I can't know a kid's thoughts un-less I am told. I don't touch or hurt. I'm strictly a "talking doctor." I like to help children with their worries. And I'll help their parents help them, too.

Reassuring talk doesn't do the whole job, however. To relax a child or an adolescent in a doctor's office, one must have a roomful of objects that are intriguing and fun. People, especially children, need to fuss with something while they talk. Spread across the tables and desks in my room are smallish objects to fiddle with. Small tile puzzles with a nice, smooth-feeling motion, a jiggling puzzle with tiny ball bearings that fall into holes, a magnetic troupe of acrobats you can pile into fantastic constructions, a smooth wooden box that opens to expose six or seven china cats and a mouse, a couple of tiny houses with babies in one and even tinier furniture in another, wooden circus figures capable of movement or dance, a rock collection, three Russian "matrushka" dolls (one of which opens to expose two smaller dolls, each inside the other), three little Japanese fantasy beasts, none bigger than a watch face, and a painted soldier whose string you can reach from your seat on the couch to move both of his arms and legs—these are just a few of the curiosities I've collected over the years.

In other words, you can fuss like crazy in my office. But I don't want you fussing so much that you can't talk. I'm a "talking doctor," right? And I'm a kind of kid myself. I love all sorts of "kid" things. I make strange little collections. All of these comfort my little charges. Sometimes the children I see, in fact, want to add to the collections themselves.

Take my rocks, for instance. Annaliese's little sister, Trudi, brought me a piece of found glass from a beach near her stepdad's airforce base. It's still atop my desk next to a chair for my patients. The heir of an old American fortune brought me an Indian arrowhead from a beach on an almost empty island his family owned in the Caribbean. A traumatized little girl from Southern California brought me an uncut watermelon tourmaline from the Pala Mines east of San Diego. There's fluorite, calcite, and hematite on my desk. There's a plastic "diamond." There are fossil fish, a cut trilobite, a whole trilobite. Crinoids from England sit side by side with baculites from regions unknown. The rocks, stones, fossils, and shells feel good in one's hand. They get piled and moved around several times a day. Nothing gets stolen, not even the semiprecious tiger eye. And kids keep adding to the collection. A little girl painted a face on a smooth stone and it's stayed there for a quarter century. Last month, a boy found a rock for me that's shaped like a heart.

My blue and white office, in its own way, is a seductive place—a place you want to come and sit down in. All around are things I cherish. I assume others will like them, too. Once, a strange and ironic event occurred around my rocks—in fact, it probably represented a childhood moment of *no* change, I'm sorry to say. A 10-year-old fourth grader, Dennis, was brought to me for evaluation because he was indulging in a number of washing rituals. I saw him a couple of times, and each time he headed straight for the chair next to my big desk where the rocks are on display. He would grab a few stones—the ones he thought looked the most like "jewels"—and stroke, eye, and admire them as he spoke with difficulty about his feelings, his family, and his peers. This was a boy in pain, and I suggested to his parents a course of once-weekly therapy, along with some medication. His mother and father, however, had distinctly different plans for his rehabilitation, which didn't involve psychotherapy at all. "We've taken a page from *your* book, doctor," his mother phoned me later to say. "We've bought Dennis a gem collection. He liked the one in your office so much, and he improved so much while he was using yours, that we think his own semiprecious stones and polishing wheel will do the trick." I tried to argue a bit, but to no avail.

The three-piece Russian matrushka doll I mentioned earlier had such a prominent head scarf that she took on the configuration of a perfect cone. There's something intriguing to a child in picking up an object that looks, shape-wise, to be an upside down ice cream cone, but that turns out to be a painted woman. Intrigue appeared to have been the impetus for 4-year-old Cammie to pick her up when she came in for her session following the adoption party. Cammie inspected Madame Matrushka and declared her to be "Lil Red Riding Huud." Her declaration came in a voice that no longer growled, but still sat a little too far south of normal.

Cammie could now easily manage the sliding wood doors to my toy shelves. Knowingly pulling them open, she took out a raccoon puppet she had never used before. She pronounced him "Wolf." Wolf pounced on an invisible "Grandma" whom we couldn't see and killed her. Next he fell upon Little Red Riding Hood and ate her up. Boy, was this grim! Did Cammie have any more of this sort of play in her? She sure did!

As a matter of fact, Cammie launched into a ritualized monthly game of "Little Red Riding Hood." Wolf killed off Grandma as an automatic event; because Grandma was never depicted by an actual doll, I figured she stood for Cammie's dead infant sister, Bethany. As for Little Red Riding Hood herself, she was bitten repeatedly by the voracious beast of the forest. Rather than identify with the poor bitten victims, however, Cammie showed me that she had developed a penchant for "identifying with the aggressor."[59] Now that she was developmentally able to employ this defense, she gloried in its use. She enjoyed herself heartily on Wolf's behalf. She licked her chops, smirking month after month, over his cheap victories. What could be more feral than this? I strove to see how we might change the atmosphere in Little Red Riding Hood's forest—and, thus, in my office—but Cammie and I needed time for that.

It helps the atmosphere in a child/adolescent psychiatrist's room if the doctor is always ready and willing to play. How many mothers and fathers can stop what they're doing to horse around, hang out, and have fun? This, therefore, represents a nice contrast between us and parents. Play sets the psychiatric office atmosphere apart from all other spheres in a child's life. The idea of infusing the spirit of play ("fun") into what one does as a therapist is so important in working with kids that sometimes the therapy won't truly begin until that particular spirit is established. In 1971, the British analyst D. W. Winnicott wrote that psychotherapy depends on a doctor who can play and on a patient who, if necessary, can be taught to play.[60]

Here's an example of what both Winnicott and I mean. It comes from a Berkeley, California, psychiatrist. Henry Massie had been asked to see a teenaged girl whose main caretaking parent, her dad, was deployed in combat in Iraq. You can imagine how frightened the young girl felt. But Dr. Massie had a sudden spurt of an idea of how to battle her extremely negative attitude.

A Pleasant Hour

CONTRIBUTED BY HENRY MASSIE, MD

Teresa, a high school freshman, was referred because of collapsing grades, shoplifting, and a relatively recent change from loving to surly. She had been caught drunk with a girlfriend on the edge of campus. Her problems began during the year her father—a noncommissioned officer—was fighting in Iraq and she, therefore, had to live in Berkeley with her widowed grandmother. Although she previously had stayed successfully for brief periods at Grandma's, she was now misbehaving badly. Teresa had grown up on army bases with her father because her mother (a teenager when she gave birth) had abandoned them. Recently, her father had become doubtful about whether Teresa could live with him again once he was relocated "stateside." He didn't know if he would be able to manage her.

In her first appointment, the 14-year-old, physically mature and wearing supertight jeans, hid inside the hood of her sweatshirt. She provided only affectless, monosyllabic utterances. Her grandmother joined us later—a duenna *dressed in black, hair in a severe bun—and she then recounted a long list of Teresa's many failings. Our key moment occurred toward the beginning of Teresa's second visit, when I decided on a new goal—make the hour pleasant for both of us. Gesturing at the toy shelf, I asked if she'd like to play. Her face lit up, but she deferred the choice to me. I sat down on the carpet with "pickup sticks"—a game of patience, skill, and strategy—at which Teresa immediately excelled. After a short silent period, she brought up the big picture (something I had avoided because of her prior reluctance to talk). She wanted to live with her father, she said, while adeptly manipulating a stick. "But I bet he will make me take a virginity test. I won't do that! I don't do sex, though." She mentioned her own virginity casually, but jumped back almost immediately to the subject of high school. "I get in trouble [there] because being cool is the way to have friends. I know it's wrong. I know my grandmother cares about me. But she keeps me in a prison." By this time Teresa had amassed the winning pile of sticks.*

MEANING OF THE MOMENT

In 1962, Peter Blos wrote about the unevenness of adolescent development, explaining that physical maturity and various cognitive and emotional capacities often leapfrog each other.[61] *It is easy to forget that there is still a child with whom to ally inside an angry, adult-appearing teen. In my moment with*

Teresa, I decided to join the "child" in play. This motivated her to lay out the nature of her problem and its potential solution. Later I met with her grandmother and explained how hard it was for a girl to grow up abandoned by her mother and stranded in a new community. Teresa worried every day about her father, who was in harm's way. This led the contrite grandmother to weep and admit that she needed to soften her approach.

Within weeks, Teresa joined her returning father at his Texas army base. Several months later, I learned that she had decorated the bungalow he had purchased in their military town. School was going well, and Teresa now owned and took good care of a horse, a dog, and a cat.

One can see how the minute Dr. Massie switched his gears to "play," the teenager matched him move for move. It created an immediate moment of mutuality of actions, goals, and regard. It literally allowed affection to flow directly between doctor and patient.

In this case, floor play was a marvelous extra, and it worked well with this particular adolescent. But it's not for all of us. If you prefer not to play on the floor, a set of space-saving "nesting" tables can be an ideal solution. In one tight package, the therapist has a group of small tables that can be lined up for car play, doll play, a tea party, or a puppet show. Consider, too, having a portable box filled with trays of cars. A "whole world" can be set up on the little tables. And, if the psychotherapist owns a movable desk chair, he or she—still seated on the chair—can move along with the child and join in the play. In Italy, I bought a collapsible dollhouse that easily sets up atop my tables. I found five fabulous dinosaurs in a museum shop. What a fight can occur on those tables! A collection of Star Wars figures that sat unclaimed in the lost and found box in our office eventually became an important part of my play space as well.

Speaking of play tables, a Jungian sand-tray table fits well into this scheme. Many therapists swear by them. The sand tray is attractive and intriguing. It's fun for a kid to add another, and another, and yet another beautiful figure into the mix. And it's fun to move the sand about with one's hand and touch all of the interesting textures available on the tray. Variety is key, however, so I wouldn't suggest relying solely on the tray.

One of my northern California colleagues, Stewart Teal, from Davis, uses a chalkboard in his office. How the child patients respond to the board depends on the particular person, however. You'd assume kids would want to draw with the chalk—but sometimes they prefer an eraser fight!

Chalk Dust

CONTRIBUTED BY STEWART TEAL, MD

Four-year-old Carson was referred to me because of his aggression toward other children. A large child, his physical attacks were so severe he was unable to be around any youngsters his age.

The parents agreed that the onset of this behavior was very sudden and had started at a Christmas party soon after his third birthday. Shy at first, he began physically attacking the other 3-year-olds, forcing his parents to stop the party. Prior to the party his interactions with other youngsters had been cordial but not very interactive. Carson's parents reacted very differently to his problem. His mother was extremely worried. She could see he was not going to be able to attend kindergarten. His father, a rancher, minimized the behaviors of their only child. He stated that he, himself, had been much like his son as a child and had been able to manage to get through school anyway. The father also acknowledged he had few friends as a child. Even now, he much preferred involvement in his work to being social.

Carson presented as very intelligent—in fact, he had taught himself how to read. But he had limited social skills, and when he became frustrated with a task he would reach for the closest toy in my playroom and throw it with great force in an unpredictable direction. When I expressed my concern about his dangerous behavior, he did not know what I meant. He seemed to have no understanding of what my facial expressions, tone of voice, and body posture were intended to convey. There was a void where his capacity for empathy should have been.

Although he was a bit clumsy, there were no defining neuro-logical symptoms.

I set out to establish a therapeutic relationship and to teach him empathy skills. I began seeing him weekly and spent 15 minutes at the end of each session with his parents. The father seldom attended.

For the first 6 months of therapy, Carson remained unin-volved. He drew high-action pictures, mostly circular scrib-bling as he narrated violent conflicts between aliens and ro-bots. When I met with his mother we discussed modeling nonverbal communication for him and using stories that em-phasized social understanding.

I have a blackboard in my office that Carson occasionally used to draw his repetitive pictures. One day, when he seemed particularly involved with his circular scribbling, I inter-vened. "Carson, those aliens are really angry today."

He stopped mid-scribble, grabbed the eraser and furiously erased the picture. He then attacked me in a cloud of chalk dust, slapping the eraser with one hand while holding it with the other. When he attempted to hit me in the face I took the eraser out of his hand and lightly slapped it about a foot from his face.

"Gently, like this, Carson," I said.

He stiffened. I gave him the eraser and held his hands in mine. Together we slapped it, raising a new cloud of chalk dust. He looked right into my eyes and a huge sweet smile I'd not seen before spread across his face. We took turns gently slapping the eraser at each other. This became a ritual, re-peated at the end of each session, for the next 3 years.

MEANING OF THE MOMENT

This interaction demonstrated a new concept for Carson— aggression could be controlled, shared, and fun. It opened a new dimension in his life, a meaningful relationship with an adult male who could help him learn the social skills he needed in order to manage his world.

When we finished treatment there was no evidence of any psychopathology. Initially I had wondered if Carson had been

*traumatized, but no history was ever uncovered. I concep-
tualized his problems as neurodevelopmental. However, in
Carson's case the treatment seemed curative. This was possibly due to the plasticity of his nervous system and the family
intervention.*

In many ways, Stewart Teal's patient, young Carson, resembles the
adolescent girl Henry Massie evaluated while her father was off fighting in Iraq. Both children were relatively fatherless, though Carson's
dad lived with him on the family ranch. I don't know whether the father's lack of involvement made the young boy particularly angry, but
it does give us another piece of data to throw into his diagnostic pot.
Whatever the diagnosis was, however, here was a situation in which
Dr. Teal's playful office atmosphere created a "moment" between doctor and patient. They mutually recognized the significance of their
moment together, and interestingly, they arranged to celebrate it
with a ritual at the end of each session that followed. The chalkboard
and erasers allowed them to miniaturize the boy's horrible battles into
smaller skirmishes marked by sneezing, powdery faces, and suddenly
graying hair.

I believe that miniaturization is one of the biggest reasons that play
works so well in coping with human problems.[62] When the world is
seen on a small scale—from above, as in "child's play," or from dark-
ness into light and from back to front, as in watching a play performed
on a stage[63]—one sees gigantic problems from afar. This enables a
person to consider the wholeness of a problem, not just the details. It
lets the person separate a bit from himself and see the world from
other points of view. It allows him to feel, not just to think, or to deny.
And rather than suffer, the person can relieve himself of the problem,
at least tentatively, by having some fun with it. The effect is a relief of
emotional burdens—a "catharsis," if you will.

All of us recognize, on the other hand, that one can't use play alone
to work out the diagnostic and treatment puzzles one encounters with
young patients. All along, you are asking and re-asking yourself about
the diagnosis and the formulation. Week after week (or with Cammie,
month after month) as you play, you also want your patient to talk.

Sometimes he or she talks about the creatures in the pretend world you have established. But all along, you are trying to discuss the real world and the child's real problems, too. "How are things?" you ask. Or, "I heard you were sick last week—tell me about it." "So school must be starting," you say, letting your voice trail off. Then you wait. Hopefully your little charge takes over with talk as well as play.

Some people, however—especially those who've had very hard lives—demonstrate a number of problems talking about real life. The therapist can respond by teaching language through the medium of play and then personally transporting this language into the new medium of straight talk about realities. My plan with Cammie, when she was 4, was to start helping her to experience human feelings while playing "Little Red Riding Hood." Through her tea parties, I had first shown her that some solutions existed for terrible events. I had allowed her to see that society helps to prevent and change bad situations. This kind of work fit largely into the scheme for fixing trauma that I call "correction." But I had yet to observe Cammie emotionally express much about the trauma she had experienced. I thought she needed to learn the particular language to express these feelings ("abreaction"). And then later, of course, we might get to what I consider the third important element of trauma psychotherapy, "context." (With Cammie, these three elements of trauma treatment took place in the order I just outlined. However, there is no set order in which they always must occur.)

First, I defined Wolf's emotions for her, as Cammie enjoyed Wolf so much more than the other characters in the nursery tale. "Excitement." "Joy." "Anger" at Little Red Riding Hood for her lack of cooperation in being killed. "Fury." "Rage." "Impatience."

And what about Little Red Riding Hood's feelings? "Fear." "Horror" as she realized she might be eaten up. "Despair" or "sadness" at realizing Grandma was dead. Cammie caught on quickly. She began to use the right words for Little Red Riding Hood—and at home, she began choosing these kinds of words in her "Sally stories," which were still going on before bed. Every once in a while, at the family dinner table, Cammie even used an emotional word to describe her own life or an immediate feeling.

No matter what Little Red Riding Hood felt, however, Wolf was Cammie's ultimate victor in my office. He monotonously killed off the fairy-tale heroine, regardless of what the little crimson-caped girl did to try to save herself.

Cammie was 5½ years old. She finally seemed ready to face school in the fall. She had a good vocabulary for her feelings. She could behave herself at the mall or on a picnic. Her voice was hitting alto range. There was a tiny fundamentalist Christian private school that had been kind to a few of the children Sandra had previously cared for. Why not give it a try?

We all felt some trepidation about entering Cammie into kindergarten. But one couldn't wait forever. We'd just have to take the plunge. Hopefully, the atmosphere at school would be "right" for her.

As you may have already noticed, there was a technical difference between the way Drs. Massie and Teal played with their patients and the way I played with little Cammie Brooks. Drs. Massie and Teal talked to their patients about their real lives as the patients played pick-up sticks and "chalk wars." With Cammie, on the other hand, I talked about Wolf, Grandma, and Little Red Riding Hood, not Cammie. In other words, I stayed inside the play and did not tie my comments to Cammie herself. The first technique, moving out of a child's play to talk directly to the youngster, is the one that was favored by Anna Freud and her followers. The second, remaining entirely inside the play, is the technique recommended by Melanie Klein, the rather unusual psychoanalyst who lived in London at the same time as Miss Freud and who is usually credited as the originator of play therapy.

Luckily for us, even though the two pioneers of child psychoanalysis would have lined up on opposite sides, we can use both techniques, sometimes in the very same session.[64] Having previously commented, "Wolf enjoys scaring Little Red Riding Hood," one might say later, "Sometimes when you fight with your brother, you get the same sort of excitement," especially if the play is not as "stuck" as Cammie's was. The psychotherapist has ample opportunities to see which of the two basic play therapy techniques, and in what combinations, works best.

Interestingly, in Stewart Teal's vignette about his angry preschooler, Carson, the therapist starts his play interpretations by commenting on Carson's aliens being angry. The little boy becomes even more enraged as he hears this interpretation (inside the play itself). Then Dr. Teal speaks directly to Carson, not to the aliens. "Gently, like this, Carson," he says. That works much better for Carson. Within a couple of seconds, the doctor and patient have experienced their moment together. They know it and celebrate it afterward, time after time.

Sometimes a child cannot relax enough in the doctor's office to play at all. Or the play may be too stilted and unmovable to accomplish much. Over the years, one sees some cases that simply *have* to be moved outside the office atmosphere. Kids are sometimes taken on walks by their doctors. They are accompanied to a city or suburban park (if it's nearby). A toy store that used to be directly across from my office served as a great place for me and the occasional child to walk, discuss, wish for, and fantasize. Over the years, various kids and I supplied my office with soldiers and war equipment from that store. At one time, outdoor glass elevators offered a unique experience, and the huge one at the St. Francis Hotel became a destination for me and the occasional youngster. In other words, one needs to improvise on one's atmosphere with the very anxious, hyperactive, or neurologically impaired child. If he or she cannot sit on the office chair—or floor—the treatment might have to be taken outside the office.

In this spirit, take a look at George Stewart's vignette about a neurologically handicapped boy who needed the fresh, "sweet" Berkeley air outside of George's office to "lighten up." Note how the world outside—the cat, the guys at the auto shop, the candy sellers—becomes, in a sense, the primary object of the child's and doctor's play. Interpretations are made about the outside world, not about the boy. The boy picks up on these interpretations and observations in order to understand his own inner world.

Xootr Therapy

CONTRIBUTED BY GEORGE STEWART, MD

Nicholas was an 8-year-old handful when he came to me. He was having terrible tantrums. Homework and bedtimes were huge struggles. He couldn't get along with his loving and consistent parents, who had adopted him as a "preemie." Nick had serious neurological problems. Rather than sitting for meals, he grazed at least five times a day while on the go. He was "a little hurricane," a thrill seeker, who set up vestibular stimulation by standing on his head or whirling. He sought cold baths to calm himself. He inevitably wet the bed. Of normal intelligence, he was a precocious reader but had difficulty with any emotional content or complex ideas. He couldn't get along with other kids. He was medicated with stimulants, antipsychotics, and selective serotonin reuptake inhibitors (SSRIs) in various combinations. His parents were not at all convinced they worked.

When Nicholas began his psychotherapy, he was being mainstreamed in a small, structured private school. The tiny, undersized boy had been given a desk separate from the rest of his class, facing a wall to decrease his stimulation. In my office, he referred to himself as "an alien." He said "no" to virtually anything I said.

After a few impossible months of trying to start some sort of psychotherapy, I decided that Nicholas and I should take our therapy outside the office.[65] I usually ride to work on a Xootr, a sturdy folding scooter with a handbrake. With Nicholas's dad's permission, the boy and I took off on the scooter for the local candy store, Sweet Dreams. It became our routine. Nick would choose a dollar's worth of candy, and then we'd cruise to the local toy store, where he'd explain the latest games and gadgets to me. The variations became endless. We met "Chalky," a cat who loped along our route, and we grieved for Chalky when he no longer appeared. We exchanged knowledge of the flora we passed. We set new coasting records. We got permission from John (of John and Tony's Automotive) to take a thrilling shortcut through their lot, sneering at the little yappy dogs next door. All along, we talked about Nicholas's week, his friends, his travails, his concerns. I taught him how to comport himself at a candy or toy counter, or when he (or I) encountered a friend.

We continue our routine to this day. If it is raining, we either drive in my car, an inferior vehicle for this purpose, or spend the hour in my office. Eleven-year-old Nicholas has become comfortable enough in my office that he occasionally loses himself from the beginning in imaginative play (which we try to discuss and understand), or in conversation about current issues (which we also try to discuss and understand). He is doing much better now with friends and at school, having made the successful transition to "upper school." He also has become able to talk effectively about his feelings. His bed wetting and temper tantrums have become rare events. Although Nicholas still needs my help facing new developmental challenges and the "politics" of childhood, his improvement has been remarkable.

MEANING OF THE MOMENT

Weekly adventures have provided a very difficult boy with containment and pleasurable physical proximity. They have presented enough stimulation and thrill to keep him engaged in treatment. Our outings have gradually allowed us to develop a relationship based on mutual enjoyment and shared responsibility for safety. Nicholas has had opportunities to learn social skills through his visits to two local shops and his engagement with pets and people along the way. These days I very much look forward to Mondays at 4:30 P.M., as does he. I'd recommend—if you don't have a Xootr—to try the same sort of adventure with the "right" child on foot!

Was there an actual moment here? I think so, though there was no meeting of the eyes or a sudden gushing from the well of talk. Here, George Stewart made a sudden, unexpected decision to take the therapy outside the office. This, I believe, was the "moment." George would share his scooter. He would share the outside environment. He would share his commentary on the relationships, feelings, and actions of the living things within the hundred-or-so acres around his office. If the child soaked up this condensed atmosphere, he would be far better able to handle the world's atmosphere.

Do we routinely help parents create playful enough atmospheres in their homes? Sometimes, I think, we neglect or ignore how important play is inside of families. And we also forget how difficult it is for busy parents, struggling to earn enough money to support their families, to provide the kinds of playful atmospheres we hope for. We must continually remind ourselves—and the families we treat—to make the time and the effort to play.

Certain activities lend themselves to the whole family's participation. Others are virtually solo. We have to help parents see that coaching soccer isn't necessarily a family activity, even though Junior may be a member of the team. A ski trip in which the parents ski the adult runs while leaving the kids in ski school is not necessarily a "family" vacation. On the other hand, if everybody fishes (and talks), hikes (and stops to look and talk), or sits on a beach (and plays around and talks), the family is truly setting up an atmosphere that encourages play. Play is "fun" by definition. It is a mental or physical activity that is directed solely at having fun. So if Dad's the soccer coach and he and Junior chew the fat several times a week about the ins and outs of soccer, it might actually be "play" after all. It all depends upon how it's done and what spirit it imparts.

Most family play is informal and happens over the dinner table, over the bathtub, over the phone, over the blankets before bed. The leading tools are the story, the joke, the playful conversation, or the song. All that informal stuff sets up an atmosphere, a tone. It not only helps us psychiatrists do our jobs, but also helps all the children we never even are asked to see.

Play is the language whereby two separate individuals can find a unity of communication.[66] Nothing could be more disparate among humankind than an adult psychiatrist (sophisticated, well-educated, worldly, perhaps of a different gender or culture) and a young child (naïve, not-yet educated, tied to home). Yet through play, these two people can find a togetherness, a singleness of purpose, a number of shared feelings, a sense of fun. Play can be used therapeutically as a neutral medium into which small phrases about life can be inserted. Play can be used as a metaphor. It can be used to teach metaphors to those who can't yet use them. All of these play functions aid in the process of childhood change. To start, however, a playful atmosphere might just be what is needed to get a kid simply to walk into your office.

CHAPTER SIX

Waiting Games

Traditionally, in doing insight-oriented psychotherapy with mildly to moderately disordered adults, the underlying idea has been to "wait the patient out." Yes, the doctor makes interpretations, linking the patient's transference to his or her behaviors, either in the past or present. Yes, the doctor also helps link the patient's current loves and hates to old hankerings or conflicts. But achieving full insight into the many ways an adult patient's inner psychology works traditionally has been left up to the person being treated. It often takes an adult months or years of therapeutic effort to achieve this kind of thorough, self-driven, personal understanding—and even more time to set up new patterns of action or to put an end to symptoms.

The customs in child and adolescent psychotherapy flow from adult practice. The fact that child work is a subspecialty of general (adult) psychiatry certainly feeds into this. As one trains as a child/adolescent psychiatrist, one spends the first 2 or 3 years treating adults. Adult treatment is the basic skill and source of knowledge by the time one turns to treating younger people. As a result of this training, child practitioners carry an innate understanding and an innate patience with the idea of the "waiting games."

One of the best examples of waiting games that you will find in this book is the case of Tim from Chapter 1. Tim, an incarcerated teenaged sexual perpetrator, was consistently given rewards and kudos by his doctor, Bill Sack. But the other striking consideration in Tim's turnabout was how long Bill waited for this boy to start changing. Rather than trying to elicit affect, in fact, Bill tells us that he simply decided to be patient until Tim showed him where he wanted to go. The doctor innately understood that pushing this particular boy would not help.

But waiting does not often fit in well with today's child and adolescent psychotherapy. The current trends indicate a quicker, more directive style of response. Waiting, in fact, has turned out in recent years to be an exception rather than the rule. With Bill Sack's patient, for instance, the rest of the staff at the juvenile institution where Tim was an inmate took an activist, nonwaiting stance with the 16-year-old. This is fairly usual. The boy was constantly looking for— and receiving—punishment and restraint from his ward workers and case managers. Dr. Sack, however, consciously decided to wait the boy out, and his wait took an entire year. It was well worth it. A boy who might have become a repeated sex offender turned completely around.

We can easily imagine the pressure a person like Bill Sack might have felt from the staff at the juvenile institution where he consulted. There is such a scarcity of child psychiatrists around the United States (and in the world!) these days that the demand for our services often outweighs the luxury of waiting with a certain single child. Larger institutions dealing with kids' lives—social agencies, educational services, courts, pediatric facilities—are unwilling and sometimes unable to settle into *inaction*. They must create ultimate dispositions for large numbers of kids. They often require from their consultants an immediate plan, based on the best guess of what would work.

A great deal of pressure to do something fast also comes from the individual child's development itself. If the march toward emotional maturation becomes curtailed in one phase of development, it will become distorted, or sometimes even stop, by the next phase. As any child takes on this inevitable march to maturity there isn't very much time to wait.

Other than the time involved in waiting a child out, there is also the question of the psychotherapeutic goal. Is it—as with adults—insight?

Heaven help us child and adolescent psychiatrists if it is! Kids are no-toriously poor at understanding what is or was wrong with them. They are notoriously poor at grasping what was done with them and to them in treatment. "We just played," is a typical after-the-fact analysis of what happened between doctor and patient. On top of that, kids are not particularly forthcoming talkers. To get them to open up, the child psychiatrist often has to become very direct—in other words, to take an active stance. The treater of young people, therefore, doesn't tend to wait for talk, insight, and understanding the way that an adult practitioner would.

All in all, today's practice in child and adolescent psychiatry is to wait less, not more. This doesn't mean, however, that we treaters of children shouldn't ever stand still. When there is no option other than to wait, the practitioner just stays where he is. The ambiance in his office becomes one of pleasant, nonpressured endurance.

Here is an example of what I mean. Ken Braslow, a young psychia-trist in training, and his supervisor assessed an angry adolescent boy who could not get along inside his family. Although the boy had gone through one trial of family therapy before, the resident physician had many reasons to believe that another try would be successful. Neither the boy nor his parents went along with the doctor's idea. Rather than offering something else, however, Dr. Braslow decided to wait the three of them out. No other options would be put on the table. Ken's conscious decision to temporize until the family achieved a certain level of insight led to a dramatic change in his teenaged patient.

Beginning in Midstream

CONTRIBUTED BY KENNETH BRASLOW, MD

Timothy, a big, strong, 14-year-old eighth grader, had been adopted at 3 months of age by two gay men. He had been abandoned by his young, single mother shortly after his birth. Timothy had begun his therapy in our clinic with another psy-chiatric resident 6 months prior to his new start with me. His diagnoses included attention-deficit hyperactivity disorder (ADHD) and severe parent-child relationship problems. It was noted that he acted extremely oppositional with both "Papa" and "Dad" and frequently "got in their face." The patient had been originally referred to UCSF by a private family therapist who did not think her family work had been successful with the trio. She suggested individual psychodynamic therapy, which had been carried out for 6 months by a male resident, while another resident on our staff managed Timothy's medications.

When Timothy was transferred to me, I was his fourth therapist in a single year. He had not made much progress. He repeatedly challenged Dad physically, and he verbally sassed Papa. When we first met, Timothy was taken aback that I asked him anything at all about his family—he said he had talked "mostly about girls" to his first UCSF therapist and had enjoyed it tremendously. He wanted us to go on in exactly the same vein so that he could begin dating. In a separate session, his fathers told me that, even though they had done all the "homework" that their private family therapist had given them, Timothy was far too hostile to accept their efforts. They wished to bow out of the boy's treatment altogether. His aggressiveness was his own problem.

Because everyone's complaints were about the family and nobody wanted to talk about it, it appeared to me that family therapy was indicated once again. Perhaps this time we could make a success of it. I surprised Timothy by requesting to see the three males together. "Do I have to?" Timothy protested. Arriving in my office, they argued on and on against the idea of resuming family work. I noticed that each time the fathers failed to validate Timothy's concerns, the boy, step by step, escalated his belligerence. When I pointed out this process, each family member suddenly appeared to appreciate the value of having me there in the room.

Our therapeutic moment came, however, the next time we met. I had again confronted them with their usual pattern of behavior when Papa announced, as if he considered this a fresh idea of his own, "Maybe we should consider family therapy." Everybody joined in with gusto. Timothy's change had finally begun.

MEANING OF THE MOMENT

Making a decision about whether to pursue individual or family therapy, especially when an adolescent is the identified patient, can be one of the most challenging considerations in the treatment process.[67] This boy's gay adoption, too, could have been considered challenging in and of itself. Moreover, it was challenging for a resident to inherit somebody else's treatment plan. The therapeutic moment with Timothy and his fathers occurred when I surprised the three of them with my approach to their treatment and we finally chose the appropriate modality for this particular boy. Over the next few months, as we worked together, Papa and Dad became able to yield more freedom to their son. In return, they received far more friendliness, maturity, and constructive behavior from young Timothy.

In this case, the waiting game didn't take long. Ken Braslow not only offered a family his idea for treatment but also gave them a vivid demonstration of what he intended to do for them all. The parents and the boy went home and—unconsciously—mulled it over. When Papa, the family leader, brought up the idea of family therapy as his own, Ken took him up on "his" idea at once—never criticizing, correcting, or competing with him. The case was now on track. It took a short wait but it was worth it.

One statement that this family made to young Ken Braslow reminds me of a problem numbers of families appear to have. The parents told Ken that Timothy's aggressiveness was "his own problem." They implied that they would wait for Timothy, all by himself, to work it out. In other words, they were willing to let Timothy create his own difficulties and then find his own ways to overcome them. "You made your own bed. Now lie in it," I suppose they might have put it.

What a fine line parents have to walk between this form of passive waiting and its opposite, rushing in and rescuing their youngsters! In certain cases, when parents don't come to the rescue, the child's problems may pile up. On the other hand, if families do function as rescuers, their children may become almost addicted to being saved time and again.

In general, a period of patient waiting is helpful where the milder problems of childhood are concerned. But lying on "beds of nails" is not the best alternative for sorely troubled kids. We must help the families who come to us find a reasonable pathway between these two choices. Patient waiting, punishing, depriving of privileges, encouraging new behaviors, rescuing—all of these are viable tactics for adults trying to tend to their families. When parents choose to wait, however, let's hope that they are not unconsciously denying that problems exist. Waiting should be a positive alternative for families, not a decision they simply have failed to make.

As a quick, relatively impatient person myself, I find the long waits inherent in getting a child to change one of the most difficult parts of my practice. I often try to bypass the long waits with play, jokes, metaphors, drawings—whatever, if it works. But sometimes you just have to wait anyway.[68] Perhaps the child may even wish to envision you as a perpetual "waiter." Perhaps he or she considers you to be a Homeric heroine, weaving a tapestry all day and unraveling it by night so that you can leave everything you do just as it always was. Such a patient almost forces you to wait.

This point came home to me recently in a very strange way. A former patient of mine—now an adult living in Europe—wanted to see his old psychiatric chart. I am required by law to allow this, but I insist that the patient and I have an hour to talk about the records (in my long career this has happened three or four times). The young man had come to me as a 3-year-old who paraded about at home, wearing his glamorous mother's perfume and pearls. It looked as if he might be heading for a "gender identity disorder." He saw me for about a year and gradually began enjoying more gender-appropriate activities and accoutrements. I was able to enlist his overly busy dad to become more involved with him, and I helped the preschooler—through his play—to accept himself as he was, a boy. His treatment dwindled off by the time he was 5, but then when he turned 8, his parents went through an incredibly bitter divorce. His powerful, wealthy father eventually married his mother's powerful and wealthy best friend. The boy saw me briefly and sporadically then, but he was sent away by ninth grade to a boarding school, making it impossible for me to help him through the maze of his fractured family and, in a sense, through the maze of his own fractured adolescence.

After the divorce, everything in this particular boy's life changed. And so, when he visited my office at the age of 30, he wanted to see me as entirely unchanged. He needed to imagine me and my life in total contrast to his parents and their lives. How do I know this? Because he said a number of things about his impressions of me that day. And what he said, unconsciously (I think), revealed a fantasy of a "Patient Griselda," somehow frozen in time, waiting for him forever in an office high above Union Square. First, he commented that I have always looked like a "female senator." Flattering as that may be, I'm too short, too casually coiffed, and too purposely funny to meet that description. Second, he said that in the 27-year interval between his first visit and his revisit at 30, I had "not redecorated." Come on! You can't run a busy downtown office and not redecorate! Of course there are constants—I am who I am, no matter how many years go by. And I have the same tastes I had years ago. But the young expatriate—hurt as he was by people whose disruptive lives seriously disrupted his own—had an inner compulsion to view me as different from his family. For him, I was an oasis of dignified, unchanging stability. He had needed someone to sit still and wait for him as he grew up. What a disappointment in reality! But what a pleasure in the mind!

My 30-year-old friend would probably have been dismayed to learn that, at about the same time he was going through his early college years, I was waiting and waiting not for him, but for Little Miss Cammie Brooks to quit playing "Little Red Riding Hood." Time after time, her Wolf gorged himself on Grandma and then saved space for a good meal of the little red protagonist. Now, in a proper little girl voice, Cammie spoke the proper feelings for the three main characters. But she couldn't stop her tendency to "put all her eggs into Wolf's basket." She felt her strongest emotions for the aggressors, not for the passive victims.

I was waiting to find a conclusion to Cammie's endless game. But in many ways, the aggressive discharge through this kind of play was giving young Cammie a chance to behave less aggressively at school.

She was "making it" in kindergarten, although her immaturity demanded that she go through the experience twice. She was not particularly mean to the other kids, though she didn't tend to hang out much with them. It was taking her a while to catch up, but as they used to say in the old feminist cigarette ads, "You've come a long way, baby."

Cammie was—for the first time in her life—drawing herself repeatedly as a little person, complete with the right gender, big eyes, and a smile. As for Wolf, I was just going to have to wait for that triumphant blowhard to get his comeuppance. I would have to be uncharacteristically patient until we could find our way out.

Are there any rules about what would impel a psychotherapist to wait a child out? As in Ken Braslow's case, you would certainly wait if there were no other viable options, no other places to divert or direct the child's treatment. You would also wait if the child's behavior or problem confused or stymied you. At that point, you'd try to consult with another colleague—your supervisor, say, or your peer. Or you might read some professional literature on the subject. You might also wait, as I did with Cammie, if the child has committed herself with absolutely stubborn insistence to a certain behavior inside your office. This possibly could mean that the behavior was of such extreme importance that it might be, in fact, displacing maladaptive behaviors *outside* the office. You would, perhaps, also wait if a child (and his or her family) consistently rejected your interpretations, suggestions, or prescriptions. The family might need more time to come around.

Do we ever recommend to parents that they "wait a child out"? There are numbers of instances when temporizing is the best bet for a family. A lover of football myself, I call it "punting."[69] Kids—especially adolescents—challenge their parents to punish them, for instance. A parent can note that there *will* be a punishment, but refuse to name it until they confer together and can ensure that they will be able to enforce the penalty. Many times it is wise to cool off before deciding what to do next. With the exception of infants and toddlers, where you have to react immediately to the situations they create, older children understand, and even appreciate, the need to temporize until careful thought, not just emotion, takes over.

We have now seen a number of case examples of how children turned around within the first couple of sessions. Reese Abright has an example of exactly the opposite. In the case he reports here, a frightened little boy made tiny, almost imperceptibly positive changes during a prolonged course of therapy. When Dr. Abright finally decided that "time was up," the boy thought about his "end date." In processing this inevitability, he suddenly demonstrated a dramatic—and probably permanent—shift. It was the very last day of his treatment. His psychiatrist had waited for this moment for 3 years.

First Hour, Last Hour

CONTRIBUTED BY REESE ABRIGHT, MD

Kevin, age 7, presented with symptoms of nervousness, insomnia, and academic achievement below his parents' and teachers' expectations. The boy often witnessed arguments between his parents, largely about him or their own relationship. In our first meeting, Kevin spontaneously made a drawing of a broken and sinking ship with people falling through the water below, where they were attacked by sharks, crabs, and other threatening sea creatures.

Over the next 3 years, I saw Kevin once weekly. His diagnosis was "adjustment disorder with anxious mood," but the condition did not clear up as quickly as the ordinary adjustment disorder does. I believed Kevin's concerns were thematic enough for us to talk them out without bringing medications into the equation. Attack by a monster was the recurring idea behind his art and play. My therapeutic interventions were focused on helping him establish increased mastery over the anxieties associated with his life inside his family. As his therapy progressed, Kevin's fantasy play gradually gave way to more realistic discussions of his problems at home and school, and his parents and teachers reported steady improvement of his symptoms and academic performance. We set a date to end his treatment.

On the day of our final session, Kevin wanted to show me a magic book, but he had forgotten to bring it. Because it was our last meeting, I encouraged Kevin to talk about what he had thought of our work together. In response, he asked me for some rope. We found a ball of twine, and he began to tie and untie it, progressively making more and more complicated knots. Then, he started tying himself up, escaping from the knots, and remarking that this was magic. In fact, the book he had been reading (and had wanted to bring along) was a biography of Harry Houdini, the magician who had been able to get himself out of knots, "even in dangerous waters." *I said that the magic Kevin was demonstrating today suggested he could now get himself out of the knots into which he used to feel tied up. He then switched to playing catch. Using the ball of twine as our object, he began festooning my office with streamers as the twine unraveled. Kevin commented,* "It's like one of those goodbye parties on boats." *I agreed.* "It's a bon voyage party." *He replied,* "Yes, like on the Love Boat."

MEANING OF THE MOMENT

The moments with which psychotherapy begins and ends are often telling. A final session may offer new perspectives on themes that emerged at the very outset of treatment. Kevin's last session demonstrated striking continuity with, yet an evolution in, the concerns evident in our first meeting. His experience of himself had changed in 3 years from an identification with helpless victims of external forces (e.g., sharks) to a sense that he could now take magic into his own hands and extricate himself from difficult situations. The sinking ship of his first session had become transformed by his last appointment into the scene of a festive bon voyage party during which he could confidently bid farewell to his doctor. These changes occurred in the context of the many previous sessions in which Kevin had explored (through metaphor) his anxieties about the grown-ups in his life and about growing up himself. In his last visit with me, Kevin's positive reworkings of previously terrifying images indicated this was indeed a propitious moment for psychotherapy to end and for normal development to proceed.

The striking accomplishment Reese Abright's patient showed his doctor on their last visit together was a newfound sense of mastery and control. This had not been a prominent facet of Kevin's psychology until the very end of his treatment. In other words, what the child/adolescent psychiatrist was looking for as an endpoint was not the "insight" the adult psychotherapist seeks—it was rather a readiness to let ordinary development propel this child toward normalcy. Reese Abright waited patiently as he chipped away, bit by bit, at his young patient's worries. Then, at last, the little boy gave him a dramatic demonstration of change. In the very act of leaving, the young lad was finally experiencing an enormous personal metamorphosis.

In recounting the metamorphoses of their various child patients, the contributors to this book have described not only the change itself but also what they have done to precipitate, catalyze, or even just nudge along this massive shift. In these moments, the young patients experienced an interval with the doctor that meant something special to both of them. The final moment I've included in this chapter, however, is an exception. Here, Henry Massie offers us a case in which the patient's turnabout occurred entirely out of the doctor's sight.[70] It was a moment, tucked away from family and friends as well. This instant of change precipitated a total personality shift in the adolescent girl Dr. Massie was treating with patience and warmth. The psychiatrist feels that his main accomplishment, in fact, was to wait this girl out. This allowed her moment to arrive all by itself.

Worthless Loser?

CONTRIBUTED BY HENRY MASSIE, MD

Eight-year-old Jane's inattentive, lackluster school performance deeply frustrated her parents. Successful marketing executives with hectic lives, they were already worried about their latency-aged child's possibilities for college. They also objected to the way Jane tried to run their household. Neuropsychological testing showed Jane to be gifted mathematically and in visual-motor skills. Descriptively, the child's diagnosis fit the criteria for ADHD, but the testing psychologist reported that she might be responding to a "hyperactive family culture." Both parents traveled frequently for their work. Their family vacations with Jane were busy, almost frenetic.

I took Jane into treatment and ended up seeing her at varying intervals for 8 years and counting. During that time, her schoolwork remained inadequate. At times, in talking about her home, her body trembled and her eyes teared up, yet she declined my psychological interpretations. Trials of ADHD medications were ineffective. Her parents resisted my attempts to refer them for family or individual therapy. The only type of help I was able to offer without resistance was support for Jane in the face of her parents' ongoing impatience. There was little I could do about her academic performance, which she explained away with the usual clichés ("The teacher lost my report"; "I thought that assignment was due next week"). The worst moment came when Jane's parents called her a "worthless loser."

After years of occasional work with me, Jane's mother and father, who had begun to relax a bit, especially on their family holidays with Jane, decided to let her go to boarding school. When she was offered the choice between applying herself at a local, private high school or going away, Jane foiled the three of us, however, with a third choice—a boyfriend. The love affair, complete with "responsible sex," lasted almost 2 years, during which time it served as yet another diversion from Jane's academics. From about the age of 14 on, however, Jane had been busy developing another distraction, which served as a healthy "sublimation" of her intense sexual and aggressive drives. She developed a "hobby": web merchandising. She was "mad for" teenage accessories—purses, scarves, and shoes. And so Jane began working on the fine points of selling them. It surprised us all when several college-level students at a highly respected fashion institute in San Francisco hired Jane to tutor them on their various computer projects. This required a newfound independence on Jane's part. It also lessened the power plays her parents could exercise. How could they ground her when she went to work? How could they take away her allowance when she earned all the money she needed on her own? Jane's parents began to retreat from confrontations. It cooled the hothouse at home considerably.

Then, when Jane was about to turn 16, two amazingly opposite events took place within 3 days, amounting to a "moment of truth" entirely out of my sight. First, Jane flunked out of private school. She received a letter stating that the school's decision was inexorable. Second, with the help of a downtown attorney whom she had hired herself, Jane signed a seven-figure contract with a major Internet company. They purchased the novel method of web merchandising she had developed, along with her on-site expertise. Jane's parents couldn't have been prouder. They have lavished her with praise ever since (and she lavishes them with trips and gifts). Now, on her own, she has hired a tutor to help her finish high school. And she pays me herself, as a "consultant," choosing voluntarily to keep up her noninvasive psychotherapy.

MEANING OF THE MOMENT

Jane is who she always was—a nonconformist with great potential. A controlling person, and highly competitive with adults, Jane allowed me to conduct supportive therapy only.[71] Over the years, she shrugged off my interpretations with "whatever" insouciance. But I stubbornly resisted overpathologizing this girl. I stuck with her despite my frustrations and moments of silent impatience. Her hobby made sense to me as a coping skill, and it became an object of my therapeutic support. I will always remember what she said at 15 years old—"I can't relax at school, but my work gives me comfort." What Jane didn't say—that she had found little "comfort" at home—confirmed my impression that she had come all those years to my office for exactly that.

This is a story of a girl who, for 8 years, did not respond to medication, interpretation, rules and regulation, or standard education. She did respond, however, to her doctor's steadiness and understanding. Thanks in part to her doctor's extraordinary willingness to wait, Jane eventually experienced a life-altering change. It proves that the waiting game, if psychotherapists and their young patients can endure it, is a potent technique in and of itself.

CHAPTER SEVEN

A Place to Talk and to Use Talk Playfully

When I gave up my stethoscope for papers and pen, when I turned in my white coat for plainclothes, when I left the scalpels and retractors back in the hospital O.R. and chose, instead, a lofty blue and white room full of toys, what was I doing? I was trading all of that wonderful equipment for something entirely intangible—words. True, I still have a prescription pad, which I use with maybe a third to a half of my patients. But the major equipment I use as a physician dealing with people's emotional problems is my language, my tone of voice, my rhythms, emphasis, gestures, grammar, and what I say—one great big category called "talk."

All a surgeon really needs from you is your body, your consent, and your cooperation. Then he or she excises the problem. All an anesthesiologist needs is a note on your allergies, weight, and maintenance medications. Then he or she puts you to sleep, keeps you alive, and kills the pain. You are but one of the actors in the drama of the operating room. And then, when you wake up, a whole new cast of characters—your family and friends—come to the hospital to help. Like toys and transitional objects[72] (blankets and bears), they serve to cheer you along your way to recovery.

Conversely, as an outpatient psychotherapist, you are all alone with your young patient. In a sense, you function as a whole operating room team—and, to boot, as that important chorus of family and friends. I've been thinking about this analogy because I am 18 days post-op today as I write. My surgery went fine, and the offending problem (thank heaven!) was benign. I loved the surgeon—she was good and followed up well. However, I figured out exactly what was being done to me not from what she told me, but from the Internet. I am grateful to the anesthesiologist not only for keeping me alive but also for keeping my brain functions working as well as before. But when I put the whole experience together—and it was the very first operation of my life—I realize that these excellent physicians hardly talked to me. Talk simply isn't their medium of commerce.

So how does what I do as a psychotherapist analogize to what an O.R. crew does? I believe that "talk"—especially about a child's emotions, but also, importantly, about cognitive issues that the kid might not yet grasp—alleviates pain. I also believe that "talk," especially about maladaptive behaviors or symptoms (and the various ways to get past them), dissects poor functioning from the healthy, with the precision of a scalpel. Finally, I believe that "talk" gives comfort the way one's family gives comfort after an operation. Talk can take on the characteristics of a pacifier, a playmate, or a toy. Not only is talk a technique, but it also creates and maintains a relationship.

I have a vignette of my own to offer at this point. Lily Anne was a toddler who, as an infant, had been used by an uncle for child pornography. She had been traumatized so severely, in fact, that she had barely been able to develop. She couldn't talk. She couldn't indicate "no." I swear, she hardly could smile. Through her play with my office baby doll, Lily Anne had to be taught human language. "You're touching her body," I'd say to Lily Anne. "Those are her arms." ("Bahd," she'd say back to me. "Ahms.") As she undressed the baby, she learned more body parts, especially those carrying high emotional impact. ("Gina," she learned to say of the doll's private part and, by unspoken analogy, her own. She liked the sound of the word *butt* and said it often. She even learned the word "ureetra" [urethra].) Here I was doing a very special kind of surgery. Rather than cutting things out, I was creating a transplant. I was putting in an organ, speech, that should have been there all along. I taught Lily Anne the words for her feelings, at first in terms of the baby doll, and later in terms of my Alice in Wonderland doll, whom she called "Princess." Words, I found with Lily Anne (as I have found with so many other children), diminish unspoken pain. Better than opiates, they also aid a youngster's cognition. The words are labels for concepts that enlighten a child and enable the youngster to accept realistic explanations. With enlightenment and explanation, their silent pain is relieved.

With Lily Anne's newly transplanted language in place, we laid a scalpel to the rest of her problem. We cut some of it out, first by finding new contexts, such as the probability that "sex will feel good when you're all grown up and love somebody" or that "you get to *choose* whom you have sex with." We cut further into the problem by locating some corrections to being abused—"A person usually goes to jail if he does stuff like that to children." All of this surgery and anesthesia was ostensibly being done on behalf of "Baby" and "Princess." But in the end it benefited the player, little Lily Anne, herself.

A Princess Grows Up

Lily Anne Doe was 28 months old when I first met her. Having discovered that her older brothers—Sam, 6, and Bert, 4—had been sexually abused and videotaped by an uncle-by-marriage, Lily Anne's grandfather, a retired police inspector, searched porno websites, tragically finding not only his two grandsons posted but also his baby granddaughter. All three children suffered post-traumatic symptoms. At 2, Lily Anne passively and quietly allowed Bert to jump on her, knock her supine, and move rhythmically on top of her. But her development was even more drastically curtailed than a PTSD diagnosis would have implied. She did not run, explore, indicate "no," or talk. She showed no inclination toward toilet training. She was virtually a silent child.

The family temporarily moved to San Francisco to work with me. I saw the three little Does for a year and a half, dividing 2 hours once-weekly among them. In many ways Lily Anne was the worst off. One might have thought her retarded, but for her ability to pretend. I watched her silently pick up my baby doll and rock it tenderly. I taught her the adult names for the baby's body parts, along with how to feed, burp, diaper, and comfort the little thing. We also worked on protecting it. In this fashion, after a few months, Lily Anne became a talker.

Our turning point occurred soon after Lily Anne stopped playing with my pink-clad baby. She had come across a gorgeous classic doll I keep in the cupboard, whom she labeled "Princess." Her mother, who attended our sessions, commented, "Lily Anne just loves princesses." I seized the moment. "Let's put 'Princess' on the potty!"

"Can't. It hurts," Lily Anne protested.

"Yes, I understand," I replied. "One of the king's men did scary things to her a long time ago." I said it matter of factly. "She's afraid because her vagina got hurt from the bad man."

"Hurt her." "Yes," I said. "Jump on her." "Yes." "Like Bert?" she asked. "He hurt Bert, too. Then Bert hurt you," I replied.

Over the ensuing weeks, Lily Anne became very angry at the king's man—for Princess's sake, of course. We also considered the King's daughter's fears. "To poop?" "Yeah." "To marry a prince?" "Yeah." "But when Princess is all grown up and really loves a prince her own age, then none of the stuff they do together will hurt. In fact, it'll be really nice." Lily Anne looked surprised, but she took it all in. Her affect brightened noticeably.

We played "Princess" for about 6 months. During that time, the little girl was able to handle her older brother, telling him to leave her alone. At 3, she considered the "facts" of adult sexuality and decided that, although Princess was too young for sex right now, it would be okay later on. Lily Anne easily toilet trained herself and excelled in preschool.

MEANING OF THE MOMENT

Traumatized children need to abreact, find contexts, and behaviorally correct for their ordeals in order to resolve them. But traumatized children also need to feel free enough to develop. Lily Anne's Princess was this toddler's metaphor for dealing with her terror of growing up. By my moving into a doll's life—and interpreting it with frankness, respect, and humor—I encouraged Lily Anne's development to get back on track. Every few years, I hear from the Does, who now live in North Carolina.

Everybody's growing up fine. The family even sent a beautiful new Fairy Godmother doll as a thank you.

This case illustrates the therapeutic value of words, a point that was brought home to me when I phoned Lily Anne's mom to ask for her permission to tell her little girl's story. Our cure had held, she told me! Lily Anne was doing brilliantly in elementary school, had friends, and was developing at a normal pace. The boys, too, were doing fine. Nobody was seeing a "shrink." Everybody was thriving.

Then Lily Anne's mom took me by surprise. "You know what still sticks in her mind about her treatment in San Francisco?" she asked me. "The way you used to sing 'Dance Lady, Dance.'"

I had forgotten all about it! Now the ridiculous little chant rushed into mind:

> Dance lady, dance! Dance lady, dance!
> Dance lady, dance lady—dance, dance, dance!

That old spoken song was just a little something Lily Anne and I did, far away from the realms of abreaction, context, and correction, my "big three" of treating trauma. Long ago, two different patients had separately given me small Russian dancer figurines, their heads and bodies perched on white plastic stands. One wore a red polka-dot babushka, and the other, a pink one. If you pushed the dolls delicately on their sides, and if they were perched just right on their little stands, they would dance for you with gyrating heads, shoulders, and skirts. Every time Lily Anne made one of the dolls dance, I'd say my crazy little poem. I had invented "Dance Lady, Dance" solely for Lily Anne and have never used it again. In fact, I'd only say it for little Lily Anne when she had the little Russian lady set up just right. As the Russian folk doll went through her madcap motions, I recited my strange little number. I was using my words as a "toy," something no surgeon could ever do with a scalpel.

Lily Anne learned that she could control the Russian doll, a true toy, and me, temporarily her "toy," too, by getting everything concerning the dancing lady exactly right. I didn't realize it at the time, but my daffy poem had been therapeutic. An apathetic, underdeveloped infant had received—as a toddler—a surgical implant through my words. Language gave Lily Anne a sense of "mastery." Playing with language inserted even more "control" into her lexicon of behaviors. Mastery and control go toward making us humans truly "human."

The next time I do transplantation surgery, I hope I am aware of it.

When we "operate" on children, we use metaphor as a surgical tool. We talk of "princesses," "roadways," "pirates," "quarterbacks," "clipper ships," and "mermaids." Early in his career as a psychiatrist, Joel Zrull, for instance, created a moment of change for a psychologically confused, mute twin by speaking to young Ken about "elevators." Dr. Zrull was making metaphors with a boy who was *acting* psychotic, while the boy's identical brother, also a patient of the doctor's, was *being* psychotic.[73] Did the nonpsychotic boy consciously know what was being done with him? Probably not. Like a surgeon, the psychotherapist left his patient partially in the dark. Not giving up the full key to the metaphor, Dr. Zrull allowed himself to be satisfied with a simple cure, not a sophisticated one with full and total understanding on young Ken's part. Joel, a teacher of mine from our University of Michigan days, did not come up with the idea of "elevators" out of his own head, in fact. He watched his patient's behavior. Then he remembered something. Before his young charge, Ken, had gone completely mute on him, the patient had liked to create playful fantasies about elevators. What was Ken doing now with the building blocks in Joel Zrull's office? Could he have constructed a twin set of elevators? And might they both be broken?

Elevator Going Up[74]

CONTRIBUTED BY JOEL ZRULL, MD

Ken was a 13-year-old identical twin. His brother, Larry, was also my patient. Both boys had been hospitalized in the child psychiatric unit where I was doing my psychiatric training. When they were together, the twins, who were short and slightly round, exhibited loose associations and spoke with clanging alliteration and neologisms. When Ken was separated from Larry, however, he became more appropriate and could sustain a reality-bound conversation. Larry could not do this. Each boy evidenced localized slowing on his electroencephalogram (EEG), but on opposite sides of the head. Ken also had a seizure disorder that was being treated with Dilantin, which was the only drug he was receiving. Larry was much more severely disturbed and diagnosed as psychotic. He was being treated with medications and supportive psychotherapy for his psychosis, but after much consideration, it was decided that Larry needed to go into a state facility where he could receive longer-term treatment. Ken remained at our hospital. After his twin's departure, Ken regressed and began taking on his brother's physical mannerisms and speech patterns. Our hospital staff began to wonder if the wrong twin had been sent to the state facility.

Ken regressed in therapy from talking with me quietly to only playing with my toys. He refused to speak outside his play. One day, shortly after Larry left, Ken was playing with the blocks. He constructed two elevators. He had fantasized about elevators in earlier phases of his therapy. But this time he mumbled that the elevators were totally broken down. Nobody could repair them. At the suggestion of my supervisor, I made an interpretation the next time I saw Ken. I told him that the elevators were indeed repairable. One required much more work than the other one, which seemed to have fewer damaged parts. I told Ken that the repairman would work and work on the better-working elevator until it was running smoothly.

In his following sessions, Ken began to talk to me again. We took walks in the area around the hospital, stopping at a sandwich shop, drugstore, and gift store where Ken could gain some social skills. Ken remained in the hospital 8 months before being discharged home and to outpatient therapy. Larry remained in the state facility for 4 years.

MEANING OF THE MOMENT

Because Ken was using the metaphor of broken elevators to represent himself, his brother, and the therapist, my interpretation was made within this context. I talked inside of Ken's play in order to reassure him that I understood him. This became a moment between Ken and me. I gave Ken hope for his own personal recovery by drawing a distinction between him and his twin. I also reassured Ken inside the elevator metaphor that I would stick with him, like the best of elevator repairmen, and not send him away or abandon him. Not only did I understand him, but now Ken could understand me as well.

Joel Zrull, who for many years served as Chairman of Psychiatry in Toledo, has told an "ancient" story here. Of course, kids don't spend 8 months or 4 years in hospitals anymore. Newer medications, day-treatment programs, halfway houses, and special education classrooms have bypassed much of that. But the mutuality created by sharing a metaphor—still feels as new as tomorrow to the youngster who experiences it. Many of us aren't metaphorical enough today, especially with disordered teenagers. Adolescents still love the metaphor and respond to analogies involving modern technology (such as cell phones or instant messaging), tales from films, the feats of superheroes, and myths. Sports talk may work well, as may talk about Ninja Turtles, sharks, or Hello Kitties. It isn't necessary to decode the metaphor and say, "That's you!" The words alone carry the power to cure. They bring understanding—"one elevator is easier to repair than the other." They bring reassurance—"elevator repairmen don't quit." They bring hope and a will to survive. They cement the therapeutic bond.

I continue to wonder what makes some psychotherapists stay entirely inside the metaphor when making an interpretation to a child—as I did with Lily Anne and Joel Zrull did with Ken—whereas others, such as Nancy Winters (in Chapter 3) and Stewart Teal (in Chapter 4), move out of the metaphor and talk directly to the youngster. I think that the decision usually comes in an insightful flash. The age of the child, the power of the metaphor, the child's repeated pleasure in that particular play theme—all of these factors weigh into the doctor's decision. But the decision comes fast and naturally.

Do parents use metaphor much in talking with their kids? There's no way to know until somebody—a linguist, most likely, who studies a number of families' speech patterns—tells us. Storytelling certainly is a grand family tradition, especially within certain cultures. Do these families then find alternative endings, make up new characters, or send out veiled messages to one another through the storyline? Metaphor is so powerful as a treatment tool, one might think that parents would have discovered it by now. But I'm not so sure they use it much, especially in terms of elaborating on the stories they tell. After all, we parents don't do surgery, except for prying out an occasional splinter in our kitchens.

Talking in metaphor, code, special "inside" languages, poetry, rap—in other words, using language in the play mode—is an extremely powerful device, not only for families, but also for individual kids in psychotherapy. Like the toddler Lily Anne who remembered "Dance Lady, Dance," other children will retain a two-line poem constructed at the doctor's office, a jazz beat, a rap rhythm. I remember learning about a group "rap-music" debriefing after a shocking junior high school tragedy.[75] The students did it all in rhyming couplets—kid after kid—to a rap beat pounded out by an electronic device. The music, the rhythm, the fact that the young people themselves had created the words—all of this made the curative potential of their rap session that much more powerful.

Metaphor can sometimes be used as a "code" between doctor and patient. Once the metaphor catches hold between these two people, it can be utilized time and again. In the next vignette, a child's frightening drawing of a mother bird pecking out the eyes of her young provided a metaphor that became a sad but meaningful communication "code" between Stewart Teal and the frightened schoolboy he was treating. (Interestingly, in this case the boy himself made the Anna Freud-like linkage to his own reality.) Ten years after Stewart interpreted the meaning of this bird drawing to the young fellow, a similar problem came up, and the metaphor was used once again. Here, then, we can see the power and lastingness of a mutually understood linguistic "code."

The Danger of Being a Baby Bird

CONTRIBUTED BY STEWART TEAL, MD

Wayne, a 9-year-old third grader, was urgently referred to me because, for 2 weeks, he had been refusing to go to school, complaining of feeling deadly ill. The ruddy complexioned, healthy-looking boy was clutching at his mother whenever she tried to get him out the door of their house. He had occasionally exhibited smaller emotional outbursts over the years, but made excellent grades and had good friends.

Wayne told me he had always been afraid to go to school, but now it was worse because of a game the boys were playing secretly called "Smear the Queer."[76] One boy was designated the "queer" and had to run a gauntlet through the playground while trying to avoid being knocked down, and thus, "smeared." Wayne believed that, if he were "it," he would be killed. I made the diagnosis of "separation anxiety disorder" (and, of course, a "school phobia"). I suggested twice-weekly psychotherapy and assigned to Wayne's father all the duties of getting him to school. At school, we set up a plan to have the boy gradually return to his classroom after friendly initial stays in the principal's office.

Three months into treatment, Wayne still was having intermittent panic attacks. One day during a session, he drew a disturbing picture. "The mother bird is pecking out the eyes of the baby bird," Wayne explained, totally without affect, as he pointed to his drawing.

"That baby bird must be very scared and hurt and angry with the mother bird," I commented, my voice purposely full of sympathy. The color suddenly drained from Wayne's face. He began to sob. He remembered something, he told me. When he was 4, his mother left him at preschool on a cold rainy day. Apparently unaware that school was closed, she drove off without looking back. Wayne struggled to open the school door and then wandered about in the rain. He believed he was going to die, never to see his parents again. Our therapy proceeded smoothly from that point on. Wayne explored his tense relationship with his mother in a number of respects. After about a year, he was symptom-free.

Our therapeutic moment happened not once, however, but twice. A few weeks after Wayne started college, he came to see me for an emergency visit. He felt terrified of the drinking he had observed in his dorm. Someone might fall out of a window!

The situation was so frightening that Wayne believed he'd have to leave the university. I handed Wayne the drawing of the birds he'd done when he was 9. Again, the blood drained from his face. He looked at me, first questioningly, and then with a smile. As if on cue, we both burst out laughing. Wayne now could fully remember the nursery school incident. After that, he made it through his freshman year without having to retreat home.

MEANING OF THE MOMENT

Two times with my help, this young man connected his current panicky fear with a traumatic preschool experience. Both times, he needed to reconsider his partially repressed trauma from a more mature and self-observing perspective. His childhood drawing of birds served as our mutually understood "open sesame." Selma Fraiberg, the great American psychoanalytic social worker, wrote of the importance of connecting repressed feelings with the event that originally stimulated them. She said in 1975, "In remembering [we] are saved from the blind repetition of the morbid past."[77]

The case of Wayne is the only one in this book, beside my "wild child," Cammie Brooks, in which two therapeutic turning points in the same patient are illustrated. These two cases have one big factor in common—they tell of long periods in the life of one patient. But the two cases are different in another regard: Each time Cammie came to a new turning point, she entered it through different means, whereas young Wayne and Dr. Teal came to both of their meeting of the minds in the same fashion, using the same metaphor. There is something pungent and lasting about the metaphor of a mother bird blinding her baby. It became an insider's language between doctor and patient. It stood for "trauma." But it also stood for a very special relationship.

Word play, like retractors and clamps, is often the key to the surgical excision of a childhood problem. Kids love any sort of game in which the words themselves are a part of the play. Speaking pig latin, for instance, hiding a message inside a drawing, a song, or (traditionally) a bottle, creating an inside joke, or making up a new riddle are methods of building and maintaining alliances. Codes are of great fascination to kids of all ages. Interestingly, you don't have to be above the age of abstraction (around 12)[78] to have fun with words. In fact, the elemental, even boorish, songs of toddler and preschool life become a bond between doctor and patient.

When I was young, my sister and I played word games galore. On bus rides all over Cleveland, we tried to speak nonsense Chinese (with a few slang American words tossed in, to give it some meaning). She was "Beebahdah" (Barbara). I was "Leenohdee" (Lenorie). My little brother was "Reebert" (Robert). I still call him "Reeb." We'd stare at the sky in front of department stores, hoping that the crowds would look up, too. We brought back a Chinese language newspaper we found in New York City, hoarded it, and sometimes tried to act as if we were reading it on the bus. When William Steig wrote his *CDB* (See the Bee),[79] my mom brought it home from the library and we were off and running on letter, number, and sign languages. We still write letters to our families in that Steig code, and I've heard that the poet Ezra Pound used the same code, long before the Steig book, to send postcards to his friends from St. Elizabeth's Hospital, in Washington, D.C., where he was incarcerated after World War II.[80] I know from personal experience that word games bring people together, stir up the joys of childhood, and even promote certain levels of mutual understanding.

In my view now, as a mature professional, if you can find a way to communicate with a kid, the words themselves aren't of primary importance. It is what both of you understand you are trying to say that carries the meaning and the bond. You could call a "rape" a "massive misunderstanding," for instance, as long as both you and the patient agreed to call it that. You might come a long, long way together through such a play on words. Here is an example of a quirky, strange, inside joke between a young convicted rapist and me. Our "word code" turned out to be the only way that this young man could bypass his own stifling anger.

A Massive Misunderstanding

A juvenile court judge from a distant Bay Area county sent me a 17-year-old boy he had convicted of rape. The boy's court sentence was "6 months of once-weekly psychotherapy with Dr. Terr." No one asked my permission. No one called me with a history.

The boy's story was that one Saturday night he had gone out with a considerably older single woman. She had a terrible reputation, and he "knew" he could have sex with her. In the back seat of his car, she had protested while he insisted. Afterward, she called the police. He was furious about having been falsely accused of what he considered consensual sex. He was angry for being sentenced to something "stupid" like psychotherapy. He insisted he was absolutely innocent.

Rather than argue with this boy about whether he had perpetrated a rape (a useless argument, given my past experiences with child-abusing parents), I decided to reframe the event in question by renaming what the boy had done. Smiling a wee bit, I said, "I guess we'd have to agree that you and the woman had a massive misunderstanding." *He nodded. I might, in fact, have caught just the flicker of a smile. I felt we had agreed to play together. I then went on to outline a treatment plan. We would spend 6 months working on any* massive misunderstandings *that came up.*

And that's what we did. We worked on his angry personality traits in the "here and now," week by week reviewing how he dealt with his friends, neighbors, working people, and enemies. I chipped away at his gripes and rages, using as much humor as I could muster as we practiced unfamiliar skills. We set up scenarios. I insisted on clear verbs, and as few insulting adjectives and adverbs as possible. In fact, it became a kind of game, though admittedly an ironic, rather black-humored one. The idea was to deal maturely and flexibly with all sorts of massive misunderstandings.

One day toward the end of a session, he rose to full height. "I've now served my sentence," he announced, this time without the trace of a smile. "Today is the last time I'll see you. I want you to know, it's been a total waste of time."

MEANING OF THE MOMENT

In a case of personality disorder, such as this, only time can tell whether psychotherapy was effective. Two years after the boy's treatment ended, I phoned his house to ask his dad why he'd never paid his bill. The boy—now a young man—answered and insisted on knowing the reason I had called. He then asked for the amount owed. "Is it okay if I send you ten dollars a month?" he asked. Over the years, he paid up completely. Many years later, he called me and we spoke one last time. "I need your suggestions about how to help my two sons through my upcoming divorce. How should I approach it?" Before I could offer him some tried-and-true suggestions, he interjected a comment. "By the way," he said, "in case you're wondering. The problem between my wife and me? It was not a massive misunderstanding!"

Cammie and I never misunderstood each other as we played "Little Red Riding Hood" over the course of 2 years. She was going to have Wolf win. She had learned to say all sorts of words for the emotions, not only for Wolf, but also for the lost Grandma and Little Red Riding Hood. In fact, she could mourn for Grandma, and therefore, perhaps, grieve inside for Bethany, her dead baby sister. But as for the general plotline, my little "wild child" simply could not change the inexorable course of events. Victims lost all.

I tried to elicit more identification in Cammie with Little Red Riding Hood asking the 6-year-old questions to rechannel her abreactions to the proper places. "How does it feel to die all bitten?"

"It doesn't hurt."

"Oh, I think Red would have to shut off all her feelings not to be aware of the pain."

"Maybe," she answered. But Red got eaten anyway, and a triumphant Wolf danced on her bones.

One day Cammie finally admitted that Little Red Riding Hood was scared—and that Grandma was, too. She was becoming more spontaneously empathetic. But Cammie still couldn't imagine a single way to defeat Wolf.

"How about a gun? Red might hide it in her picnic basket," I suggested.

"No way!"

"How about poison? Red could make poisonous sandwiches at home, and pretend they're for Grandma."

"No! No! Grandma will eat them!"

I wondered if some contextual thinking would help. I couldn't figure out, however, how to take this approach.

Then, one day, it just came to me. "Why *do* wolves do such things?" I asked, as Cammie's Wolf began to stalk his ever-suffering victims once again.

"Wolves are mean," she said. "They don't care."

"True," I replied. It was hard—well nigh impossible—to find motivations for Cammie's birth parents' actions. "Wouldn't a wolf in the forest rather eat deer meat than little girls?" I mused, almost as if talking to myself.

"Yes," said Cammie. "But *this* wolf wants girls!"

There it was! In thinking about *this* particular wolf's weirdness, as opposed to all other wolves in the forest, Cammie finally had been able to say aloud what was wrong with her family of origin. They were outliers. They were "beyond the pale." They were deeply disordered people. They did not fit in with normal human beings. Cammie looked at me. I looked at Cammie. She had discovered a context, a meaning, a whole new understanding of what her parents had done.

Now she could find her own correction to her Red Riding Hood saga. "How does wolf soup taste?" she asked almost immediately.

"I bet it's *delicious*!" I laughed. "Let's try some."

With gusto, we slurped our imaginary stew.

That remarkable interaction was Cammie's third turning point. She could now join the world of little girls, of kindergarten kids, of children. Her first "moment," our mutual birthday, had led her to join with me. Her second "moment," the tea parties, had allowed her to join humankind. Now she was free enough to join the world of school-age youngsters, of daughters who fit into their adoptive families. I thought, perhaps, we could end her therapy soon. She was far more sociable. She was beginning to learn at school. She was beginning to like dinosaurs, as does almost everybody in kindergarten. After that day,

Cammie never played "Little Red Riding Hood" again. Her game had been cleanly excised.

It doesn't really matter how an operating room looks, as long as it's sterile, well-organized, and well-equipped. And the O.R. people all look the same anyway—clad in green or blue, well-scrubbed, space-agey. But the therapy office is different. As psychotherapists, we must create an environment tailored to the unique needs of the child. We must be willing and able to wait—and sometimes a long time—for youngsters. We must love to play and share this love with the kids we see. Above all, we must use our words like the deftest of technicians. And we differ from the surgeon here, too. Rather than sending the patient off silently as soon as a bad spot is cut out, we forge alliances that work over time. We find words that carry lasting meanings. We want our little charges to find their own ways before they have to leave us.

I will end this part of the book about the psychiatrist's atmosphere with a limerick I once wrote for a bright girl who couldn't spell. I wanted her to see that spelling, although important, wasn't everything. I used a quote from the Book of Matthew in it, and she knew the *New Testament* well enough to get my little inside joke. The idea was to have fun with a problem that ordinarily was no fun for her at all. A playful spirit is still one of the world's most potent medicines. It infuses our atmospheres with hope.

> I once saw an old sikh by the parkh.
> And I followed him in as a larkh.
> I'd wanted to sayh,
> "Have a nice, pleasant dayh,"
> But I lost him there diep in the darkh.
>
> One day with the sikh still in mindh,
> I spotted him two steps behindh.
> I told him the tale
> Of the parkh where I'd failed,
> So he said to me, "Sikh! Ye shall findh."

Part Three

"GETTING" the CHILD

"I like bananas and you like banahnahs."
— George & Ira Gershwin, from "Let's Call the Whole Thing Off"

CHAPTER EIGHT

Following a Child's Lead

Yesterday, the rainy season hit California. Earlier in the week, cirrus clouds had gathered for 4 whole days. Then, one night, the sky completely cleared. I pronounced the gathering storm a false alarm. But my rain-predicting abilities proved rusty from 6 months' disuse—somehow, the storm pulled itself together once again. Then I made an even bigger blunder in the game of outguessing the rain. Noticing in the early morning yesterday that the wind was coming in from the south, I figured it would start to rain in a couple of hours. That should have happened—it usually does. But instead, it took many more hours before a drip even dropped. What a slow, lazy storm! And what a lousy weatherlady!

I learn from my mistakes. And nature is the best of teachers. Not every storm is alike. Each has a "mind of its own." Even with a number of weather satellites up in space and a weatherperson on every news channel, the particular storm does exactly what it's going to do. Just as with a child in psychotherapy, you can't jump too far in front and guess. You must always follow, and watch.

And how did the people around my office take the first rain of the season? They, too, behaved in their own unpredictable fashions, showing distinct individuality. There was no way to accurately guess what they would do. When, in the morning, I asked Sandra Brooks how she was going to drive her long way home in the storm, she said it would be no problem. In fact, she could hardly wait to get back. "At home," she said, "we'll sit on the porch, and get all fluffed up in blankets, and watch and listen. It'll be so nice." Richard Willets, 13 years old now, was back in my office late yesterday afternoon for a post-traumatic "booster shot." Puberty had intensified his early memories and horrors of his pedophilic neighbor. Richard and his mom cell-phoned from their bus ride downtown to say that the rainy-day traffic was making them a bit late. You'd think Richard would arrive aggravated, but no. "I'm glad it's raining again," he told me. "All the ugly, brown dust will be gone." A real Californian, this boy! But not Jim Genzale, my office assistant. Jim moved here from Boston 3 years ago and hates our winter rains. "They went on *so* long last year," he remarked over lunch. "I thought California would be much sunnier." At the sight of the first rain of the season, disappointment was written all over Jim's young, ordinarily sunny face.

Like impending storms, individuals are "individual." You have to watch them and listen carefully to what they say if you are to figure where they are coming from and what they're going to do. People cannot be entirely predicted. Diagnosis helps. It determines a trend. (Diagnosis: "You live in California?" Trend: "Well, you're going to have to expect a season of winter rains.") However, trends don't tell the whole story. A formulation (the psychological explanation for the child's worries and behaviors) makes our predictions more reliable. But the individual child may still behave in an unexpected way or mumble an out-of-context phrase. Our job is to follow. Many times we must improvise in order to stay on the child's path. We need to remain flexible enough to drop our predictions and to pick up on the hard-to-decipher signal that a young person may be sending.

A couple of short examples from traumatized children I have evaluated may help here. The first is sad and gruesome; the second, oddly funny. A sister and brother were brought from Wyoming by their grandparents after the school-age kids discovered their mother murdered. It had been about a year, and their father, who was found to have arranged for someone else to do the killing, was in prison. After the first couple of assessment sessions in which I saw each child alone,

I saw the siblings together. As we talked and drew pictures, I noticed that the traumatized pair said something to each other about "Mama sleeping." I took them up on it. "What do you mean, 'sleeping'?" I asked. "She wasn't dead when we found her. She was snoring," the little girl answered. "Then," her little brother added, "she died."

"Did your mother used to snore at night?" I followed their thinking.

"No. Just then," they agreed.

Now I could understand. The two youngsters had heard their mother's Cheyne-Stokes breathing when they found her. It was a death rattle. I explained to them that they had discovered their mother when she was barely alive. She was breathing her last breaths, which sound like snores. There was nothing an EMT, ambulance, doctor, or hospital could have done. And the helpers certainly did not kill her, nor did the poor children who had discovered her in this condition.

You might think that such a morbid discussion would have further shaken these two fragile young mourners. But no. They were relieved. They could not have saved their mother, nor could have anyone else. They left my office a little less gloomy and clouded over.

My second example about following a child's lead has to do with a nonverbal signal I received from a young patient who reportedly had been sexually abused. It was during the late 1980s, when everybody but me, it seemed, was using "anatomically correct" dolls to diagnose childhood sexual abuse. I thought the dolls were too explicit and might intrigue a child into playing "sex" even if the child hadn't had an actual sexual experience. In fact, that month I was writing a debate column for our child and adolescent psychiatry journal about whether or not to use anatomically correct dolls.[81] When the 6-year-old patient was brought to my office for evaluation, I showed her the toys and other curiosities in the room. Was she interested in my unexplicit dolls? No. The rocks? No. The kittens and dogs? No. Cars? Dinos? Puppets? No, no, and no. My, my—what was it to be?

The little girl pulled off one of the blue and white plaid cushions from the back of my couch. Nobody had ever done that before, but it was okay. She placed it on the floor. Then she pulled off a cushion from the seat of the couch and dragged it until it could be put, seam for seam, on top of the other pillow. I said nothing and just watched.

Then the rubbing started. Back and forth, back and forth. The top pillow moved slowly at first, and then rapidly—all the while vigorously rubbing against the bottom pillow. It took no genius to follow this kindergartener's meaning. She didn't need an explicit object to be provided by a mental health professional. She had enough sexual worries and preoccupations to find sex wherever she could. All I needed to do was understand.

Children have trouble insisting that adults get their gist. They'll try to tell us something, but often they say it just once. If we don't get it, they may never say or demonstrate it the same way again. Of course, we can still count on "the repetition compulsion," Freud's magnificent discovery about conflicted or traumatized people's need to refeel, retell, redream, and reenact.[82] But with youngsters, the repetition compulsion takes so many forms that it may be lost in translation. Our best bet is to ask our young patients to tell us what they mean at the time they drop one of their undecipherable clues. Okay, so we look dumb! But who cares? Kids think adults are dumb anyway.

One of the best examples of a beautifully executed attempt to follow a child's lead comes in the following vignette from a grand lady of southern California child and adolescent psychiatry, Rita Rogers. Rita is one of those unusual people who exudes a kind of magnetism, whether you know her well or not. But what tools—beside herself—was Rita going to use in order to handle a little Iranian boy who had decided not to talk?

An Extended Doll Family

CONTRIBUTED BY RITA ROGERS, MD

Reza was a 5-year-old boy referred to me in the spring of 1979 because he had stopped talking. The admission diagnosis was "elective mutism." Both parents were physicians who had emigrated from Iran; the mother was Muslim, and the father was Jewish. Only English was spoken in their family. Both parents insisted that their son had a completely normal development and they knew of no reason why this handsome, naturalized American boy had suddenly stopped talking at home, in school—in fact, everywhere.

Reza's mother and father wondered how I would talk *to this young man who did not talk. When I told them that I would* communicate *with him in the playroom, they looked at me questioningly. When I asked who Reza's most favorite person was, they replied in unison: "We are."*

In the playroom, Reza did not seem particularly interested in the mommy, daddy, or sibling dolls. He seemed to be looking for additional figures. I helped him in his search, but he dismissed every figure. So I fabricated a rag doll. Reza immediately fashioned a little kerchief for the rag doll and held it close to himself and took it home. On his next visit, he came very close to me and whispered in my ear, "I speak Farsi."

I now learned that Reza had been especially attached to his maternal grandmother, who stayed behind in Iran when he moved to America. Because of the Iranian hostage crisis, she could not come to visit. During subsequent sessions, Reza, while holding onto the rag doll, played out his anger at his family for bringing him to the U.S., where he could not have his intimate Farsi talks with his beloved grandmother.

After 3 months of play therapy, Reza started to talk. Whispering in my ear, he told me to tell his parents that he wanted to talk on the phone to his grandmother. I insisted that he would have to tell this loudly and clearly to his parents in my presence, which he did (while holding onto the rag doll). When he arrived at school the next day, doll in hand, he declared to his class, "I speak Farsi." The class accepted his entirely new speech nonchalantly, even though they did not know exactly what he meant.

MEANING OF THE MOMENT

We must follow children's leads no matter whether we are playing, talking, or medicating. This young boy presented virtually no psychiatric history, but he came to therapy with a background replete with cultural motifs.[83] As Reza searched for a doll, I realized we would have to tailor an object to suit him. He then decided that our finished project was "Grandma." Through using his self-designated transitional object, Reza became able to break his silence.[84]

This is an example of setting up a perfectly nondescript, nonleading item for a child and then waiting for the youngster's response to it. The item itself crossed cultures. Rita Rogers originally comes from Hungary, and the boy, from Iran. Rita survived the Holocaust; the boy emigrated from a country that currently disavows the Holocaust. Yet doctor and patient understood each other. The piece of fabric, for both of them, *was* Grandma. The adult and child spoke the same language, the language of love. It didn't matter that the young man had decided to be mute. His doctor knew how to watch and "listen." Once Reza could show Dr. Rogers his concerns, he became able to speak once again.

Consider, if you will, how similar the first three examples of this chapter are. Each child was eager to indicate his or her problem to the doctor. It just took the very general stimulation of a pleasant office, an adult who obviously wanted to learn about the child, a willingness to play or draw, and a problem crying out for expression. We cannot let these expressions fall on deaf ears and closed eyes. What children say and do is significant.

One of the tragedies of our busy, busy times is the fact that parents often don't hear what their children are saying. Something very important may be minimized or even denied. Children want their parents to know if trouble is brewing. It's a desire that may be masked by disdain and ridicule on the part of the kid. But underneath everything is the old, innate wish that somehow, in some way, a parent will get the message and understand. Everything we grasp as parents cannot be gleaned in retrospect. Some predictive and prospective actions must occasionally be taken. If we accept the cues we receive from our kids, we'll be that much better off.

I can't help thinking in this respect about a Washington, D.C., political problem that came about because a child's statement had long gone unheeded. After he left the Congress, a 16-year-old boy, a page to the House of Representatives, tried to tell the congressman for whom he had worked (a Louisiana representative) that Mark Foley, a Florida representative, had been writing him "sick" emails. The boy's former boss didn't do much. It was a "political" decision, most likely. The boy must have felt unheeded. Then the emails, along with the boy's complaint, found their way to the House leadership—the Speaker of the House, the Republican fundraising chair, the Majority Leader, the chair of the committee on pages, and probably a number of others. But rather than acknowledging the page's characterization of Foley's behaviors as "sick," a few of the congressmen renamed the behavior as "over-friendly," warning the Florida representative to behave himself in the future. The House leadership virtually dropped any investigation they might have undertaken. This, too, must have been an attempt to "save political skins," but psychologically, the adolescent boy once again must have felt ignored. After about 10 months, old instant messages from Foley to a number of other 16- and 17-year-old pages arrived in Washington. Tony Snow, the President's Press Secretary, mischaracterized them as "naughty." He, too, was "denying" away the import of what the children meant to say. But one after another, enough instant messages and accusations arrived until an avalanche of evidence buried the delays, the inaction, and the excuses that the adults in high places had made. No one meant to do psychological harm to boys, I would guess. The motive was to mitigate political harm to Congress and the Republican party. It turned out to be one of those telling examples of what happens when adults cannot or will not attend to kids. Someone alerted ABC News. ABC listened.

By the time she turned 7, Cammie Brooks was valiantly trying to act "normal," but unfortunately, she was experiencing serious problems listening and paying attention. In her classroom she exhibited signs of ADHD, which were probably related to the horrible shakings that Nick and Bonnie had subjected her to as an infant. She would need medication to learn, to function at school without running around and talking, and (later) to do her homework. Cammie's neurologist and I agreed to give her methylphenidate (Ritalin) two to three times a day. Cammie also developed "absence" seizures, during which time she mentally derailed, made barely noticeable facial movements, and then became stuporous. Once, Cammie's neurologist needed to test her under anesthesia. The 6-year-old emerged from unconsciousness, growling in basso tones at Sandra, "You bad!" and "Trow away." I rushed to the hospital in response to Sandra's urgent phone call. In her disoriented post-anesthetic state, Cammie was reliving her traumatic infancy with Bonnie.[85] Sandra felt relieved once she understood Cammie's "displacement."[86] The little girl's seizure disorder, like her ADHD, became relatively easily managed with the proper medications. She had become frightened, however, of all these health problems and their attendant interventions. And, unfortunately, this was just the beginning.

I still thought, despite all her health problems, that Cammie might be "normal" enough to quit her psychotherapy in about a year. She was drawing herself as a regular little person. She saw herself as "usual," not weird. To prepare her to leave my care, I asked Sandra and Tom's permission to tell Cammie what had happened during her infancy. We arranged a sequence. First, Sandra showed Cammie photos of her old house, the baby's grave (weed-covered and unmarked), the hospital E.R. where Cammie had been taken the first day she arrived at the Brooks's house, and her birth parents. Then, I told Cammie the facts of her infancy as I understood them. I told her about her injuries, both mental and physical. She took it well, without any visible shock or distress. In fact, I concluded that Cammie might still remember bits and pieces. Yes, infantile amnesia masks most event memory from before a person turns 3 or 4. But trauma, with its shocking specialness, may break through this kind of amnesia. A feeling tone, a physical sensation, a sense of something terrible, a wordless (or one- or two-word) memory, may be retained. We must remind ourselves that at age 2, in fact, Cammie had been able to tell me, "baby die, die baby," all by herself. So her calm reaction to what I told her now, as a 7-year-old, did not surprise me.

Planning along with me, Sandra and Tom drove northeast in the Central Valley to check out Bethany's gravesite. They cleaned up the disreputable little burial plot, planted groundcover, and ordered a tiny stone. The graveyard keeper remarked to them, "I've always wondered if somebody would ever come out here to visit this poor little baby." And then, with Bethany's marker on order, Sandra, Tom, and I went into the waiting mode. Would Cammie indicate that she was ready to leave me? Would we "get it" when the moment came?

Children set up various kinds of leads for us to follow. Some point to a certain defense mechanism, such as Cammie's post-anesthetic displacement from her birth mother to her adopted mother. Some direct us to an actual event, such as the little Wyoming siblings' indication that their murdered mother had been alive when they found her. Other leads children offer us have to do with a wish—for contact with Grandma, for instance. Or they deal with a complaint (the page's communication to his former boss, for example). A few, in fact, relay messages about the child's own self-image. ("I'm just a lump of shit," from Aubrey Metcalf's vignette in Chapter 4.)

Spencer Eth, an expert on childhood trauma whose research work I have long admired, gives us an interesting therapeutic "moment" here. It hinges on his recognizing a classic childhood defense, "denial in fantasy." Dr. Eth, like me, was dealing with a child whose mother had been murdered. But in his case, Spencer had the privilege of treating, not just assessing, the youngster. When the child inadvertently threw out a dramatic hint as to his defenses, the doctor took him up on it, and the boy's post-traumatic condition instantly and dramatically began to turn around. Of course the young man would always have to live in the shadow of an awful family tragedy. But he would also be able to stand up proudly now, and enjoy some of the better moments that life might offer him.

When the Dead Become Alive

CONTRIBUTED BY SPENCER ETH, MD

Andre experienced a tragedy that no child should ever endure. He was 2 when his parents separated, and afterwards he rarely saw his father. When he was 3, Andre's mother became involved with Joe, a jealous and violent man. After the affair was over (from Andre's mom's point of view), both mother and son tried to avoid Joe. But one day when Andre was 5, Joe found the boy and his mother and forced them to accompany him to a motel. Joe ordered Andre to stay under the bedcovers. The boy peeked out, however, and saw his mother being beaten to death. He was an eyewitness to murder. The next day, Andre was placed with his father. Four months later in our first psychiatric session, Andre drew a picture and told the story of a racecar driver who won a race and received a trophy. In doing so, however, he angered the other drivers. This story evolved into another about a racecar driver whose car spun out of control. The driver was burned and had to go to the hospital. As we spoke about hospitals, Andre firmly announced that he did not want to talk about someone being dead. He picked up a toy telephone and repeatedly dialed home, complaining, "There's no answer. No one is at home." Andre was eventually able to talk about what had happened to his mother and how he had taken a "big look" from under the covers. He felt afraid to do anything at that time, "because Joe might whip me." The little boy then picked up a toy gun, saying, "I would like to be able to shoot Joe." He added, "You wouldn't whip me, would you?"

In the session following his sixth birthday, Andre described the party his father had thrown for him. Everyone was there, and he had received many fine gifts. Andre announced solemnly that his mother was not at the party. He then added quietly that she wouldn't be at his seventh, or eighth, or any other birthday party, either. At that point, on the verge of tears, Andre heard my office telephone ring. He shrieked, "Is that my mother calling?"

MEANING OF THE MOMENT

Andre's poignant lapse into wish fulfillment (that his mother was still alive) contrasted sharply with his acknowledgment immediately before that of the terrible reality that she would never appear at a birthday again. This moment in therapy illustrated the power of the defense mechanism "denial in fantasy." Anna Freud wrote that: "the fantasies helped [a World War II–traumatized London boy] to reconcile himself to reality . . . conscious insight into the inevitable played no part here."[87] I was able to show Andre that he had shut out reality by means of imagining that his mom was still alive. He was thinking of her "living and well, on the telephone." The idea might help

him for a while, I told him, until he could sort everything out.
As Andre considered this over several weeks, he became far more
able to accept his own traumatic bereavement. He eventually
gained considerable strength from his psychotherapy, and
when asked, he testified powerfully in court for the criminal
prosecution against Joe.

The therapeutic distance one finally is able to go with a child whose parent has been murdered may turn out shorter than the distance one gets to travel with a less disturbed child. One has to gauge the type and severity of the original condition when one considers the extent of these magical moments of change. I think of Dr. Eth's young patient, Andre, as a very seriously affected survivor with miles and miles to travel prior to arriving at true "wellness." Dr. Eth's discovery of what Andre was trying to tell him—that he had peeked during the murder; that he continuously feared another attack, this time on himself; that he refused to allow himself to believe that his mother was gone; that he told himself she'd be on the phone—helped the doctor explain to young Andre the mental mechanisms he was using. The doctor expressed willingness to wait for the boy to give up on his defensive maneuvers. But the boy, in response to Spencer Eth's interpretation, turned around within the course of a few weeks. He accepted bereavement, the first step in the long, long process of childhood grief. He went to court and faced Joe, a sign of extreme bravery, especially after almost being murdered by Joe himself. All this was accomplished because the psychiatrist was acutely attuned to following the child's lead. Dr. Eth then provided the linkages and explanations to account for what the little boy revealed.

I believe that a child with a milder condition than Andre's (and, perhaps, with a condition that just recently was discovered) will come closer to normalcy than Andre did after his "moment of change." A child with recently discovered problems may even look totally well following his moment. Such was the case with a newly disturbed and definitely untraumatized 4-year-old boy who fell into the hands of New Orleans child and adolescent psychiatrist, Martin Drell.

All Talk and No Play Makes Jack a Dull Boy

CONTRIBUTED BY MARTIN J. DRELL, MD

Once, under severe time constraints, I tried to save my clients money by doing a quick two-session evaluation on their 4-year-old son, Jack, who had suddenly begun to have terrible temper tantrums. I met first with the parents and then with the young boy. I was active. I was structured. My questions came quickly and furiously. At the end, I had tons of data and not a clue as to what was going on. Why was Jack so suddenly angry at his family? After a few fruitless attempts to contort the data into a usable formulation, I realized that my concerns about money and competence had gotten in the way. I vowed to jettison my idea of a brief assessment and return to what I was comfortable with—a longer evaluation in which I was less active, kept my mouth shut, and let the child show or tell me what was going on.

This strategy worked. At Jack's next visit, after a short pause in which I invited him to play, he went over to the two-story dollhouse, which he began to arrange to approximate the floorplan of his own house. The family dolls were then set in motion, with the father and mother dolls yelling and screaming while the little boy doll lay still in his bed, pretending to be asleep. After the parent dolls fought, the father doll was banished to the downstairs sofa while the mother doll stayed in the upstairs bedroom next to the bedroom of her frightened son. Variations on this theme pervaded the entire session. At the end, I called Jack's parents into the office. With their little boy's permission, I proceeded to recount the events in the dollhouse. Jack's parents were flabbergasted. They had no idea he knew of their recent marital troubles. They had tried their best to argue after he had gone to bed.

MEANING OF THE MOMENT

Jack fully knew what was worrying him. But he hadn't been able to tell me in ordinary language. He needed to use the symbolic idiom of play. And he needed a little time to relax. Once I relaxed us both, he could demonstrate his problem brilliantly.

Jack reminded me that a child often can hold up his end of therapy,[88] *especially if the process is not interfered with by the therapist's anxieties and doubts.*[89] *As the Bible says, "and a little child shall lead them."*

This case shows just how important it is to give children enough time and space to take the lead. Dr. Drell found that when he took over the assessment process with total control, the little patient would give his doctor nothing. As soon as he let up and allowed the young fellow to "show and tell," there was no further problem following the preschooler's lead.

Unlike congressional politicians who need to be elected every 2 years, we psychiatrists and mental health practitioners have no reason to deny or disregard what we learn from children. Yes, a child, especially with a custody dispute hanging over his head, may have a preplanned or adult-imparted "agenda." But these agendas lack the spontaneity of a comment like, "You wouldn't whip me, would you?" They lack the liveliness of a dollhouse filled with fighting adults. To me, adult agendas in the mouths of children sound just like what they are, a talking-points memo from Mom or a smear campaign from Dad.

For reasons of space and continuity, I cannot go into great detail about separating the true childhood lead from the false, or implanted, one. But I will give you a small example here before leaving the subject. A very young boy, the object of a nasty custody dispute, came to my office to try to convince me that he should live with his dad. He gave me a whole list of reasons, some of which sounded sophisticated and rehearsed. But the child was genuinely enthusiastic about how much more fun he had with Dad, especially at the races, when his father competed in the stockcar events.

"Tell me more about the races," I requested, following the lead I was receiving from this boy's emotional tone.

"I sit with Dad's friends. We laugh. They put pink powder in their noses. They get the powder from Dad. He puts it in his nose, too. We all have fun."

"Show me the color pink," I asked innocuously. He pointed at my white walls. He showed me a white book. Following this little boy's lead had taken me to a weekend activity loaded with cocaine, or something like it. It did not bode well for his father's custody (or visitation) wishes.

If a child fails to talk at home about a crucial issue—like how she thinks she looks, for example—that doesn't necessarily mean the subject lacks importance. It may mean that the child does not have parental permission to discuss the matter. Or that the parents are too pained by an issue to open it up. Or that someone feels jeopardized, or guilty, or even humiliated, about what this particular child might say.

Children often come to our offices with something so painful to say that they can only tell *us*. It may be, in fact, their only chance to let it out. We must give them enough space to "say their piece" or "play their piece." The best approach is to expose the entire problem, to get it out into the open. And then we must deal with it.

Michael Brody, an expert on the mass media and its effects on children, found himself treating a depressed mother who had given birth to a little girl with facial deformities and partial deafness. The mother, a beautiful woman herself, felt absolutely devastated at having such a strange-looking and impaired young child. Dr. Brody, realizing that his adult patient could not allow her daughter to say how she felt, decided to assess the little kindergartener himself. The poor child was having problems at school separating from her mom.

Watch how an experienced psychotherapist follows this little girl's lead. Watch, too, for how this particular mother exhibits "blindness" and "deafness" to her own child's cues. We well understand the reason here. It is a maternal sense of failure.

Barbie Versus Mr. Potato Head

CONTRIBUTED BY MICHAEL BRODY, MD

Sarah was born deaf, with incomplete development of the ears and a deformed face. She came to me at 5 years old, suffering from severe separation fears and a pending school phobia. Her mother had begun seeing me years before over depression for bringing "such a child" into the world. Sarah's mom had decided not to send the little girl to nursery school, for fear that she would be teased. When I first met her, it appeared that Sarah had internalized her mother's disgust and anxiety. She could not stay in kindergarten without her mom. The teachers were growing impatient.

The little girl looked sad, very small and immature, and had badly distorted facial features. I could barely understand her speech. Around her neck, she wore a device for hearing, and at first, she only interacted with her mother. I asked her mom to show me how they played together. Hesitant at first, her mother went to a pile of dolls, some of which were Barbies and some of which were generic dolls. Sarah's mother selected two blonde Barbies who looked quite like Mom and nothing like Sarah. "Hey, let's go to school," she prompted her little daughter. There was a long pause. I said nothing. Sarah looked bored and her mom stopped talking.

Then it happened! Sarah spied something of interest in my pile of toys. She pulled out Mr. Potato Head. Busily, she began picking up some small plastic pieces: a nose, a lip, and an ear. Slowly, and oh so carefully, she attached them. Sarah began telling us, not just her mom, about "Willie." She was going to make "his face . . . put this here . . . get him his nose," she said. Busily, she worked on correcting the poor old potato's deformities. After about 15 minutes, Sarah's mother left us. We worked together for a few weeks—always using Mr. Potato Head—until the little girl could stay at school alone.

As she grew up, Sarah went through a number of corrective surgeries. I continued to work with her mother. I also saw Sarah about every 6 months to check on her developmental progress. Her mom gradually recovered from her depression and began using her renewed energy to care for and stimulate her daughter. During her sophomore year of college, I met directly with Sarah once a week. She talked about various problems of young adulthood. In a voice that had become far more resonant and clear, she spoke while manipulating old Mr. Potato Head. In fact, she picked him up just about every time she came.

MEANING OF THE MOMENT

Our moment, when Sarah was 5, demonstrates that a child will choose the right toy to tell her particular story. Control and mastery were the most obvious themes of Sarah's kindergarten-age play, but identity was also a central issue.[90] *She identified with the ugly Potato Head while simultaneously trying to be the person, like a surgeon, who could refashion old "Willie's" face. Mr. Potato Head not only provided the spark for 5-year-old Sarah's healing play (creating a new self-image), but also became just the right metaphor to anchor our relationship while Sarah attended college.*

In the previous chapter, Stewart Teal's vignette told the story of how one drawing served as a link between a boy's problem with his mother at the age of 9 and his return of symptoms upon going to college at 19. Here, Michael Brody's story presents a similar situation—a young girl who played with the same toy, a Mr. Potato Head, in two periods of treatment about 13 years apart. Each time, a certain picture or a specific toy was especially meaningful to the patient. Each time, an early "moment" was created by following the youngster's lead. The difference, however, is that in Dr. Teal's case, the same stimulus was used to set up two discrete moments. In Dr. Brody's case, the moment occurred only once—on the first psychiatric appointment when she was 5. Later, the college-aged girl fussed with Mr. Potato Head during a series of appointments, but she did not experience a second moment of change through using this metaphor.

I think if I had had a young child patient who was going to need repeated plastic surgeries, I would have gone out to buy a Mr. Potato Head, or something quite like it. If I were treating such a child, I would have hoped, in fact, to find three different toys of that type, so that the youngster could pick a favorite among them. I remember once evaluating a little girl who had been "scalped" by a lion at a Texas antique fair. I didn't have any lion figurines or stuffed animals in my office at the time, so I went across the street and bought three hand puppets, a lion, a raccoon, and a bunny. The little girl refused my new lion with great distaste, handing him off to me. But she took the other two puppets in hand and then interacted, with significant personal revelation, with "my" lion. It was well worth the triple purchase, and, as you already know, my raccoon spent 2 additional years being Cammie Brooks' Wolf.

By the time she turned 8, Cammie had long since given up Wolf. She went on to play "Tyrannosaurus rex," because she, like the rest of her first-grade class, enjoyed the world of dinosaurs. Unfortunately, however, T. rex psychologically resembled Wolf for Cammie. He liked to steal and eat the other dinosaurs' children. I set myself to help Cammie find "corrections" for T.'s horrible behaviors. We played out reactive beatings from Stegosaurus's plates, gorings through the use of Triceratops's horn, lashings with Brontosaurus's tail. Cammie enjoyed these dino fights and even allowed her T. rex to temporarily lose. But the beatings, gorings, and lashings didn't totally daunt the toothiest dinosaur of them all. By the end of each session, old T. rex rose again!

A "moment" of change, however, was on the horizon for young Cammie Brooks, and this one, unique among her eight turning points, would take place well beyond my sight. A sweet little gravestone for Bethany had been installed north of the Brooks's home. The dead infant's plot was beautifully cleaned up and replanted. Even Bethany's graveyard keeper looked happier. It was time to take Cammie to go "see" her baby sister.

On their drive up and across the Central Valley to the cemetery, Sandra, Tom, and Cammie stopped at a florist shop and bought a bouquet. Then they went straight to the cemetery. A very pretty and proper 8-year-old girl by now, young Cammie was visibly moved. She stooped down and set the flowers near her baby sister's name. Then she said something entirely unplanned and unrehearsed. It was magical in its own way. "You died," Cammie addressed her words to Bethany. "I got to live," she went on. "I promise you I'll have a good life."

Not only would Cammie be a person, not an animal—and a civilized "usual" person at that—but now, she was vowing to be "good" as well. This was a shared moment between an innocent survivor and an innocent, but dead, victim. It was an episode of great promise. Although I was only tangentially involved (having told Cammie the facts of what had happened, and helping Sandra and Tom plan her cemetery visit), I consider this a therapeutic turning point for Cammie.

CHAPTER NINE

Passing a Child's Test

Western literature is chock full of stories in which a young person (almost always a male) must pass a special test in order to prove himself worthy. In fairytales, it's the young upstart prince, or even a simpleton, who wants to marry a certain princess and win half the kingdom. But first he must climb a glass hill, slay a wicked dragon, climb brambles, enter a ghostly castle, and ride his stallion "east of the sun, west of the moon." If you prefer classics, the would-be hero must clean the filthiest of stables, win at Troy, journey the Aegean and Mediterranean Seas, and fly on a winged horse or two. Happily, in Greek mythology, we find a test-taking female as well, young Psyche. In order to win back her lover, Eros, Psyche must complete a series of difficult tasks and travels.

In real-life Western history, we find that test-taking knights were expected to joust and to keep vigils. Younger sons were sent out to seek their fortunes on the high seas. Even during America's golden period, there were difficult tests for the young and ambitious. John Adams, who as a boy had struggled with languages, was forced to learn Latin (a formidable task) in order to gain admission to Harvard.[91] George Washington had to prove himself repeatedly to his peers because he did not have the opportunity to go to college.[92] Proof, proof, proof. Test, test, test. It never stops in Western literature and history.

Today, all of us mental health professionals go through considerable advanced schooling to end up, finally, in our chosen careers. You'd think those pop quizzes, midterms, final exams, and term papers would have ended by graduation time. On top of that, however, each one of us has had to pass a number of qualifying exams—even requalifying exams—in order to practice in the particular state and with the particular certificate we want.

The psychiatrist might like to sit down and relax after all that test taking, right? But no. If we work with kids, our test taking will go on forever. The only difference is that we're not always certain we're being tested. The youngster in psychiatric treatment is not likely to announce, "Today is test day!" Like a terrorist who remains quiet after the bomb explodes, the child silently puts you through your paces, all the while watching to see if *you* explode. In other words, child-given tests are sneaky and subtle. The exams are all about the therapeutic relationship. "Does this therapist want to work with me? Do I want to work with her? How much does she care?"

Interestingly, the parents of our young patients test us, too. But we are almost always conscious of the fact that we are being examined. "What are your qualifications?" a mother and father want to know. "What psychological 'school' do you follow? Are you eclectic? Do you specialize in something? Will you make sure to keep young Colby off medications? Do you *have* to tell Shelly's school that you are working with her?" These are tough questions and require straight, honest answers. Sometimes your answers may sound "wrong" to the parents, and you still do your best to explain yourself as "right" for their child. But you will not be able to pass such parental tests each and every time. You will know, even in the worst possible case, however, that you have been examined. It is clear that a test has taken place.

As opposed to the adult-administered test, a child-driven exam does not usually come in question form. There are no out-and-out confrontations. Rather, these are subtle, or sometimes not-so-subtle, attempts to throw you and the psychotherapy off track. Why should a kid be so eager to derail a program that, in the long run, is likely to help? Because psychotherapy usually functions as a kind of deprivation. You are chipping away at defenses, deviant actions, and even fears that feel ordinary and sometimes quite acceptable to the child. You are doing slow surgery, cutting out dysfunctional parts while your little patient is unanaesthetized and fully awake. It hurts. It stings. Why can't you attack someone else? What would make you give up? How might you—involuntarily—be sent away?

A "test" is a great method of ridding oneself of a "geek," a "nag," or a "dolt," children think. If the doctor flunks the child's exam, the test administrator can tell mom or dad not to pay the bill, or to stop bringing him, or that the therapy is "all screwed up." The kid might also mock the doctor at school, exaggerate, or create an "incident" for others to hear with comic hilarity or even alarm.

All and all, then, it's crucial to be on the alert for child-initiated tests while conducting psychotherapy. Most of these come early in the sequence of treatment. The youngster is examining whether it is safe to enter the relationship. But a number of tests, may be organized later, too. This is one of the main places we see, and may be able to interpret, transference. It is important that we ask about, comment on, and sometimes willingly take these tests. At times, too, it is important that we play along in silence.

Basically, there are two types of response one might consider to the child-initiated test. The first is interpretive; the second is participatory without interpretation. A young Portland, Oregon, psychiatrist, James Powers, who practices in the same office suite with our vignette contributor Mike Deeney, offers us an illustrative vignette here. It tells the story of a teenaged girl who had slipped out of treatment with James a while back and had returned for a possible second course. The patient put Dr. Powers into an impossible bind early in the period when he was trying to reinstitute her psychotherapy. The test was set up as an announcement. The doctor's response was set up very deliberately and with entirely conscious planning.

The Test

CONTRIBUTED BY JAMES POWERS, MD

Sixteen-year-old Taylor came unwillingly to my office for a second attempt at therapy. It, like her first attempt at 14, came at the request of her grandmother, who was concerned about Taylor's tendency to speak and dress provocatively, to get involved with "bad" boys, and to take chances with fast crowds and fast cars. She had a working diagnosis of "conduct disorder." But that didn't tell half her story.

Taylor's father died of a heroin overdose when she was 5 years old; soon afterward, she was removed from her mother's custody for severe neglect. Taylor was then placed with her 20-year-old sister and her sister's fiancé. She lived there for 9 years until, once again, she was found to have been neglected. After a brief placement with her grandmother, who did not have the energy to keep up with her, Taylor went into the custody of her next-older sister, who by then was 20 and had a live-in boyfriend. This arrangement continued for only a year because of chaos at the sister's house. Taylor was then placed with a paternal cousin. The net effect of this neglectful early life was that Taylor was often left to fend for herself. When she experimented, her guardians often rationalized the risk-taking behavior as ultimately being in her best interests. They refused to have any struggles with her around limits. Taylor considered this a fine way to achieve an intoxicating sense of freedom.

I originally met Taylor during the period in which she was living with her middle sister. We worked together a short while, but she dropped out without explanation when her sister's boyfriend was arrested for a racially motivated assault. Two years later, her grandmother insisted that Taylor return to therapy. After about 3 months of begrudging compliance, the girl requested that we decrease her once-weekly sessions to every other week. I felt uneasy about it, believing that if I agreed, Taylor would slip between the cracks once again and be lost to therapy, this time forever. I was aware of a conflict, however. If I said a plain "no," Taylor would probably throw me into the hated role of an authority figure who was limiting her autonomy. That could easily rupture any trust that might be developing between us. Thus, I did my best to navigate between the Scylla and Charybdis of neglect and authoritarianism. I told Taylor that if she wanted to decrease the frequency of her therapy, I would not stop her. But I also needed her to know that I didn't

*think it was in her best interests. Taylor then tried, with the full
arsenal of her persuasive abilities, to convince me that it was
both in her and in my best interests. I persisted, saying I would
not prevent her, but I would not be persuaded to say something
I thought was untrue. We left it unresolved. By the next time
Taylor came (2 weeks later, of course), she announced that she
had decided to visit me every single week. From that time on,
Taylor has engaged me in a lively, unambivalent, open way.
She seems to trust me, in fact.*

MEANING OF THE MOMENT

Children who are neglected often test.[93] *This has little to do
with their diagnosis. Instead, it rests on their need to gauge the
therapist's ability to protect them. By indulging in risk-taking
behaviors, such kids repeatedly and unconsciously manipulate the hypothesis that they are unworthy of achieving their
developmental goals. In any adolescent, the wish to be cared for
often comes into conflict with an opposite wish, to "do what I
want." This conflict may be exaggerated in a neglected teenager.
During Taylor's therapeutic turning point, I was able to demonstrate my concern and incorruptibility without making her feel
that I was limiting her ability to make her own decisions.*

We've seen enough examples of instantaneous, spontaneous therapeutic moves now that James Powers's careful deliberation and refusal to
leap one way or the other looks fresh and entertaining. When you
think about what the doctor actually did, you find that he simply refused to make any move. He "danced on the head of a pin." He carefully spelled out the nature of the patient's test for her and then refused
to take it. He played the "waiting game."

In response, the patient made it seem that she had won some sort of
victory—by breaking a week off from her psychotherapy schedule. But
when she returned, it was on Dr. Powers's terms, not hers. The psychiatrist's patience had paid off. The problem was well interpreted, and
the girl—because of it—could better understand her other important
relationships. She was really the one who benefited from her test. Like
the lightbulb in the old joke, it was now *she* who "wanted to change."

With older teenagers, it's interesting to note how many of these important tests occur in the last seconds of an hour. After the psychiatrist has said something like, "We've run out of time, so I'll see you next week," comes the adolescent's test. Often it is posed as a question—"Can we change my meds?" "Can we make it in 2 weeks?" "Do you mind giving me your home phone number?" "Your cell?" "Your pager?" Newspaper reporters and television producers have told me (informally over the years) that they can count on this same sort of thing happening after they've closed their notebooks, laptops, or stopped the cameras from rolling with an "expert." One is still "on the record," and this last-minute material usually gets "in." As a test taker, the psychological professional can't be too careful.

Usually the successful psychotherapeutic tactic with young patients is to put off last-minute tests until "next time." Then we can really discuss the issue with our young charges. Unless a crisis is involved (the patient indicates a bad reaction to a medication, an urge to commit suicide, a suddenly developing problem at school), the child's test must wait. The psychiatrist, like James Powers, makes sure to bring up the patient's last-minute test as this "next time" comes around. And during this second session, there will be enough space and breathing room to interpret the patient's transference, as well as the test that was administered.

The silent or unstated test and its nonverbal answer is another equally important type of child-initiated exam and its psychotherapeutic response. We've already seen three very good examples in earlier vignettes, as a matter of fact. Recall Henry Massie's adolescent patient whose father was off fighting in the Iraq War (Chapter 5). The young girl virtually refused to talk to Henry the first time she met him. Throughout that first hour—in a sense—Henry took her test. In her view, he might have failed, or passed (through his patience), or come out in a gray area. But in the subsequent session Henry suggested that the two of them play. That was a delayed but A+ response to the girl's silence of the week before. It cemented their relationship without interpreting it at all.

When the adolescent patient of Dr. Mike Deeney caught the psychiatrist driving his "cool" Jaguar into his office parking lot, that, too, looked like an instance of patient-initiated, though inadvertent, testing (Chapter 4). The doctor had already ducked questions about whose car it was. So he might have been construed by his young patient to be dishonest or, at the least, evasive. But Dr. Deeney handled the exam in a straightforward way. He answered that the Jag was, indeed, his car, and then he threw in a bonus for the patient. Would he like to go for a ride? No interpretation was offered but none was required. Their relationship turned positive from that moment on.

The third uninterpreted test you have already read about came from the 6-year-old incurably leukemic girl who, mysteriously, was not walking (Chapter 1). Here was a very young child who, like an adolescent, needed to test her new doctor, Ronald Benson, to see if he could "take it." Little Darlene needed to know if an adult male professional could bear hearing her thoughts. So she studied his demeanor—and probably his eyes for the glint of a tear. After Ron proved himself strong enough, she engaged him in a crucial conversation. It forged enough of a relationship to sustain Darlene for the rest of her short life. There was no need to interpret what had just taken place. Tests, well-taken, are often self-explanatory. They require no commentary from the observer. One simply moves on.

As Cammie Brooks moved on from her fourth "moment," her visit to her baby sister's grave, I considered ending Cammie's treatment. We were enormously optimistic about the progress Cammie had made from animal to human, and then to a committed, "good" human, as well. But even at 8 years old, pretty and petite that she was, there were a few "failed tests" that concerned Sandra, Tom, and me. For "Show and Tell" in her small, first-grade classroom, for example, Cammie brought her pet gerbil, "Mousie," to school. Unfortunately, she returned home with a dying animal. She had squeezed poor Mousie too hard.

Cammie insisted on burying Mousie in a little cardboard box under a giant oak tree on the Brooks's property. She cried with genuine regret. It was an important lesson in death, burial, and ceremony. But I remained concerned about Cammie's "squeeze." Was she still using too much "identification with the aggressor" (all that T. rex play) and "passive into active" (never, never a victim again) to get along in human society?[94]

On top of these emotional problems, by the middle of first grade Cammie was academically behind by 2 full years. She had begun the first year of what turned out to be a childhood spent in tutorials. Both reading and math needed continuous bolstering. By the time she began reading on her own (with difficulty), Cammie used her pictorial reading materials, especially those about animals, to shake herself to orgasm. Polite person that she was trying to be, she would excuse herself gracefully to her room. Then the whole Brooks house would virtually rock to the increasingly violent rhythms of her self-stimulating shaking.

But the *coup de grace* to our plans to terminate Cammie's psychotherapy literally came from her brave, but troubled, heart. Cammie developed wild, fast-paced heartbeats that would last for a day or two at a time. It was an electrical conduction problem. She was taken to UCLA, first for diagnostic studies and then for cardiac ablation procedures. Apparently, Cammie's heart contained several locations that generated, or picked up on, aberrant rhythms. I talked by phone with the leader of the pediatric heart team. I told her how regressed this "wild child" might become under anesthesia. I said how essential it was to have Sandra or Tom with Cammie at all times.

Then I let the heart team do their work. At the same time, I realized that terminating Cammie's therapy would be unwise. We were going to have to stick with once-monthly psychotherapy for the foreseeable future.

You may wonder which of Cammie's many physical problems directly stemmed from what Nick and Bonnie had done to her, both in and out of utero. The ADHD and seizures were apparently directly connected to being shaken as an infant. The learning disabilities also directly related to the "shaken baby syndrome" from which Cammie suffered. The cardiac enervation difficulties, on the other hand, which took up much of Cammie's next couple of years (and the gastrointestinal tract enervation problems, which showed up as she became an adolescent), could not be explained through the traumatic shaking and biting meted out to her as an infant. There was another possibility, however, although we could not prove it. Bonnie may have used street drugs during her pregnancy with Cammie. An ongoing fetal bath in cocaine, methamphetamine, or a similar "upper" might have accounted for this kind of electrical conduction abnormality. It would have been a relatively rare effect, but it is occasionally noted as an intrauterine complication.[95]

Unfortunately, the cardiac ablation procedures done on Cammie did not completely work. They helped, but many of Cammie's elementary school days were marked by the times she was unable to go or to stay at school because of a racing heart. This certainly didn't help her learning problems. Nor did it make it easy to medicate her for her ADHD. Given extra homework to try to catch her up, Cammie developed screeching tantrums when her academic energies were depleted. This pretty and sweet young lady, when faced with a tough homework assignment, was capable of sounding like a wounded beast. She was also capable of administering a "test," as you shall soon see.

Parents are kid-tested more frequently, but less dramatically, than we psychiatrists are.[96] The temper tantrum is an early test, a battle of wills and control. The parental response, hopefully always the same, is to move the small preschooler or toddler away from the place where the conflict started and to divert the youngster's interest to something else. Refusal to join the battle is the best parental response. More problematic behavior is stimulated, on the other hand, when two parents handle the same situation differently, or when one parent cannot remain consistent with his or her behavior.

The next great group of tests often comes up around preschool and kindergarten "triangulations." Because normal Western kids watch their parents for cracks in their togetherness, anything that splits a mother and father apart may be tried by a youngster. Again, despite differences in how each parent may want to react, they must work out a unified type of response. When both parents work, when the family is divorced, or when there is a single parent (and, perhaps, a grandmother or a hired babysitter), the unified response has to be coordinated between all the child's caretakers.

Children became "legalistic" by the time they reach latency age. Parents must sometimes (not always) hear the arguments out. On the other hand, the test is whether the parents will get lawyerlike, too. They need to find other means. In fact, by school age and for the foreseeable future, children become varying and enterprising test givers. Just look at the tests my colleagues and I have reported up to now. The type of test becomes more variable than anything ever thrown at us psychiatrists by teachers or professors. The idea is for parents to remain consistent, unified, patient, and flexible enough to change their overall plan, if necessary. One easily can "punt" (delay) and then come up with a plan later. And, thankfully, even if a good parent flunks a few child-administered tests, he or she will probably graduate with honors from the largely self-taught "School of Parenthood."

I was unaware of Cammie Brooks as a test giver when she started playing "Dinosaur" in my office at 6½ as she was going through her second round of kindergarten. For about a year or so, we indulged in one-on-one fights between T. rex and the other dinos, who in sequence were trying to protect their babies. I knew that the traumatic theme (biting infants to death) would continue unabated until Cammie's trauma could be more fully worked out. It was such a terrible, life-altering trauma that it would not retreat with ease. When Cammie was about 8, I decided to try pitting organizations of dinos against T. rex. This was an attempt to prove to her (without many words) that societal institutions, like firemen, police, armies, and governments, had enough power to defeat the outliers, like Cammie's birth family. We built dino-made cliffs for T. rex to fall off. We invented an all-dino police squad and an all-dino reform school for juveniles. She let T. rex lose. We laughed a lot. We found foster homes for the neglected dino young, and we constructed orphanages whenever there was a mass slaughter of adults. We felt sad for the survivors. Whatever we did to understand (context) and fix (correct) the dinosaurs' behaviors, however, old T. rex inevitably rose again. Like Lazarus, he could, in fact, rise from the dead.

Just after Cammie turned 9, she was dealt an unusually bad hand in the game of life. First, an 8-year-old girl down the street, whom Cammie didn't know, disappeared. A couple of days later, she was found raped and murdered. The local sheriffs captured an itinerant handyman in short order. But all the talk around town left Cammie feeling terrible. In fact, one day after drawing herself as a ballerina literally floating on air inside her house, she drew one of the most miserable, unhappy, pessimistic self-portraits I'd ever seen. It was the day after her unfortunate little neighbor disappeared. The drawing showed huge rain clouds over Cammie's house, buckets of tears falling from her eyes, and a face blackened with smudges and frowns.

Within a week or so, Cammie's situation became even worse. Her birth father, Nick, was released on parole from prison. He had served 6 years for murdering an entirely helpless human being, his own infant girl. I guess you might consider 6 years a "baby sentence for a baby killer." Nick knew (through Bonnie) exactly where Cammie was living. So he decided to hang around the Brooks's place for a while.

Suddenly, the whole adoptive family came under attack. A dead rat showed up in Tom's office mailbox. Strangers were spotted at all hours in cars and vans parked outside Sandra and Tom's house. The Brooks kids had to be warned. Phone threats were made by a number of different voices, claiming that the family cats were about to be killed (the Brookses raised dogs, not cats). Cammie was shown another picture of her dad and advised to run if she ever saw him. I spoke with her about it, too.

I felt it necessary to phone the judge who had sentenced Nick to prison in the criminal case. He said he couldn't directly participate in the parole process, but he promised to figure "something" out. Within days, Nick moved away. Within months, in fact, he violated the terms of his parole and was put back in prison. As far as I understand it, he broke his parole three times. But he was "out" for good in less than a year.

All of this wreaked havoc with Cammie's sense of security in her adoptive home. But the worst situation of the year—from Cammie's childhood perspective—had yet to come. And it would lead to Cammie's one-and-only "test" of me.

George Stewart, one of my Northern California colleagues and the rider of the Xootr you read about in Chapter 5, was tested to the limits by a small, weak boy named Danny, whom he was seeing during his years of residency training at UC Davis. The little boy, a younger brother, had found himself in perpetual disfavor within his family. In comparison to his slightly older sibling, Danny was less muscular, powerful, and aggressive. Because of this, Danny invented a unique test for his young doctor. The resident psychiatrist watched Danny's test repeat itself. What was this child trying to prove? Dr. Stewart consulted with his supervisor, Harold Boverman, who is still a distinguished child psychoanalyst himself (in Oregon). After much thought and discussion, the young doctor found himself alone, once again, with the boy. Tested as usual, George blurted out a comment without pausing to think. For this little boy, it was exactly the right answer to an unspoken test. Dr. Stewart had "aced" his examination.

That's a Really Great One!

CONTRIBUTED BY GEORGE STEWART, MD

Danny was a 5-year-old when I began to see him. I was a first-year child psychiatry fellow. My training director had been asked to see Danny at his kindergarten. On that visit, Danny was in fetal position under his desk, remaining there all day despite entreaties from the teaching staff. In addition, at times he bit other children, spoke very little, and was extremely fearful, especially of bodily injury. For example, when he scraped his knee and it bled, he was terrified, thinking he was a fluid-filled sack and he would flow away through his wound.

Of note is the fact that Danny had a hyperactive, daredevil older brother just 15 months his senior. He also had a set of depressed parents, living through an unhappy marriage.

Danny quickly came to life in therapy. He talked, drew beautiful pictures (his father was a commercial artist), and developed rich representational play. His recurrent themes were the biting animals and their victims. As our relationship deepened and Danny drew and played out his conflicts, he became happier, less fearful, and surprisingly chatty with his mother.

Toward the end of 2 years of therapy, Danny began to use the bathroom during our session, claiming he had to pee. When he would not return to the office, I would seek him out. Invariably, he was standing with his fly open, his erect penis in full display for me, and an expectant look on his face. I was a bit flummoxed

*as to what would be a useful therapeutic stance, so I would sim-
ply tell him to zip up and encourage him to return to the playroom. Later, my supervisor was similarly unclear as to the
meaning of Danny's behavior, or what I should do to proceed.
Because I was videotaping the sessions for supervision, he encouraged me to stand behind the camera if Danny exposed
himself in the playroom.*

*One day, when I pursued Danny into the bathroom, perhaps
for the fifth time, I saw him standing on top of the sink! His pants
were draped around his ankles as he gripped his erect penis. He
smiled expectantly at me. I heard footsteps in the hallway, could
imagine how this might look, and saw my future career vanish-
ing in my mind. I said impulsively, "Danny, that's really a great
one!" He beamed at me, pulled up his pants, returned to the
playroom, and never went back to the bathroom again.*

MEANING OF THE MOMENT

*Danny's therapy with me concluded in the next few months. He
spent the last several sessions drawing a magnificent pictorial
series of dinosaurs, depicting his experience in therapy. The
story proceeded from the struggle of fierce carnivores and vul-
nerable vegetarians to include an X-ray machine that discovered "love" inside the brain of the fiercest carnivore. The meat-
eating dinos then became friends with the vegetarians. All of the
dinosaurs were sweet and generous with each other and wist-
fully said "goodbye" to each other in Danny's final drawing.*

*Our turning point in this boy's therapy was my affirmation of
Danny's masculinity in a very direct response to his invitation
to note his erection. My response derived from my unconscious
empathic attunement with him. It was almost instantaneous.
Because of the dramatic nature of Danny's request and my
anxiety about it, it had taken this young boy several tries to elicit
what he required of me. Then, it came in a flash, and with it, our
instant of mutual understanding.*

It is clear from the example George Stewart gives us here that Danny's
child-initiated test had to do with transference. Would his therapist
think him the same sort of weakling that his parents did? Would

Dr. Stewart behave similarly to Mom and Dad? Could the doctor be impressed with Danny's masculinity?

A therapist cannot simply choose to be the same or the opposite of a child's parents. He or she must think out the dilemma—sometimes aloud in front of the patient. The decision is made not on the doctor's behalf, but on the patient's. Sometimes, as in Dr. Stewart's comment to Danny, the decision is almost immediate and seems to well up from the doctor's unconscious. Rather than an interpretation, a remark is made—within seconds—that immediately settles the issue. Sometimes, on the other hand, as in James Powers's response to his teenaged test giver, a full, well-deliberated interpretation is offered, allowing the patient to act as an observer and a conscious thinker, as well as an on-going participant in the testing process itself. No matter which type of therapeutic response is made, however, it is clear that these child-initiated tests are highly important to the young patient. In taking them "correctly," we set up new patterns for the therapeutic relationship.

I had yet to see a test coming from my hard-pressed "wild child," Cammie Brooks. The end of her tenth year of life was turning out to be about as bad as the beginning. Nick was back in prison, and Cammie had become more sociable, interested in her peers, and funny—as a matter of fact, her sense of humor was sensational. But practicing at her newfound social skills while suffering from ADHD didn't make Cammie a favorite at her small, rigid school. She simply talked too damn much. She could not stop whispering. One day, in the midst of such activity, her infuriated third-grade teacher called her up in front of the class. She slapped the little girl hard, as everybody else watched. The poor child was more humiliated than hurt.

Sandra heard about it that very afternoon. She immediately confronted the parochial school principal. The director of the school stood up for the teacher, not Cammie. The next day, Cammie rode the bus to her new school. She would attend the local public schools from then on.

And whom did the new girl in school meet on that very first day of taking the school bus? A kindergarten boy who followed her around and continually insisted he wanted to have sex with her. What a year! No wonder the test took place soon afterward.

One pleasant spring day, I decided to see how well Cammie knew her times tables before letting her take out "her" dinosaurs once again. There were myriads of new ones she had inserted into my bottom desk drawer. She had recently brought me a bag from the Central Valley because, she said, I didn't have enough "babies." Well, Cammie couldn't do any of her times tables that day, not even the simplest ones. I checked her for the concept of multiplying. Yes, she understood. She just hadn't practiced enough, I figured. So I suggested that every night before dinner Cammie do five "multiplies" for her mom and dad. "This way," I said, "you can sing for your supper."

Cammie hated my suggestion. She let out a groan, then a moan, and then a growly yell. Next, she threw herself onto the floor and started kicking at nothing. Rolling around and screeching, she settled into one of the loudest, most animalistic, yuckiest fits I've ever seen. I talked a little. I asked her to settle down. I asked for her to tell me what she wanted. But there wasn't a thing I could do. I wound up reading a little mail, straightening up my desk, and making a couple of comments. In general, however, I ignored her.

My office door is sound-proofed. My ceiling looks like popcorn, it's so acoustically "correct." But Cammie stayed so loud and so wild for her whole psychiatric hour that I knew she was affecting our entire medical suite. What was I to do? I stayed passive and relatively nonreactive. I certainly wasn't going to behave like Wolf, T. rex, or, worse yet, a mean and particularly uncomprehending third-grade teacher!

I knew at the time that this was a test. Who was I?! How would I take the real Cammie Brooks at her worst?[97] But I wasn't sure of the right answer to her test. I couldn't back off from demanding multiplication from her—Cammie *had* to learn it. But she didn't have to learn it this very minute. I couldn't act tough, either. That was a given. And I couldn't be a "weasel" and go tattle to Sandra. I was just going to have to sit there and take it. So the "wild child" screamed and screamed while I sorted my mail and thought about her. When the hour was up, I said so. Cammie stood up and walked out. There wasn't a tear on her cheeks. There wasn't a destroyed item in my office. I turned Cammie over to Sandra and said a polite goodbye to them both. Sandra winked. She had heard it! Of course, my soundproofing had failed me.

But had I failed or passed Cammie's test? I didn't speak with Sandra by phone all month. That was on purpose. I waited to see what would happen. At the next appointment, Cammie hid from me, as she often did, behind Scott's desk. Greeting me with her usual big smile when I "found" her, she came into the office and dove for the bottom desk drawer where all the baby dinos were kept. Grabbing the rest of the dinos from the toy cabinet, she set them up on small tables. We were off and running, once again, with the murderous T. rex.

Had we come to a turning point? It certainly felt like one. In fact, I can say now in retrospect that it was the only time Cammie Brooks ever showed me negative transference. What she learned that day, I think, was that I was safe. No matter what, I would refrain from attacking her.

Following our moment, I would be allowed to push Cammie verbally. She'd let me push her hard, in fact. But now she knew, once and for all, that she could count on me, trust me, safely *be* with me.

Within a month, I learned something from Sandra that convinced me that Cammie's tantrum had represented a moment of change between us. Cammie's test question was, of course, "Will I be able to allow myself to be intimately attached to people?" Within weeks, Cammie's answer to that important question had arrived in question form. After school, Cammie asked Sandra—it seemed out of nowhere—whether she and Tom had written a will. The answer was "yes."

"What will happen if you both die together?" Cammie inquired.

"You'll have a guardian. Your big sister, Marla," Sandra replied.

"But what about Dr. Terr? Who'll take me to her for my appointments?"

"I don't know."

"Find a person to drive me there, and write it down in your will. I'll need Dr. Terr's help. And I'll need to go there once a month. So I want you to write it down."

Sandra and Tom revised their will. They told Cammie when they did it. I apparently had passed a big, big test. Like Psyche, I had proved myself worthy.

CHAPTER TEN

Delving Into a
Young Person's Interests

I once met a preschool girl whose main interest—at the time—was Walt Disney's *The Little Mermaid*. As she sat in my waiting room that first day, she drew a picture of two "little mermaids," one colored brown and the other, red. The small child had traveled a great distance from her Arizona ranch to see me. Her personal experience certainly warranted such a trip. A ranchhand, seeking revenge upon her father, had extracted his vengeance from her. The little girl's horrifying story had become expressed in her mermaid drawing. Everything, in fact, that had happened to her—being stolen from her own bed at knife-point, being bound and gagged, being taken to a trailer where the man raped and sodomized her, being cut in several places with his knife, being left to die in a tree, falling out of the tree, wandering in a field miles from home, being picked up by strangers, EMTs, police, a hospital E.R., and finally, finally being reunited with her frantic family—all of this was emotionally expressed in highly condensed form through The Little Mermaid.[98]

Her brown and red fish girls were drawn lying face-up on a bed. One mermaid, she told me, was so scared that "she [could] only say, 'Brrrrrr, brrrrrr.' " "That's how she shouts," the 4-year-old child explained. The second mermaid, colored red, was "all cut up—she can't say anything." Hovering over the entire drawing, which depicted the mermaids' bedroom, was a huge, bright-yellow monster, a male. (Here the girl veered away from the Disney film script, which features an evil female.) This little girl's psychological experience put a unique cast to the whole issue of "little mermaids." The scariness and urgency of her tale came entirely from her own mind. Would she have shown me her unique expression of terror as quickly or as effectively without her interest (and my interest, therefore) in heartbreakingly beautiful young ladies-of-the-sea? I doubt it.

The normal enthusiasms of children have a great deal to teach us. Avid interests, in fact, provide us with singular entry points to a child's inner being. I remember many of these almost obsessive enthusiasms from my own life as a child. I developed the enthusiasms myself, but then others helped me expand and explore them. This is where my mom fits in. She was a children's librarian.

Mom worked at a library within walking distance of our house. She had a distinct philosophy about childhood reading: "Follow your loves." To follow your interests as a child, of course, you might have to delve into "adult" books, and that was absolutely fine with my mother. In fact, if she had to get a *very* adult book for me from the back of the library where they were hidden from view, that was okay with her. Stashed books sometimes contained filthy words. But I never read for that particular pleasure—I had heard much of that language out on my elementary school playground. Some of the books in the back contained sexual information and explanations. I read a couple, but quickly lost interest. The best of the books from the backroom, I found, contained human stories. In fact, in that dark little room behind the stacks, the ladies of my mom's library system had hidden Boccaccio's *The Decameron*. What a book! And what a place to keep it!

I developed so much interest in human stories when I was 9 and 10 that I tried to read anything I could find about the great natural scientists, like Pasteur, the Curies, Koch, and Louis Agassiz (my favorite). By sixth grade, I wanted to read everything I could find on psychiatry— and so, I read the only three textbooks that they kept in the branch library where my mother worked. And another piece of my Mom's philosophy on reading fits in here: She didn't require that you read every single page. "Just what interests you," she said. In fact, Mom loved it if you discarded a book after a few pages—that particular act showed you were a "discriminating" reader. So I read the three (now very old) textbooks of psychiatry only for their authors' case vignettes. I didn't care much about Grinker's or Strecker's or Lillienthal's (or was it Lowenthal's?) theories and explanations. It was their patients who spoke to me.

Did I stay with psychiatry after sixth grade? No, absolutely not. By then I had discovered an array of new and different interests: bird identification, then the flowers, and finally, world stamps. I never became spectacular—or even fully competent—at any of these identification pursuits. My interests, I suppose, didn't hold long enough. The way Mom and I looked at it, however, I was doing all that reading "just for fun." My childhood interests were a source of play, and they eventually became a large part of who I am.

So what do kids like? And how do we psychiatrists follow these likes? Certain subjects—dinosaurs, for instance—fascinate almost all kindergarten-age youngsters. Some youngsters, like Cammie Brooks, don't give up their interest in old T. rex for years. Some, like my younger brother, move to a spinoff, like present-day reptiles. Rob has stayed interested in snakes and lizards all of his adult life. Most kids, however, have given up on the dinos long before Little League Baseball, swim teams, or 4-H Club projects take over their enthusiasms. Childhood interests, unique and amazingly varied, keep on coming. And these interests are exactly where we psychiatrists can venture in order to establish meaningful relationships with our patients and to make meaningful metaphors and analogies for them.

Of course, we must inquire. How does anyone know what a child's interests are without asking? And sometimes we must educate ourselves—read a handbook on butterflies, for instance, or rent the DVD of a well-loved film. Whatever a child's focus of attention and enthusiasm is, we must delve into it a little. Not only will the psychiatrist learn something, but he or she will also probably enter into a moment of mutuality with a young patient.

Wild enthusiasms, typical of latency age, affect considerably younger kids as well. One doesn't ordinarily think of a preschooler, for instance, as harboring this kind of avid interest, but it actually happens quite a bit. When the "right" kind of film comes along, or the "right" kind of song, poem, or costume, a 3- or 4-year-old child may take on the "rabid fan" nature of an early teenager. Under these enthusiasms, there lies a psychology, a genetic predisposition, a stage of life, gender issues, the family, real wounds—a host of complex influences already at work. But they enable us to "see" and then to "follow" the child.

Consider, for instance, a very young boy who was being treated by Theodore Gaensbauer, a Denver psychiatrist who specializes in preschoolers and who is deeply interested in trauma. Dr. Gaensbauer often prefers to see the young child along with the child's mother. He does this so that the parent can offer information, participate in sessions, and take the same treatment approach at home. In Dr. Gaensbauer's example, we find an almost 4-year-old boy, Mark, who had become obsessed with George Lucas's *Star Wars* series.[99] The young fellow's interests, in fact, were a little "over the top." By following Mark's enthusiasm, and then by asking three questions that this interest elicited, the doctor, the boy, and the boy's mother came to share a moment of understanding.

Three Little Questions[100]

CONTRIBUTED BY THEODORE J. GAENSBAUER, MD

Mark came to me when he was 3, after showing continued anxiety, temper tantrums, and post-traumatic play related to hospital treatments when he was 22 months old. An IV infiltrate had ballooned Mark's arm, necessitating a series of painful surgical procedures including a skin graft. Mark fought the bandages he was forced to wear for several months. His parents, in fact, had to consistently tape a sock over his hand.

My treatment of Mark took place over 15 months and involved 21 sessions. Mark's mother actively participated. Through play, art, and storytelling, we helped Mark express his traumatic emotions and gain a more coherent understanding of what had happened. He was making progress when, shortly before his fourth birthday, he engaged in a playful sword fight with his mother. I noted aloud that he was directing all of his thrusts at her hand. Mark's mother then remarked that he had been watching Star Wars *and especially liked "the part about Luke getting his hand cut off."*

I asked Mark, "Did watching Star Wars *give you some of your old hospital feelings?" "Yes," he said, as if it were self-evident. My second question was something I had not previously considered, given the fact that at the time of his injury he was so young and speaking only single words. "Did you worry that your hand would be cut off while you were at the hospital?" Again very calmly, he answered "yes." Mark's mother now interjected a third query. She remembered aloud how desperately, at 2, he had tried to pull off his bandages. "Did you used to take your bandages off to make sure your hand was still there?" Mark still looked entirely unfazed. "Yes," he said, in that matter-of-fact way. Following this session, Mark's remaining symptoms resolved quickly and he moved rapidly toward finishing his treatment.*

MEANING OF THE MOMENT

Taken together, our three inquiries about Mark's play constituted a classic psychoanalytic interpretation. They linked Mark's past to his present and helped him (and his mother and therapist!) to understand his old behaviors. They also allowed us to reassure Mark about his present and future fears. As opposed to Luke Skywalker's, Mark's hand was in no present danger. Most impressive to me, however, was the notion that Mark's concern about losing an arm had not retrospectively crystallized around the developmentally expectable mutilation fear one often sees in 4-year-old boys. Rather, at 22 months Mark was already able to consciously appreciate that his arm, not his genitals, was truly at risk. An essential element of psychotherapy is helping the patient, no matter how young, to integrate his past and present experience. Entrance into the inner world of infants and toddlers is a special challenge. Moments such as this one confirm that such access to a small child's inner life is indeed possible.

The marvelous example that Jerry Dodson gave us from the fictional land of "Elm Street" comes to mind here. Like Ted Gaensbauer's young patient, Jerry's sleepless boy had found himself obsessed, in a highly unpleasant way, with Wes Craven's film series. After a couple of attempts to learn what was bothering his young charge, Dr. Dodson voluntarily watched *Nightmare on Elm Street* himself. Without understanding the film, the psychiatrist could not see himself understanding the patient. Then—and only then—was he able to think up the idea of writing a letter to the film's writer, Wes Craven, on the boy's behalf. And because Jerry Dodson had entered his patient's field of interests, there was no problem afterward in enlisting his young patient's attention, imagination, and even identification.

Dr. Theodore Gaensbauer similarly elicited eager cooperation from his very young patient. The boy's secret—that he had feared his hand was cut off by his doctors—emerged fairly easily once Ted dipped into the boy's cherished story of the character Luke. Once this character became pulled into conversation, the little fellow's secret popped right out. Here, the doctor could ask interpretive questions, linking the youngster's past to his present and future. They could then share their moment of revelation as a trio—Mom, Ted, and little Mark. It all followed from Mark's avid interest in Luke.

At 10 years of age, Cammie Brooks, too, had developed an avid interest. Unfortunately, it all rested with a sex-obsessed kindergarten boy. Cammie, still pretty and petite, was being pursued on her school bus by a little fellow who had apparently pinned all his hopes for some sexual activity on her. Do such kids smell each other? Animals do. I can't figure it out, but apparently the boy, Andy, had some immediate pheromic awareness of Cammie. Once the "wild child" entered his "scene," he couldn't let her go. He bugged and bugged her, following her everywhere, declaring his love, and spying on her through his older sister, who was in Cammie's third-grade class. Andy proposed various things to Cammie, not just once, but time after time. First it was "Let's get married." Later, after a number of refusals, it was just a plain "Let's have sex." Cammie was Andy's entire field of interest. Cammie's interests were narrowing down to Andy, as well. She confessed to me that she'd "kinda like to have sex with him," although she also confessed that she didn't "know what 'sex' was." Maybe she should try "sex" as an experiment, she said.

Unlike my mother, I didn't have a library backroom to which to refer my little "wild child." I was going to have to be the whole library myself. So I asked Sandra's permission to tell Cammie the "facts of life." We needed to put a stop to young Cammie's (and little Andy's) current interests. This field of youthful enthusiasm was not going to get Cammie anywhere, other than horrified, perhaps, all over again. I had a strong suspicion, on top of all else, that young Andy might have had a story or two to tell about his own early life. Traumatized children are impelled to repeat in action what was originally perpetrated on them. Sometimes—like Cammie—they stay passive in their latency-age behaviors. Sometimes—like Andy—they take the active, "T. rex" stance. Whatever it was, this was a field of childhood interest that, at least for now, had to be curtailed.

Explaining the "facts of life" to Cammie helped her to see the difference between sex connected with love and forced sex, infantile sex, autoerotic sex, and sex with kindergarten pests like Andy. We glanced at each other a number of times through our little discussion, and we laughed a number of times, too. My explanation, quite a short monologue, I guess, was connected with a far more extensive and relatively enjoyable dialogue. It lasted only one psychiatric hour.

This hour became Cammie's sixth moment of change. I knew it only later. My recognition of the moment came because of Cammie's response to our little talk about "sex." First of all, she brought me a number of picture books the next time she came to the office, for me to "keep a while." They were all of animals. She "shook" to them, she confessed shyly. Animals excited Cammie sexually, especially, she said, when they fought to the death and showed their claws and teeth. She wanted to get rid of the pictures that ordinarily aroused her.

Next, Cammie asked me to help her get little Andy "off her back." She no longer wanted to try nature's grand experiment with him. She was at a loss, however, as to how to get rid of him. We brought Sandra into Cammie's session and asked her if there was anything Sandra could do. Cammie suggested that Sandra call Andy's mom. We readily agreed. The moms would have to take care of it.

Finally, Cammie told me a nightmare she'd been having all of her life. It was of looking into a dark "tunnely" space that seemed to her to expand in a terrible way. She didn't know what it was, but it scared her and awoke her from sleep. This, too, sounded sexual in origin. But it was uninterpretable until we could learn more.

The thrust of Cammie's sixth moment was that in informing Cammie truthfully and graphically about sex, I helped her diminish her interest in the subject to more normal and manageable levels. This turning point, therefore, was marked by an exchange between us. As I gave Cammie sexual information, she gave up some of her sexual repetitions. She came out ahead. She would no longer be sexually uncontrollable. From now on, she could talk with Sandra and me about sex, and let us help her. I wanted Cammie to look forward to making love, I told her, but in the future. Both Sandra and I sincerely hoped for her to eventually enjoy her love life as an adult. But not now!

Sandra phoned me after her call to Andy's mother. She told me that Andy had been "called off," and that Cammie was visibly relieved. Sandra learned from Andy's mother that Andy and his sister had been adopted that past summer. Both had been permanently removed from their home of origin—and a couple of foster homes, too—for various kinds of adult sexual abuse. Andy's mom would make sure, Sandra said, that he stayed away. She didn't want a "wild child" in her newly adopted son's life any more than we wanted him in Cammie's. Interestingly, however, Andy's big sister must have indirectly enjoyed her sexual "spying." It also, I suppose, was a form of post-traumatic repetition. She bullied, teased, and gossiped about Cammie at school for the next couple of years.

As the sexual situation developed between poor Cammie and little Andy, their childhood interest in one another could not be "nipped in the bud." Nor could it even be "cut off in full flower." Thankfully, however, this interest never came to fruition. I guess one would have to say that every single interest of childhood cannot be indulged. As with all else, even items of intellectual and scientific curiosity sometimes carry limits.

Although the stage of latency is the great one for childhood enthusiasms and healthy obsessions, these interests can and should develop during the older phases of child and adult life as well. Staying eagerly enthusiastic and committed, in fact, is one of the secrets of aging with grace, no matter what stage of life you are in. So when you meet a kid who is not actively engaged in something, you are probably meeting a kid with problems. Perhaps, in fact, he is "dysthymic," our psychiatric term for nonbiological, but significant, unhappiness, *ennui*, depression.

Such was the case with a boy I met last year, whom I'll call "Edison" in honor of one of the more interested, curious boys in American history, Thomas Alva Edison. My young Edison was brought by his mom with one specific question in mind—"Can he be treated without medicine?" Edison had been given three different diagnoses over time at the well-reputed child psychiatric clinic he attended. Going "by the book," they had medicated him for years with drugs to match each of the three diagnoses they had given him. I suspect nobody really got to know Edison at that particular facility. Whether any of their diagnoses were truly "right" at the time they were given, I cannot say. I doubt it. But one thing was certain—no matter what drugs the doctors administered or what short course of counseling they prescribed, Edison had been absolutely unable to "thrive" under their care. I suspect it was because no one at that clinic truly followed young Edison's line of thinking.

Army of Elephants

Edison was 12, almost 6 feet tall, and slouching into puberty when I first met him. His mother and grandfather drove the sullen seventh grader to my office from their rural area about 2 hours north of San Francisco. Ever since kindergarten, Edison's grades had ranged from Ds to Fs. For years, he attended daily, hour-long classes for the learning disabled. He had recently been tested at the third-grade reading level. His peers either ignored him or argued with him. In earlier years, he had attracted all sorts of negative attention by grimacing, clowning, and making terrible throat-clearing sounds. A local psychiatric clinic diagnosed him with Tourette's disorder and treated him unsuccessfully with the appropriate medications. Later, they rediagnosed him as having ADHD and again, using proper medications for this diagnosis, saw no therapeutic changes except for the side effects. He was kept on these medications, however, until he was rediagnosed as suffering from juvenile bipolar disorder. The correct drug protocol for that, along with a number of counseling sessions, did nothing to help. In 6 years of psychiatric treatment, Edison had been treated "by the book." But he had never been given a course of psychotherapy.

Edison's parents had long been divorced. Together with his younger sister, he rotated homes every week. His mother and father, hard-working and decent people, had virtually no time for their kids. Unattended, Edison spent hours watching the Cartoon Network, playing videogames, and squabbling with his sister. Occasionally, on a weekend, he went somewhere.

The boy qualified for the diagnoses of dysthymia (lifelong sadness) and learning disorders. I would be allowed to see him every other week. I began by urging each parent to speak more with him, help him find some books he liked, and spend time. We kept him off medications. I taught him a few words for feelings, and joked with him about the human condition. Ironically, Edison was a quick learner. He began greeting me with a big smile. His almost silent grandfather usually brought him to sessions, and I asked the elderly pear rancher to begin speaking with him. "About what?" the old man seemed at a loss. "Weather, animals, the price of Bartletts and Boscs, farm machinery, whatever." Their discussions eventually settled on tractors, and Edison got to ride on Grandpa's big one.

But our therapeutic "moment" happened over elephants, not tractors. And it came because Edison's history class had begun studying ancient Rome. Edison voiced admiration for Julius Caesar ("cool") and for Rome's earlier enemy, Hannibal of Carthage ("a smart planner").[101]

I moved into Republican Rome right along with the boy. "What was Caesar like at school, do you think? Did he horse around?"

"No!" Edison looked aghast. "Caesar showed dignity and leadership, even as a kid."

"Oh," I paused, letting the young man's idea float about the room. "And Hannibal—do you think his elephants traveled on impulse?"

*"No," Edison laughed. "That took strategy. Do you know—
those elephants marched all the way up and over the Alps!
They're high, like the Sierras!"*

*For the next couple of sessions, we applied Caesar's states-
manship and Hannibal's war tactics to a number of situations
in Edison's world west of the mountains. And then it was over.
The history class had moved on to the European tribes and
Mongolian hoards. It was becoming obvious to me, however,
that the modern-day boy was moving even faster. By semester's
end, he had earned only a C+ in history (because he couldn't
sustain interest in barbarians) but he got an A+ in math, with
a B average. His reading scores leaped by two grade levels to
"high fifth." He developed a friendship with a boy who liked to
"talk things over" with him. A popular girl was rumored to like
Edison, and at Edison's "preplanned" suggestion to her, they
slow-danced at a school party. He needed more psychotherapy
to solidify his gains, but all things considered, I had rarely witnessed such a rapid and sure-footed childhood turnaround.
The magic lay in perceiving that Edison,. like the best of ancient
Roman youth, needed enough attention and care to develop
pride in himself.*

MEANING OF THE MOMENT

*If a psychiatrist discovers a child's love, this love, however
transitory, can be used to the youngster's advantage. The psychiatrist may buy a specific toy or ask the child to bring in a
favorite object. Best yet, the psychiatrist may translate the child's
love into a metaphor. Metaphors are powerful medicines—in
Edison's case, quicker and more powerful than a cabinetful of
psychoactive drugs.*

After Edison received his miraculous set of grades, I saw him only two
times. His divorced parents seemed unable to coordinate a schedule
to get him to me. His mom's job moved him even further away from San
Francisco. His parents' significant others suddenly felt comfortable raising him. And Grandpa, so essential to the whole scene for a while, told
me he was no longer being called upon to help. The improvement must
have held, at least for that year. I deeply hope it will hold long past then.

All in all, I miss Edison a great deal. Once he woke up and allowed his interests to take over, I found him a fascinating, entertaining young companion. Most of all, I remember the great smiles "hello" he gave me, just before we experienced our moment together. Julius Caesar provided Edison with an awakening. And adults, like me, certainly love to see that happen.

So how might a child and adolescent psychiatrist counsel parents around exciting their own children's interests? First of all, it would be nice if parents could share their hobbies and interests with their kids. If they fish, take the kids fishing! If they love hiking in the woods, take the kids along. Perhaps a set of parents who like ballroom dancing might feel that young kids would intrude. But in actuality, nothing would eventually please such a mother and father more than seeing their offspring become accomplished dancers. A certain pair of siblings might prefer the tango to their parents' cha-cha, but all things considered, it would bring the family together in a healthy partnership.

A second way to know children better is to share family meals. This has become very difficult in some middle-class American families because of complex work schedules. (It has always been difficult in upper-class families because such parents are often inclined to dine more formally, and later in the evening, alone.) Let's say a family can eat together only two or three times a week. If all the participants at the meal spoke of their day, of the days of others, of the nation's day, of what nature did today (of a bird they spotted, of a storm that never came in), of a new interest—and if one or two others would join in so that it wasn't a matter of delivering sequential monologues but rather more a matter of conversation—well then, I think families could know each other, and love each other, better.

Then there's the matter of libraries. Booksellers are going to hate me for saying this, but if at all possible, parents should take their kids to libraries. Why? So that children can discard books. So they can browse. So they can share their interests with a librarian or two. So they can look at something just for the illustrations. So they can read something else just for the laughs. It's difficult to discard a book you've paid for. The books we give kids "for the fun of it" should not, and cannot be, "required reading." When you start forcing youngsters to read, you've got a reluctant reader in the making. And that's not where parents want to be vis-à-vis their kids.

I wish that parents—and their interests and enthusiasms—could draw their children in. It unfortunately doesn't always happen like that. Children, especially adolescents, are prone to find interests in items diametrically opposed to what their parents stand for, like, or even tolerate. The Internet today poses an enormous challenge because it brings the library backroom forward into the preteen and teenage culture at large. The problem is not so much in meeting up with the backroom books, but rather that there is no librarian in charge. Again, family conversation represents an extraordinary opportunity to learn about a child's interests and to actively engage a child in discussion of those interests. If one is willing to talk—on and on, if necessary—about a subject of interest to a young person, this dialogue, or trialogue, or quadralogue will help open the doors to the young person's true nature. Some talks are uncomfortable. But they lead to important moments between people.

The following example from Victor Fornari, psychiatrist of the "monkey in the middle" child in Chapter 1, is a case in point. In the earlier case, Victor's benignly objective "doctor persona" was just what that particular little boy needed in order to feel comfortable enough to share his feelings. This time, however, Dr. Fornari offers us a vignette in which he wished to enter into a difficult, and potentially self-damaging, teenage boy's inner world. First the doctor used his sense of humor, sharing laughs with his patient about the psychiatrist himself. But ever-mindful of the adolescent's interests, the doctor sojourned further. He asked the young man how one goes about dying one's hair. This, in fact, carried a paradoxical twist. Victor Fornari is handsomely—but totally—bald.

Comedy of the Purple Hair

CONTRIBUTED BY VICTOR FORNARI, MD

John was almost 18 and ready to graduate high school when he was urgently referred for "self-mutilation" and "dissociation" by his school counselor. He had made six cigarette burns along his left arm and three on the right. Blond and fair, John came to my office with blue-green hair. Prior to that, he had dyed it black and then "cut it all off." On other occasions, he, dyed it orange, purple, and pink. He'd had no prior contact with a mental health professional. Of note, John's parents had divorced when he was 18 months old, and he had never seen his father again.

When he first walked into my office, John seemed distant and aloof. I pointed out that he looked like he'd rather be almost anywhere else. He did not reply. I then suggested that he might not know how to respond to me because, for a long time, he had not had a relationship with an adult man who cared about him. He peered at me as though I was crazy. I commented on that, too. He acknowledged the truth of it and we both laughed. I then said that his hair looked as though he'd put a great deal of effort into it. I thought it "looked really cool." He glanced up at me and asked if I was joking. I assured him I was serious. He proceeded to discuss the process of coloring his hair—how his friends had helped him, and how much his mother disliked it. I told him I bet it was important for him to "make his own mark" and "be his own person."

I am bald. It's an obvious fact about me. With a serious tone, I asked John, "How do you think I would look with purple hair?" He nearly choked with laughter. We chuckled together for several minutes. (I wanted him to realize that we were more alike than different.) With a mixture of humor and self-disclosure, I told John, "I liked to rebel as a kid and be my own person." (I wanted the boy to know I valued his creativity and individuality.) As an older person now, I noted how lucky John was to have "any hair options." He let loose a big horse laugh. When I told him that we would need to end the session soon, I asked whether we could continue our conversation another day. He smiled and agreed. I was not sure he would ever return. But I wound up working with him three afternoons that first week. Our initial encounter was the beginning of a 5-year, once-weekly course of individual psychotherapy. John is now working full-time for an information-technology firm and has a long-term girlfriend. He pays for his sessions himself.

MEANING OF THE MOMENT

*John did not have a dissociative disorder, nor did he need med-
ications. He needed someone to help him sort out his identity.*[102]
*He needed a man to talk about his life with, to tell about hair-
dye experiments, to assess girlfriends, careers, and the politics
of young adulthood. He also needed a laugh or two. When we
shared our "comedy of the purple hair" together, we got off to
the best of starts. It became a crucial relationship at a crucial
time in a young man's life.*

It's appropriate to note here that Victor Fornari's patient needed to
"test" his new doctor early in their first session together. "Are you serious?" he asked Victor incredulously. "Yes," Victor answered in truth,
later delivering a joke at his own expense. When Dr. Fornari tells this
particular story aloud (as he did at one of our medical meetings), the
listener recognizes how potentially difficult it must be for a doctor to
share himself as readily as Victor did. The moment they experienced
became apparent to the psychiatrist afterward, not during the seconds in which it took place. By fully entering the life of a hair-dying,
rebellious teenager, Victor Fornari fully entered into his patient's
inner space. The moment, apparent only in retrospect, cemented
their five-year relationship.

There are times when one's expressed interest simply doesn't work.
I remember a very unhappy 14 year old whose friends lived miles from
home (on the Internet). The first time she came to my office, she tried
to discuss Harry Potter with me.[103] I knew a little about Harry, but the
girl, wearing a single dark brown braid and horn-rimmed glasses,
wanted our discussion to touch on her interests in such detail that I
looked like an unteachable student in the field of "Potterism." She
had written J. K. Rowling, the author, and had picked up both the
British and American versions of the books for comparison. The
teenager's discussion, in fact, was so specific and so dependent on
knowing every word Ms. Rowling wrote that it wasn't possible to find
out what Harry really meant to Marissa. I asked her, if she had tried
writing a Harry story herself. Yes, she had, but she wouldn't share her
tale. I think our failure to link up came because this girl hid so

deeply behind her interest in Harry Potter that she refused to show me the specific meanings that Harry carried for *her*. She could have sat there absolutely silent for all she really said. That was the only time I had the opportunity to meet with young Marissa. I regret my failure. Had I been actively following the Potter craze, maybe I wouldn't have been so ill-prepared for this particular child's obsessive interest. Perhaps there would have been a moment between us. But we simply couldn't connect. And as opposed to my Little Mermaid enthusiast, Marissa never did draw her own, individual portrait of Harry.

Cammie Brooks, too, discovered and loved Harry Potter. In moving away from overt sex, both autoerotic and child-consensual, she had become far more intellectually alert. An interest in Harry brought Cammie's reading level up considerably. I now felt that, with a full range of "concrete operational skills" at her disposal, Cammie should be able to negatively compare her old hero, T. rex, to her newly emerging and far more human self. And so, I took it upon myself to change our game of dinos. I wanted to interject the "context" of civilized humans into our reptilian wars. After all, humans—like Cammie—were "brainy" and T. rex was "stupid." Humans, bright creatures that they are, can plan ahead. T. rex could only act and react.

If Cammie and I used our heads, I told her, we might defeat the reptilian baby-killer once and for all. We inserted a human army that I keep in my cupboard. We added human scientists. We even decided to wage a nuclear war. The idea of the superiority of an educated human mind was a revelation to young Cammie Brooks. "Do you think I can become a child psychiatrist?" she asked me, black eyes veiled in deep concern.

"Of course! You'll be a good one!" I said, certain by now that she could if she wanted to.

In fact, Cammie was beginning to use conversation as her primary therapeutic device by the time she advanced toward her eleventh birthday. We would set up T. rex and all his cohorts at the beginning of the hour. Then we'd talk, and talk some more. Then, by the end of the session, we would take the dinos down. I noticed that, as the months went by, Cammie would carefully place the dinosaurs on my tables, along with some rocks and other pretty items, saying that she was setting up a science museum. Then the monsters would just sit there—bleached-white bones in whispery, quiet hallways. Our talk was becoming livelier. Simultaneously, Cammie's dinosaurs were beginning to die.

At home, the "human" context was helping Cammie a great deal. She was reading the Harry Potter books for fun, and she could identify with Harry as a fellow human being. But she also realized what a traumatized character he was. He became her special peer. In fact, a number of the self-portraits she created at the time depicted Cammie as a Harry Potter look-alike. She was a very fine artist, a top comedienne, and a role model for the younger children at UCLA's yearly, end-of-summer "Heart Camp."

Then, the biggest "congratulations" of all arrived: Cammie was taken into the State of California's Gate Program. Here, Cammie's school officially acknowledged the "wild child's" intelligence, talent, and creativity. You can't qualify for Gate unless you are "gifted." Cammie had come a long, long way from her old diagnosis of retardation! We were really proud of her. But best of all, she was proud of herself.

I wish we child psychiatrists could "get" all children. Time limits us. Sometimes our cultural diversity makes "different" children difficult to decipher. Then, too, parents don't always know their youngsters well. They miss the boat—at various times—about kids' symptoms and suffering, and then they convey these mistaken "observations" to us. There are some children, like my adolescent Harry Potter expert, whom you just can't get around. And in those cases you wish they would be able to find someone else with whom they might work. All in all, however, I think we do pretty well in evaluating kids and recognizing their problems, both diagnostically and psychologically.

What I have tried to demonstrate in this part of the book, however, goes well beyond figuring out what's wrong with a child. If you can discover what's "right" as well, you may find yourself promoting a youthful moment of change. If you figure out the object of a child's love, you may help to create an instant of personal transformation. If you follow a child's lead, to "heaven," for instance, or to an Iranian Grandma, you may make the paralyzed walk, and the mute speak again.

Many of the incredible moments of change illustrated so far have depended to great extent on nonverbal communication. But some, too, are verbally explicit. Perhaps in giving a youngster the "facts of life," or perhaps in creating a visual picture of a bald man with purple hair, two pairs of eyes, "old" and young, meet in understanding. Perhaps two pairs of lips move into a shared smile. It happens because we "get" one another. I remain consistently amazed that these moments occur in child and adolescent psychotherapy as much as they do.

Part Four

REACTING in a TIMELY, PUNGENT FASHION

"Take the utmost trouble to find the right thing to say, and then . . .
say it with the utmost levity."

— George Bernard Shaw, from *Answers to Nine Questions*

CHAPTER ELEVEN

Making a Meaningful Comment

Last night, Halloween, half the kids of San Francisco were in my neighborhood canvassing three famous blocks—the streets of Washington, Jackson, and Clay—for treats. Some of the side streets, like mine, are so hilly that we expect very few trick or treaters, so in the past few years, we have put out a big basketful of assorted candy bars on our doorstep, with a "Happy Halloween! Help yourself!" note attached to the basket handle. We leave the front light on and hope at least a couple of kids will stop by.

The real "scene" takes place up our hill on the long, relatively flat blocks. There, children from all over the city come to parade in their costumes and take in the sound and light shows that our neighbors put on. There are eerie, squeaking doors, witch cackles, howls, and screams. There is music. A number of intensely flickering strobelight shows may unluckily preclude a few kids with seizure disorders from coming around. Treats include magic rings, fluorescent collars, and all other kinds of gimmicky stuff, in addition to the ubiquitous sweets. Out on the sidewalk, I heard plenty of Spanish being spoken, some Japanese, and a couple of urgent-sounding cell-phone business calls to and from guys in suits. I heard a distant shriek from a toddler who must have gotten too close to a monster or ghost.

As my husband, Ab, and I walked around the neighborhood, we noticed that this year, many of the parents going around with their kids were fully costumed themselves. They traveled in packs. I spotted a father-ballerina dressed in a tutu, at least ten vampires, a slim, wrapped mummy with a gorgeous figure, and a number of witches of both genders. The cape was almost ubiquitous. Baby strollers with wide-eyed, uncostumed infants jammed the sidewalks.

So that was the scene of last night. But what of the kids whom the holiday is all about? Children particularly love Halloween because it allows them to "be" something other than themselves. Some brave ones can even take the chance of "being" the bad side to themselves, like a bloody pirate, a ghost, an ugly witch. Many more kids want to "be" something good, like a dancer, fireman, soldier, princess. They all get to "be" adults, which they feel (without grasping the inherent responsibility) is really "cool." What's so exciting for kids about this particular holiday is its permission to emphasize a side of yourself that you don't ordinarily acknowledge. When you think of adult surgeons and O.R. nurses dressed up as vampires (of which I'm sure there were a couple last night), or lawyers dressed as policemen, or psychotherapists as witches and sorcerers, it's enough to make anybody laugh. So kids get a kick out of "being" adults, regardless of whether they're good or bad ones. And adults enjoy being opposite from themselves, whether or not they're even more scary the rest of the year.

I'm not so sure all kids love the "scariness" of Halloween, though. I remembered that one distant shriek I'd heard earlier. I saw something, too, that, for just a second, frightened me. I was standing in front of a darkened house that seemed to have two dummy figures, an ogre and a witch, lying on the ground on two different sections of pavement. It was arresting. (They were such good dummies!) And dark. I looked for a while because they were so strange and entertaining. Then, as I started to walk away, I sensed motion in the corner of my eye. My god! They were rising! They were alive! The master and mistress of a house on Washington had taken me totally aback!

A little boy, 5 years old maybe, came around the corner just then. "There's something scary back there!" I recommended to this little Superman.

He looked at me piercingly. "*How* scary?" he asked.

I was at a loss. "*How* scary?" indeed. What had been scary to me was in its own way, funny, too. Ironic. The master and mistress of a house near my own had brought me up short, surprised me, left me speechless. If the little boy saw what I saw, on the other hand, what would he think? What would he feel? Did he know at age 5 that people can look like dummies, and that dummies can resemble people? Did he know that being "dead" meant just that, and there was no unbiblical way for the dead to rise? Did he know that the inanimate could not turn animate? Would he see the witch and ogre standing up—as I had left them—or lying down and darkly harmless as he walked by?

I could not answer this little boy. I could think of no adequate words to equate my "scary" with his "*how* scary?" We would have no meeting of the minds on this moonlit night. I looked down for him. Where was he? In the couple of seconds I had struggled for an answer, the little Superman had taken off. My meaningful comment—if there had been one inside of me—would have fallen on a baby stroller, newly plowing onto Washington Street. Twins. Wow. Relief hit me, however, following my failure to speak to little Superman. I heard no piercing 5-year-old shriek behind me at the corner.

A second relief hit me when I arrived home. My entire basket of candy—the one on my doorstep—was empty! Somebody else—not Ab or me—was going to have to indulge in those sweet, gooey calories. Happy, happy Halloween!

My problem speaking to the young Superman reflected a few of the difficulties any psychotherapist needs to overcome. First, we must know a child well enough to calculate whether what we might say would be "right" for him. This was my main problem with the tiny kindergarten-age Superman. Second, we must time our comment properly, hopefully staying in context or within a colorful metaphor, so that our remark sparkles with interest for the child. Third, if we plan to link the child's past with his present or future, or to link her behaviors to her transference, the comment must still be simple enough for the child to understand. Fourth, some of the best and most lasting comments made to kids are full of "levity" (as George

Bernard Shaw put it). Many of these comments just "pop out" of us. Counterintuitive and unexpected as they sound, these bursts from an educated unconscious probably amount to the most pungent remarks of all.

Historically, the psychoanalytic or traditional psychodynamic psychotherapeutic "way" to make an interpretation, or a strong and meaningful comment, to a child has been to emphasize the linkages of a number of elements. Past, present, transference, habitual behaviors, fears—all of these become connected and explained. A good example is Ted Gaensbauer's vignette about young Mark (Chapter 10). In asking three questions in an hour, Ted linked Mark's current obsession with Luke Skywalker's hand to Mark's fear (of losing his own hand), his past distrust (maybe, he thought, his parents knew his hand was off, but he didn't know), and transference (he wasn't quite sure whether to trust Ted, who, like a surgeon, was also called "doctor"). Subtly, not overtly, all three elements lay in Ted Gaensbauer's questions. How could this "doctor" ask such a question, for instance, if he was truly in complicity with evil surgeons? Ted's questions had also broken an old barrier in psychoanalysis—the traditional assumption that castration anxiety and the Oedipus complex override just about everything else, including trauma. By leaving his questions to Mark's hand alone, Ted respected the boy's trauma and let it stand for itself (not as a symbol of a "more important" concern). These were all built into what seemed to be relatively simple questions. The meat of the questions, in fact, lay in some of what remained unspoken.

Today, psychotherapeutic comments, interpretations, and remarks to children are much more relaxed and less firmly linked up to all of the possible elements. Good comments, in fact, are often purely educational. This, of course, is very important in the "cognitive" therapies, but for children and adolescents, it cuts across all the other psychotherapies as well. Other good comments, such as Nancy Winters's remarks to her young girl patient with feeding and control issues (in Chapter 3), may sound more "in your face" than interpretive ("You wish for a boy therapist, don't you?"). Yet they work, too, if one knows the child well. In contemporary psychotherapy, some of the more "classic" interpretations, like Ted Gaensbauer's, actually come in question form. Some even sound like "scenarios." The doctor feeds the patient a "line," and the patient then thinks about it, perhaps coming up with another "line," as if they were both actors in a miniature play.

Such was the case with Geri Fox, who heads the training program in Child/Adolescent Psychiatry at the University of Illinois, Chicago. What interests me here is what Dr. Fox said to her patient. Her comment was particularly short and meaty. But for anyone other than this one remarkable girl, it might have sounded a bit too brief and rather mundane. What comes through to me in Geri's vignette is exactly what flummoxed me on Halloween with my little Superman. One must really understand the individual child's particular psychology before making a pungent, powerful remark. Otherwise, what you may say comes across as trite, banal, perhaps even hurtful.

Thanks, But No Thanks

CONTRIBUTED BY GERI FOX, MD

At the age of 17, Emily felt sad and confused about her direction in life. She had recently developed bulimia. A school counselor suggested psychotherapy. The girl had been a spectacular, Olympic-bound swimmer until she turned 14 and developed an osteosarcoma, requiring total replacement of her left femur. During her subsequent chemotherapy, she could not hold down food and became almost skeletal. She then developed into another "star" of sorts. She became an inspirational public speaker for childhood cancer. Gradually, she began gaining weight to the point of mild obesity.

Emily started her self-induced vomiting a few months before she met me. Taking this new "fork in the road"[104] seemed to create in Emily a sense of shame and alarm. She hated herself. But her vomiting persisted, even after her weight returned to normal.

I learned that Emily's family constantly focused on food. Her brother was a chef. Her mother loved to cook. Her father emphasized the importance of not wasting food, and he routinely finished the leftovers on others' plates. Emily was frequently in conflict with her dad over eating (and other topics in which he attempted to control her behavior).

One morning in her psychotherapy session, Emily spoke about a bulimic episode from the day before. She had been at a luncheon she did not want to be attending, at a time she was not hungry, with food she did not enjoy, coupled with an antic-ipated visit to her relatives' home that evening, where she would have to eat once again, and be polite to boot.

I said, "Sounds as if your body knows what you want and don't want. Wouldn't it be easier just to say, 'No thanks'?"

MEANING OF THE MOMENT

Emily had taken a "good girl" approach to much of her life, wanting to please others, especially her father and coaches. She now struggled to define herself as a separate human being. She had finally entered the normal, but delayed, developmental phase of adolescence. I believed that Emily was painfully try-ing to forge a new identity other than "athlete" or "cancer sur-vivor."[105] She needed to tune into her own internal signals and affirm them. My commentary said so. I was advocating for Emily herself, no matter what her family, coaches, charity groups, or peers might say. In order to listen to her own voice, Emily first needed to hear strong approval from me. It gave her permission to say "no" to others. In the long run, Emily would have to realize it was completely okay to become her own per-son and make her own decisions. Eventually, she would have to become her own advocate.

By our next session a week later, Emily told me she had com-pletely stopped vomiting. She came in wearing an attractive, comfortable-looking outfit she had purchased by herself. She reported holding her own in a disagreement with her dad. There was a hiking club she had decided to join. She went on to mention some career options she was considering. No longer a symbolic "hero," Emily was enjoying the sensation of becom-ing an ordinary, not-to-be-duplicated girl. The turnaround was one of the quickest and most dramatic I have ever seen. And it happened because I gave it "permission" to begin happening.

One of the particular points of interest I found in Geri Fox's vignette is the way she anticipated "the future" with her brave young patient. Rather than mopping up the past (the way older analytic methods would have instructed us), Geri looked wholly forward. I also love the way that Dr. Fox's comment was presented as if it were a line of dialogue (for a film? play? sitcom?). Geri's 17-year-old former athlete and cancer survivor saw her doctor's comment as an utter revelation. An adult was asking her to follow, of all things, her own instincts. This new instruction—different from that of any athletic coach, cancer publicist, or parent she had dealt with—floored this one particular teenager. She showed a momentous change within a week's time.

The idea of commenting on kids' futures is a new and powerful concept in child and adolescent psychiatry.[106] We need to ask all of our young patients about their anticipated lives. As early as the assessment-evaluation phase, we need to know how they project themselves forward in time. Then, our comments—even in anticipating a future only a few days ahead—may carry an important message. It has also been found helpful in the child and adolescent psychotherapies to suggest new behavioral modifications, new cognitive choices, new patterns with which to redirect bothersome thoughts. If a child has a strong philosophical or spiritual side, that side may also be talked to, far into the future, once the doctor knows what it is.

Another type of commentary that has been found helpful—if done carefully and with a strong therapeutic relationship to back it—is to confront a child with his or her unconsciously derived behaviors. A metaphor may help the young person to swallow the bitter taste of a "here and now" confrontation. But it's not always possible to displace such an issue far away from the child or adolescent himself.

A distinguished colleague, Joseph Beitchman of the Medical School at the University of Toronto, has written an excellent example in this context. Dr. Beitchman was working with a little girl with whom he felt a confrontation would be necessary. Aware that his young patient seemed to be intensely enjoying her sense of being "haunted" by a ghost, Dr. Beitchman decided he must face her down with an acknowledgment of the pleasure her symptom was affording her.

The little girl stopped speaking to her doctor for a couple of weeks. But she kept coming to her scheduled sessions. Let's consider how her therapy then evolved.

Betty and the Old Lady's Ghost

CONTRIBUTED BY JOSEPH BEITCHMAN, MD

Betty was 10 when she began her individual psychotherapy. She was afraid to sleep alone, fearful that she might become possessed. She imagined herself turning into a mean, devil-like figure. By the time her treatment started, she'd been sharing her parents' bed with her father, while her mother slept by herself in Betty's room.

We were beginning to make progress with the sleeping arrangements when Betty suffered a setback. She and a friend, Lynn, went to visit Lynn's grandmother and discovered the poor woman dead. Betty believed that the ghost of Lynn's grandmother would haunt her forever. She returned to the parental bed, forcing, of course, her mother to abandon it once again. Fixing all her anxieties on the ghost of Lynn's dead grandmother, Betty seemed unable to explore the meaning and the source of her worries.

After many weeks of therapy, as Betty chatted on animatedly about the ghost and the many, many people who were trying to convince her that Lynn's grandmother's spirit would not be harmful, I deliberately took the little girl aback by saying, "It must be fun to have a ghost around. After all, it gives you lots of attention, considering all those people who like to talk about it." Betty sat bolt upright. She looked shocked. Then I added that because of the ghost, Betty got to sleep with her father and maybe even liked that, too. Maybe she even preferred sleeping with Dad, compared to Mom.

Following her initial surprise, Betty became furious at me. I was telling her lies, she declared. In her next session, she stayed completely silent, with her body and face deliberately turned away. During the following appointment, however, Betty confessed to having a crush on her dad and feeling that her mom was upset about it. Soon after this, she decided she would be able to sleep in her own bed. Miraculously, the ghost of Lynn's grandmother evaporated without a trace.

MEANING OF THE MOMENT

As long as Betty "was afraid" to sleep on her own, she could share her parents' bed and satisfy her Oedipal wishes guilt-free. After all, she was "sick" and could not help herself. As soon as the secondary gain afforded by her symptoms emerged in my surprising delivery of a confrontative statement, a window opened to Betty's conscience. She realized she had to conform to more mature expectations.

Betty's and my "moment" involved my stating aloud an action, wish, or habit of hers that previously had been ignored, avoided, or was entirely unconscious. This amounted to a "confrontation." It was a very strong and surprising gesture from me, and could be considered from two angles. From Betty's perspective, it was my sudden, unexpected attempt to get her to face something she was avoiding. From my perspective, it was a move that produced a strong emotional reaction and started her thinking. The confrontation led to significant changes in Betty's behavior and attitudes. It worked because we already had a positive therapeutic alliance. It also worked because I wasn't expressing negative countertransference with my gesture. I took care to proceed with tact.

I have found that skillfully employed and strategically timed confrontations are extremely helpful in treating kids.[107] *One has to be careful, but it works.*

What Joe Beitchman had to say to his "haunted" young patient was surprisingly direct. There wasn't an ounce of subtlety in it. If I were the patient, it would have caught me as breathlessly off-guard as those two figures that rose from the darkened passages in my San Francisco neighborhood. Dr. Beitchman knew his little patient, however. He had listened to Betty go on and on for weeks. He had calculated his timing. He calculated his plan. He determined that a confrontative remark would be helpful. And then he said it. He turned his young patient around, first in a catch-your-breath surprise, and later, in understanding.

Does the understanding of a recovering child have to be "conscious"? I have already tried to show in many ways throughout this book that it does not. Children do not consistently remember what occurred in their therapies, and I'm quite certain that if we asked them, they wouldn't remember their specific turning points. There is a fleeting meeting of the minds, a give and take, a mutuality of experience, perhaps a mindless "flow."[108] Then, there is change. Was it some great thing we said? Sometimes. But if there's ever a "Bartlett's Quotations" for psychiatric sayings, we'd better compile it ourselves. Our young patients will never commemorate our "brilliant" remarks, nor will they even recall them.

A lack of memory for commentary, however, does not take away the fact that spoken interventions give children the chance to cognitively grasp the ins and outs of their psychological dilemmas. The moment, in fact, may capture something that is immediately understood unconsciously but later can be thought out in full consciousness. In other words, the impact of an implicit moment, experienced almost nonverbally between two people, may subsequently be translated into an entirely conscious, cognitive framework with the youngster.

When you think about Joe Beitchman's patient in this regard, you realize that, at first, Betty became extremely angry at Joe. She responded with surprise and then fury. She accused her doctor of being a liar. Did she know what was happening? I doubt it. She could hardly see beyond her own shock and anger. Young Betty needed two weeks to think. Then she delivered a "confession," followed by a decision to relinquish her Oedipal symptoms. One of her symptoms, however, simply disappeared without any discussion. This particular piece of improvement reflected the power of unconscious, unknowing repair in children. The lost symptom was the "ghost" who had haunted young Betty for weeks. The weird, spooky subject of the doctor's verbal confrontation had disappeared without a "boo!" or a whimper.

How can we advise parents about talking with their own children? Certainly, one cannot expect mothers and fathers to go around interpreting unconscious conflicts to their kids, or to link up a child's general behaviors to the child's particular behaviors with one of them.

If such parents worked with us psychotherapists behind the scenes, however, and if we knew their child well enough to help, there might be times when we could suggest a path of verbal inquiry and commentary that would aid the child a great deal. Here the therapeutic statements to be made to the child would be suggested by the therapist to one or both parents. Then the parents would administer the commentary directly to the child.[109] It's an interesting technique, and a few bright, knowledgeable parents (and their children) respond well to it.

More generally, however, what kinds of verbal comments might an ordinary parent use to help an ordinary kid? "Here and now" situations are the very best ones to respond to verbally at home. But first, the parent has to listen to a complete child-given scenario. So kids must first be taught to tell a true tale, not just by reciting the characters but also by delivering the "plot." Then the parent must listen, follow, and comment. What might the child do? What might he do the next time a similar event happens? What are the feelings involved? Does the situation sound "big" or "small"? Hopefully there is a meaningful interchange. Hopefully it becomes a real dialogue. Even if there is— as yet—no practical solution, the family demonstrates that living with suspense is not horrible per se. If we weren't "in suspense" or "in motion," we wouldn't be defined as "alive." The plotline of life does not come to a complete stop until life is over. So we might as well live in the episodic adventure format we've been given. And we might as well listen long and hard—and then add our own commentaries—to our children's ongoing "soap operas."

We offer contexts to our kids by giving them new pieces of information we have learned and reflecting on some of the old ways that childhood went in "our day." We offer them scientific, historical, anthropologic, and political perspectives. We ask them to suggest their own potential corrections to a problem. If something they say sounds too aggressive or potentially destructive to their own reputation or self-image, we kick the idea around a little. The point is to let kids discover their own solutions, but to protect them, too. Because the discussion (often ongoing) is just in words, nothing damaging can come from it. The family relationship becomes stronger. The child tries out life— verbally—and comes up with increasingly mature means of handling it.

Parents rarely think of the "perfect" thing to say. But neither, for that matter, do psychiatrists.

I'm amazed at how far the old-style psychodynamic "interpretation" has come these days. In "olden times," a child psychiatrist might have been too embarrassed to let other professionals know what he or she actually said to turn a child patient around. The psychiatrist might have been blasted in a small meeting or a grand rounds, for instance— abjectly humiliated, I would say—by older, stricter, rigid, rule-bound colleagues who wanted the child's conflicts interpreted in a certain prescribed way. Today we are writing and speaking more openly with one another about how we talk to our young patients, without sounding embarrassed in the least. That's half the battle. We can share our treating experiences without attacking our peers. Thus, we can ask for and obtain more advice. Then, too, we are able to talk to youngsters today in a leaner, cleaner fashion. We don't try to wrap up everything about a child into a single piece of commentary. Rather, we sometimes tie the transference to only one factor. Or we tie the present to some "here and now" behavior. We stay inside our metaphors. We make up poetry, "scenarios," rap music, rhyming couplets, games—and then stay inside of them to create our pungent commentaries.

With the simpler kinds of interpretations that we make to children these days, we don't have to reach the heights of a Sigmund or an Anna Freud. Instead, we can reach for the "levity" of a Shaw, or we can aim at the "surprise" of a Houdini.

As a matter of fact, when I think about the next two examples, I realize that they elicited the same sense of intense surprise that Dr. Fox's Emily exhibited, or that Joe Beitchman's patient, Betty, demonstrated at his confrontation. The first of these word-smithing examples comes out of Los Angeles from a young child/adolescent psychiatrist, Susan Donner. Dr. Donner was trying to deal with an angry boy who was barely managing to control himself in her office, waiting room, playroom, and hallway. Trying to physically deal with her patient's explosion was hard enough. Yet in the middle of it all, Susan found a couple of lean, clean—and highly meaningful—phrases to say.

A Comfortable Place to Hate

CONTRIBUTED BY SUSAN DONNER, MD

Janus was a 6-year-old first grader when his frustrated parents came to me. Over the previous 2 years, they had sought help from several clinicians for their son's relentless misery and anxiety. His diagnoses ranged from "oppositional defiant disorder" (ODD) to "generalized anxiety disorder (GAD) with tics." His mother and father believed they had failed as parents. Initially a colicky, inconsolable infant, Janus had turned into an angry, easily frustrated toddler. As a preschooler, he often viciously attacked his mother and younger brother, but he also could be extremely anxious and clingy with them. He developed fluctuating tics (blinking, stuttering, licking his lips) and nervous behaviors (chewing his collar and sleeves) by the time he was 5. Janus presented a very different side of himself at preschool and elementary school, leading teachers to see him as a shy but intelligent and well-behaved youngster. In my office, the tall, handsome boy kept his head down as he shuffled slowly from my waiting room into the consultation room. He took little joy in the play activities I offered him, and he demonstrated little empathy for the various animal and human figures with which we pretended.

About a year into Janus's treatment, in which much of his lifelong aggression and its accompanying anxiety had become channeled into therapeutic play,[110] the boy seemed to have a setback. Once again, he was acting enraged at home. Inquiring as to what was going on, I learned that Janus's teacher was about to go on maternity leave and that his babysitter had suddenly departed. When he came for his next session, Janus refused to leave the waiting room. At my urging, however, he finally entered the playroom. Grabbing a ball from the cabinet, he started to dash it against a wall. We needed to make sure about safety, I said. We needed to control the ball, not batter it. Furious, Janus ran out to join his mom and brother. He told them he wanted to leave the "stupidest doctor in the world and never come back." His mother calmly said he was not leaving. Before he could respond, I added, "Unlike his teacher or babysitter, I am not leaving either." Janus looked stunned. My comparison—obvious to everyone but Janus—took the boy by surprise.

He asked to come back in. As I opened the door, he picked up another ball and threw it at the ceiling lights. I grabbed the ball in midair, again reminding him it was my job to help him control himself. Running out of the room once again, he started "bouncing off the walls" of the corridor of our suite, stopping only when his body hit a wall or door. I said, "You need something strong outside of yourself, like my words, or these walls, to make you feel contained and safe." As if shot by a magic arrow, he threw himself face down, arms outstretched onto the carpet. He hugged it. "I am so comfortable here!" he yelled. "I am so comfortable." A few moments later, with his face still muffled in carpet, he choked out, "I hate you. I hate you. I hate you. I like you. I like you."

MEANING OF THE MOMENT

Caught between his own and his parents' "good" expectations for him and his "bad," aggressive, hateful fantasies, Janus had felt overwhelmed for years. In my hallway with his face buried in carpeting, he finally found a safe space to express his ambivalence. He came to his therapeutic turning point when he felt "comfortable" enough to verbalize it. The teacher's leave of absence and the babysitter's departure had brought Janus's love-hate conflict to the boiling point. With my remarks about abandonment, safety, and self-control, he could finally face his own two-sided feelings. He would be able to deal with them— now and in the future—with words.

"Janus," the boy whom Susan Donner named for the Roman god with two faces, loved and hated just about everybody. But before Janus could accept his two-sided problem, he had to recognize that important people in his life would unconditionally accept him. In a flash, and largely on pure instinct, his doctor told him, "Unlike your teacher or babysitter, I am not leaving either." I count only 10 words here. They tie the boy's transference to Dr. Donner to his present experience (loss of two important people). The words do not trace the

history of Janus's conflict, nor do they tie the transference to his office tantrum. So the words are simpler than an old-style psychodynamic interpretation, yet they are intoned at the very moment of
highest intensity for Janus (and his doctor). The timing is so good, in
fact, that it brings the boy up short. Susan's commentary lets him,
within a few minutes, intone his own intense ambivalence. At last, the
problem is laid out for both of them to see.

It's important to note how stunned Dr. Donner's young patient appeared to be. What everyone else had taken as a "given" (the comparison between a pregnant teacher, a babysitter, and a young woman
psychotherapist) was so far from this boy's consciousness that he
reacted to its intonement with a startle. This psychotherapeutic commentary seemed so extraordinarily quick and counterintuitive that it
took the young patient by storm.

The next example comes from my own practice. It represents one
of the youngest patients I have ever seen for "talking therapy." Marcella
was only 2 years old when she came to me. One particularly interesting thing about this very brief psychotherapy was the dual nature of
what I said—not only was I offering information and hope to a horribly
traumatized toddler, but I was also shocking (and hopefully opening
up new avenues of thought for) her parents. There was no way to perfectly "time" my remarks in this instance—during each session that I
saw the youngster, her parents behaved as if it would be their family's
final visit.

Meet Bill Denby!

*The shell-shocked-looking, 24-month-old Marcella lay in band-
ages on my office floor. She had been discharged from the hospital a week earlier—she suffered from a rare condition in
which her feet had turned gangrenous following an operation
to release bilateral, congenital contractures. She had just been
through a double amputation of her feet. The child lay virtually motionless while her unhappy parents—on my couch—
whispered to me. They believed that no one, in or out of the
hospital, had told Marcella what had been done to her. This
apparently was my assignment.*

*The toddler looked up. My plan was to offer her "good news"
right along with the "bad." I said, "Do you know what was done
to you at the hospital?" Not a flicker of movement. "The doctors
took your feet off. Right?" She nodded solemnly. Her parents
looked shocked. "The doctors did it to stop all the pain you were
having. And your feet had turned black. That meant they had
to come off." Again she nodded. She was bright. She already
knew. "There is something wonderful you need to hear about—
artificial feet," I told her. "And there's a man you must watch on
TV—Bill Denby. He has them."*

*I told Marcella's parents to ask DuPont Chemical Company
to send them their commercial featuring an athlete, Bill Denby,
who had lost both of his legs in Vietnam. The commercial showed
Bill playing basketball on artificial limbs. I explained artificial
feet to the toddler and asked her to watch the tape that her parents would show her. She must understand what could be done
to correct her condition before she would be able to mourn the
loss of her feet.*

*By the time the family returned the following month, Mar-
cella's parents said she had already watched "her" tape at least
a hundred times. The little girl, still lying on my carpet, looked
far more animated. She smilingly told me about Bill Denby's
feet "made by DuPont." Her mother and father, however,
seemed confounded about some questions Marcella had recently been asking. "What is soon?" for instance, and "Why is
soon not now?"[111] I explained that Marcella's questions concerned her new hopes for the future—the artificial feet. She
needed adults to help her understand "time" in that context.
We all went on to talk about "time" and how long "time" sometimes takes.*

*During Marcella's third visit, her parents were terribly con-
cerned about how much she had been mentioning the word
garbage at home. When I asked, "Do you think the doctors threw
your feet into the garbage?" her parents looked mortified. But
Marcella said an adamant "yes." As her mother and dad continued to cringe at our conversation, most likely sure that no one
should ever speak to children of such terrible things, I explained
to Marcella the idea of hospital bottles filled with formaldehyde,*

pathology slides for looking into microscopes, and little feet that no longer would grow. Her feet might help doctors understand how to work with other children's painful feet some day. I asked her parents for one more visit. With extreme reluctance, they agreed.

MEANING OF THE MOMENT

I had shocked and upset a set of good, but fastidious, parents by delivering the unexpected to their toddler in a series of talks about amputation, artificial limbs, "time," and the disposal and preservation of body parts. These commentaries were meant not to shock but to provide a very young, traumatized girl with the chance to abreact, to fully understand the context of her trauma, and to find corrections for it. The last time I saw her, Marcella came to my office to demonstrate her new "chemical" feet. (In a phone call beforehand, her parents had said they objected to the red shoes she wanted—they wished for something unobtrusive like brown or buff—but I had insisted she exert her only vote in the entire process.) That morning, as she showed me that she could walk, the beaming little girl in the ruby slippers lit up my room—and my life.

In looking back at this case, there is no question that young Marcella underwent a moment of change, probably most strikingly, in learning a "new" fact—that artificial feet can be manufactured and used by people. But when I think about it, too, a few other moments of shock and surprise in my office were deliberately engineered by calculated statements on my part. Marcella's mom and dad needed to learn to follow her lead and then to speak to her about it. They needed to understand that what children say—about "time," "garbage," and "red shoes"—must be heeded. And so, as I spoke to this tiny little girl, I also carefully chose words that might help the "audience," Marcella's folks. I was trying to demonstrate to two people who hadn't even been able to discuss with their daughter that her feet had been taken off that they must steel themselves to talk about anything at all with this youngster. Thus, I was not only interpreting to them, but I was also "modeling" for them how they might act in the future.[112]

If you took word-for-word notes on what I said to this little girl and her so-shy-and-shocked parents, my phraseology would never have made it into a book of quotes. My words were not beautifully crafted, nor did they convey the "utmost levity." (They couldn't have. There was nothing ironic or funny about amputating a toddler's feet.) But as I think about those old moments with Marcella, I can assure you that—as Shaw put it—I did "take the utmost trouble to find the right thing [for these three particular people] to say." As opposed to the little Superman of Washington Street, Marcella and her parents were well-enough known to me that I could insert what they needed into my very brief comments. Beautiful or not, they worked. The child left as a beaming, happy little human being. Like Dorothy in *The Wizard of Oz,* she had become magically transformed.

In the meantime, Cammie had become magically transformed by her own adolescence. At 11, she got her first menstrual period, and with it, an uncontrollable storm of hormones. I had hoped that Cammie's menarche would have arrived later. She might have grown a little taller, and would have had a little more latency time for me to work intellectually with her. But such was not to be the case. Cammie began her journey into adolescence by bleeding 3 weeks out of 4. After a few months, she once again required the help of the UCSF gynecologist who had examined her under anesthesia when she was only 4. After the exam, the doctor gave Cammie hormones, and she quickly improved.

Cammie's eventual height fell just short of 5 feet. She went to a physical therapist for a few months to correct her tendency to thrust her head forward and slump. It apparently came from heavy tension in her neck muscles. The neck problem yielded nicely to physical therapy, and Cammie came to look prettier and prettier. She was popular. Boys liked to flirt with her and she flirted right back (with extremely good humor). She developed a few close friendships with girls. She also had to learn to fight the subtle, competitive wars of adolescent girlhood. None of this seemed to daunt the slim and very petite young teen. After all, early adolescent boys and girls were nothing compared to that indescribable first year of Cammie's life. (At least, so I thought for a while.)

What did relate directly to that year, however, was a resurgence of the old problems with the electrical-conduction circuitry inside of Cammie's body. Her cardiac rhythms ran amok once again. Even worse, parts of her colon stopped propelling wastes. There were terrible backups. She repeatedly had to endure gastrointestinal interventions to get her gut moving again. The procedures were uncomfortable and humiliating.

Cammie now recognized that using her brain was the very best way to prevail. We had finally defeated T. rex through human ingenuity. She had also learned the value of human ingenuity from Harry Potter's fictional victories, many of them based on Harry's brainy approach and practiced skills at magic. Cammie's schoolwork caught up to the level of her peers, and her conversation hit an even higher level. She preferred "romance" to sex and began to tell me about the films she loved, romantic teenage stories like *The World of Henry Orient*, *The Parent Trap*, *The Princess Diaries*, and *Finding Forrester*.[113] In fact, Cammie no longer used her sessions with me to manipulate handfuls of toys. She played with words, instead.

Once, at 13, she came to my office, speaking in grunts and snorts about a fieldtrip her middle school class had taken to a protected estuary at Ana Nuevo State Park, south of San Francisco Bay. There, herds of elephant seals mate and rear their young. It was mating season, and Cammie and her class had gawked at a number of examples of raw animal sex. "It was *gross*," Cammie said, making a disgusted face.

I wanted Cammie to understand the evolutionary context of sex. I wanted her to see that sex kept the world a-goin'. Although it had been painful and "gross" for her as an infant, sex was expected and okay for adults. After she left, I made up a little word game for her, based on William Steig's *CDB* (See the Bee) letter language.[114] It would be a pungent comment in code.

The next time Cammie came to the office I said, "Cammie, remember the fieldtrip to Ana Nuevo? This is what I think about it—in *CDB* language." (Cammie already knew, through her tutors, how to read CDB.)

I handed her this:

> C D C? I M C-N D O-C-N. (See the sea? I am seein' the
> ocean.)
> D L-F-N C-L S N D O-C-N. O! O! D L-F-N C-L S F-N 6! O.
> G. (The elephant seal is in the ocean. Oh! Oh! The ele-
> phant seal is havin' sex. Oh, gee.)

The whole idea of this silly little memo was that sex—in the wide
scope of things—is no big deal. "Oh, gee." Once she read it a couple
of times and "got" it, Cammie and I had a big laugh. She giggled at elephant seals, at sex, and best of all, at herself.

Once, when Cammie had just turned 13, she confessed to squeezing
Zito, her brother's dog, too hard. She had done it a number of times, in
fact, and Zito was actively avoiding her. "It's not like Mousie," Cammie
tried to assure me, needlessly reminding me of the squeezed gerbil
who was buried under the family's old oak tree. Adolescence, in and
of itself, often inspires post-traumatic reenactment. So I was particularly concerned about this turn of events.

We brought Sandra in, with Cammie's permission, to hear what had
been going on with Zito. Then I suggested a remedy. "No contact with
Zito—nothing—for a month." That meant no feeding, no petting, no
play—zip. Cammie complained. "So long?" she asked. She already felt
deprived. But I wanted Cammie to know that animal mistreatment
was a first step to human mistreatment. As a person who now owned
a full grown body, she couldn't allow herself to act this way. The long
deprivation worked. No further episodes of this type took place.

During Cammie's middle school years, she battled an identity conflict. Was she animal? Was she human? She drew self-portraits at home
of a young lady, Hispanic and proud of it, sweet, proper, dignified.
Within a few days another almost-twin self-portrait would emerge off
her desk, bloodied, sharp-toothed, claw-handed, and furious. At times
she drew herself as "Bloody Mary," an evil figure who, like Freddy
Krueger, could attack you in your sleep. Another day, she'd be a
serenely female Harry Potter, with just a bit darker skin. She was
proud to "be a Mexican," yet her little-girl crushes were mainly be-
stowed upon the blondest, most Nordic of boys—lads with names like

Tristan, Trevor, and Trent. Some of them were boys she met at the UCLA Heart Camp, the one-week getaway in which she served to inspire many a younger child. She wrote a few kids from camp all year long. Others were boys she found at school—a half-Japanese young fellow and the sandy-haired son of a rancher. Although she was concerned with her own identity, she strongly avoided identification with her birth parents, who, she learned, had gotten back together and were raising an infant, her full brother. Cammie stayed thin, thin, thin, avidly avoiding the obesity of her birth mother. And Sandra asked the authorities to keep a close eye on Nick and Bonnie's new son.[115] Who knew what might happen to him?

Then, one day, Sandra arrived for her usual solo 5-to-10 minutes before Cammie came in with a distressing announcement. A few days before, Cammie's junior high school principal had phoned, saying Cammie was going "Goth"! There was a small group of black-clad, spiky-haired, semi-angry kids at school, the "Goths" (named for the barbarian tribe?), about whom the teachers were complaining. Within the past few weeks, Cammie had started joining them at lunch and in the halls.

Cammie entered her appointment wearing black and studs. She had fixed her hair into spikes. "I hear you have a new group of friends," I said with a twinkle in my eye. "Oh yes," she replied. "I've never been more comfortable. I feel *so* at home."

Here, then, was my chance for a classic child-psychotherapeutic interpretation. It would link past to present, exposing Cammie's unconscious. The only difference was that I didn't even pause to think. "I'm sure you *are* comfortable," I said in a conversational tone. "After all, it's what you grew up with in your first home—your first year of life!"

Cammie looked shocked. Our eyes met. Then, without another word, she burst out laughing. It was a moment between us, the seventh. Afterward, she gave up mixing with the antisocial elements of her school—and at the high school in the new district where her family moved the following year. My pointed, timely comment made Cammie's unconscious—behavioral memories that she would never fully be able to grasp[116]—available for our deliberate inspection. Boy, oh boy, did that comment work! She still refers to it, laughingly, today.

Incidentally, Cammie went back to wearing her best colors that spring—aqua, cream, and pink. Over her Easter vacation, her older adoptive brother from the Brooks family invited her to be his "date" at his formal military school dance in Southern California. She went, dressed in a long, pink, tulle gown. It was clear to a number of onlookers that the tiny, highly civilized, young lady in pink was the belle of the ball.

I saw the photos afterward. For me, it was better than *Cinderella*.

CHAPTER TWELVE

Solving a Childhood Mystery

Each individual child represents a mystery. What is the diagnosis? What is the psychological formulation? And what shall therefore be done? What medications, if any, are needed? What toys might be appropriate? What shall be said? Sometimes, the solution to the mystery belongs to the parents alone, and the task of solving it is assigned to them. But when a psychotherapeutic detective puts the solution to a dilemma into a simple verbal framework, sometimes the effect on a child is just as magical as if the great detective Hercule Poirot himself had engineered it.

Take a slight, but significant office mystery I noticed last week, for instance. It comes every year at the same time. It was around the beginning of November, and each of the five depressed adult patients I saw those 4 days were getting worse. Why? Why all five at once? Why did I have to increase their antidepressant medications, mood stabilizers, or both?

The answer was both biological and psychological. We had changed times, moving back to standard time at the very same time that the sun was getting the furthest from us Northern Hemisphereans. As a result, everything was dark. And depressed people suffer more when it's dark, dim, and drizzly. So I told all five of my patients to put their lights on timers and get them fully on 15 minutes before waking-up time and 15 minutes after going-to-bed time. I told them to amp up

the wattages in their lamps and ceiling fixtures. And I suggested buying more lamps if they needed them.

A second mystery, again slight and perhaps overly simple, lay before me, as well. And it was related to the first. Why were my former
patients—even old correspondents—getting back in touch? Two former patients took me out to lunch these past 2 weeks. One came back
after a yearlong "cure." Another showed up in town from Seattle and
saw me 2 days in a row. Another wrote me with a number of questions—I hadn't heard from her in 6 or 7 years. Why?

There are those "big four" holidays, every year all in a row—
Halloween, Thanksgiving, Christmas, New Year's. Let's say a person
used to have wonderful holidays at home. But between then and now,
perhaps somebody died. Maybe someone important moved away.
Maybe the wonderfulness is less wonderful now. That makes for nos-
talgic sadness. On the other hand, let's say the holidays of childhood
were never much fun. Perhaps there was too much alcohol at home,
too much fighting, even a wish to get the holidays over with and get
back to school. That makes for "anniversary reactions." I don't close
my office this time of year. And I know why. But I keep in mind that
not all psychotherapeutic mysteries are so easily solved.

Childhood mysteries are more hidden and intriguing than grown-up
ones. First, kids are unable to tell you much. Then, too, they lie, especially if put on the spot. That's why such mysteries are so much more
difficult, and fun, to solve. I produced a small solution to a childhood
mystery this very week, in fact. A handsome, dark-haired, 10-year-old
athlete from Kallispell, Montana, came 3 days in a row for an evaluation and some brief treatment, if possible, for his "rage." Ian often ex-
ploded at his mother and three sisters. Occasionally, a school peer felt
his out-of-control ire as well. Ian's father, an avid mountain biker, golfer,
swimmer, hockey player, and runner, rarely had time for his children.
In fact, Ian's dad preferred the company of adult males and often left
his family to fend for themselves. They were here in San Francisco on
their own. Dad was "working." They were visiting Mom's parents in
Pleasant Hill.

Was this young fellow feeling as lonely as some of the adults seeking
me out to relieve their "Novemberitis"? If you looked at Ian, especially

at first, he seemed far more angry than sad. Perhaps, though, he was so sad and lonely that he had to deny it and rail at other people. I asked the sullen-looking young fellow if he played golf.

"Of course."

"Well, how many golf dates did you have with your father last summer?"

"I don't know—ten? Eleven?"

"Two," his mother corrected him from my couch. He glared at her. Would he hit her? No, but he hated her for the moment. He was diverting his rage—from his dad to his mom. After all, she was safe. She loved him "no matter what."

"How many times did you play one-on-one hockey with your dad last year?" I asked. The boy was an elementary division hockey champion and lived in a town that loved the sport. He might actually be fun to skate with.

"Dad doesn't like to play with small guys," he answered, more honestly than before, but not quite. He now looked sad. This young man couldn't admit out loud his intense disappointment—and resultant rage. Instead, he defensively denied, and then, through displacement, lashed out at the women in his family. I guessed that I would have to diagnose him as suffering from ODD, a condition marked by childhood anger. But the diagnosis wouldn't even begin to solve half of Ian's mystery. His psychological formulation would. "Loneliness and anger over a self-centered dad and a fractured family" came much closer to Ian's core problem than ODD did. Indeed, a psychiatrist needed to know both aspects—medical and psychological—to assess any child. But the formulation in this case related the solution of Ian's core mystery.

This is how I started to solve it for him. In fact, I could tell the solution was beginning to work because Ian left my office following his final appointment feeling better. The 2006 national elections had just occurred that Tuesday, and Ian told me he had followed them closely. He knew that there had been a Democratic victory in the Senate and House of Representatives. So I asked him, when we met alone, if he had seen how President George W. Bush had acted at his press conference on the Wednesday morning after the elections. "Did he stomp his foot?" I smiled. "Punch somebody out? Yell? After all, his party lost big!"

Ian laughed. He said he liked and admired President Bush. I went on, chuckling a bit, "Maybe Mr. Bush will go home to the White House and kick Laura. Or scream at his two daughters." Now I was metaphorically explaining my solution to Ian's mystery—his constant anger at all the wrong people. I smiled again, not mentioning an athletic boy from Kallispell or a father who seldom seemed interested or available.

"When I go back to Montana," he surprised me, "I'd like to remember that picture." He laughed. He loved the idea of President Bush raging at the First Family.

"And think of me, too," I said, "especially when you're mad. Maybe I'll be able to put a funny idea—like the President having a hissy fit—into your head."

"I like to laugh," he said, laughing heartily.

"Joking helps with anger," I said. "So does 'talking' instead of 'doing.' You've got a great sense of humor, Ian, so use it as much as you can. Okay?" I meant it. This kid was smart, and he could give and take a joke.

Would this ever represent a true moment of change? I wondered. Ian came to San Francisco an angry, angry boy. And he had yet to deal consciously with the painful issue of his father's disinterest in him. He certainly hadn't begun to deal with the issue of whether his family could survive this way. Through metaphor, we had forged far enough ahead in our four sessions that it might represent a turning point. But I didn't know whether it really would amount to a moment of change.

"Will you come back and see me over Christmas if you visit your grandma and grandpa?" I asked him.

"No," he said with real regret. "I can't. We're going on a long bike ride in Florida. But I'll come in the spring. Okay?"

I believe Ian left my office looking forward to it.

One magical-detective doctor, dealing with very sick kids, is Louis Fine, who does brief psychotherapy, consultation, and medication management at Children's Hospital in Denver. He works as a team with the pediatricians and surgeons there, who tend to youngsters with serious physical illnesses and congenital disabilities. Because of the length of their treatment, many of these children stay at the hospital unaccompanied by their parents, who may be working, at home taking care of other siblings, or living in a town far away. Years ago, Dr. Fine began to notice that children with operations to correct life-long deformities or malfunctions didn't seem particularly overjoyed with their successful surgeries. In fact, a number of these kids looked downright "blue." He offers us two cases here, each presenting the same sort of medical mystery. Each child was miserably depressed after a highly successful piece of surgical magic. Dr. Fine's verbalized solution to their mysteries turned these kids around. If they hadn't been changed psychologically, they couldn't have gone on to cooperate with their long and painful "habilitations." Here, Louis Fine shows us, once again, that understanding a youngster's psychology some-times outweighs the diagnostic name you put to the youngster's con-dition. (Don't forget, however, that you have to do both!)

The Dilemma of Getting Better

CONTRIBUTED BY LOUIS FINE, MD

As a consultation-liaison psychiatrist[117] at a large, high-tech hospital, I have been given the opportunity to see children after surgeries that were meant to improve or correct congenital ab-normalities. Some of these kids significantly regressed, not pro-gressed, after their "successful" procedures. What had happened? Given the opportunity to do only brief evaluations and treat-ments, I gradually learned that these little postoperative patients held a psychological theme in common. To show this common-ality, I will present two different children with two different surgeries. Our moments in therapy happened when I spoke to each one about the same sort of psychological dilemma.

Case I. Stefan, age 12, was born with a meningomyelocele, causing paralysis of both legs and confining him to a wheel-chair. Of normal intelligence, he received praise for his aca-demic successes and social involvement. The surgery was meant to improve his cardiovascular status so he could ambulate on crutches. Postoperatively, however, Stefan refused to use his previously mastered skills. He would not cooperate with physi-cal therapy. Seemingly suffering from postoperative depres-sion, he stayed in bed. To me, he talked with anxiety about his

*current status: "Sometimes I don't know who I am anymore. . . .
If I do anything for myself, my mom will think I can do everything for myself and then she'll think I don't need her anymore
. . . I'd better not do anything." I told Stefan he had just described a personal dilemma. It was a conflict between staying
the way he always was and allowing himself to get better. I suggested to him that if he told his mother his fears, they might be
able to explore some new things they could both do together. By
the next time I visited him, Stefan had done some thinking,
and perhaps some talking, too. "I'm going to like my crutches,"
he smiled.*

*Case II. Mary Frances was a bright, attractive, verbal 10-year-
old who, due to neonatal complications, was hampered by a leg
that was 3 inches shorter than the other. She wore a special
thick, heavy-soled shoe to give her balance. Her technically
amazing surgery involved the implantation of a gradual leg-
lengthening device. Postoperatively, the child was withdrawn.
She would not walk. She looked sad and apathetic. I decided to
talk with her, not medicate her, for at least a while. With regret,
Mary Frances reminisced about how extraordinarily powerful
her old shoe had been. She said, "No one would mess with me
because I could kick them so hard." Now Mary Frances felt
empty and lost. We talked about her conflict as I saw it. She had
actually liked her bad leg! We needed to focus on mourning the
loss of her misshapen body so she could adapt to a newly balanced one. When Mary Frances began to talk about what type
of cool tennis shoes she might wear at school, I knew she had
taken a huge step.*

MEANING OF THE MOMENTS

*Psychiatrists have long observed the difficulties medical and
surgical patients encounter when they lose their previous functioning. On the opposite end of the spectrum, "habilitative"
surgery—aiming at improved functioning—can also be a
problem. The recovering child may actually qualify for the
diagnosis of depression. The surgery has threatened the young
person's cohesion of mind and body. The child originally developed his personality around a congenital defect. Now the floor*

has been swept out from under him. Explaining the "dilemma of getting better" is a way in which the psychiatrist can help the postoperative child reorganize a sense of identity. Putting this dilemma into words for the child (and for the child's surgeon) shows the young patient that his ideas about himself—and his relationship to others—used to depend heavily on diminished function or deformity. Now, a conflict exists between the old and the new. Appreciating the moments in which this kind of conflict is revealed represents one of the rewards of doing brief psychotherapy with hospitalized children.

In a very different kind of case, a little boy with mutism, who looked as if he belonged somewhere along the Asperger's spectrum of disorders (related to autism), came to visit Ajit Jetmalani, a clinician who practices in Portland, Oregon. Dr. Jetmalani treated the mute little fellow with the gloomy diagnosis for 6 months, yet nothing worked. But the detective in Ajit Jetmalani did not give up.

To Swim, To Sing, To Speak

CONTRIBUTED BY AJIT JETMALANI, MD

Jimmy was a 6-year-old waif of a boy. His parents brought him for evaluation of developmental delays and refusal to vocalize in public. Over his lifetime, he had suffered mild fine- and gross-motor problems, speech-articulation defects, and limited interpersonal relationships. Now, he did not talk to anyone outside his immediate family. Both parents were kind, bright, but reserved professionals who, like Jimmy, displayed awkward interpersonal skills and kept largely to themselves. Jimmy had no medical issues or traumatic history. In my initial play evaluation and in each weekly visit during the 6 months that followed, Jimmy drew pictures of boats, water, swimming people, and fish. He did not make a sound from the time he arrived in my waiting room to the time he left. My working diagnosis was "pervasive developmental disorder NOS" (PDD) with elective mutism. My treatment plan was play therapy one to two times a week (usually alone, but periodically with a parent), and monthly parent meetings to support increased playful engagements and social opportunities at home. I prepared myself and the family for a long, tough haul.

At the 6-month mark, Jimmy was still not talking. I vacillated between wanting to find meaning in his drawings and wanting to categorize them as the kind of "perseveration" (meaningless repetition) one sees in PDD. I began to struggle to stay actively engaged. Jimmy's total silence, broken only by the infrequent squeak of a crayon or my occasional comment, hung like a banner proclaiming the failure of my approach. As he would/could not talk with anyone outside his family, I did not refer him for psychological testing. Curbside consultants, considering Jimmy's mutism to be a form of social anxiety, suggested medicating him. It was tempting, but I waited. I kept feeling I was missing something very important. Then, one day, while watching Disney's The Little Mermaid *with my own children, I recognized the source of Jimmy's pictures! The story is about an evil witch who offers an impossible choice to the mermaid: "Give up your beautiful voice and immortality, and in exchange, I'll make you a human being who cannot speak." Jimmy was drawing pictures of the film.*

At our next session, Jimmy was lying upside down on my couch, staring at my feet. I said I had just watched The Little Mermaid *and was thinking about his drawings. The little mermaid had really wanted to speak with humans, I said, but she was so afraid of the witch's curse that she couldn't make a sound. Jimmy began to hum. I went on. I was happy, I said, because the mermaid found a way to beat the witch and save her voice, too. Upside down, Jimmy made eye contact with me and said, "Yup." He then began to talk. During each session that followed, we conversed and enacted themes from the film, and within 3 months, he began to speak in other settings.*

MEANING OF THE MOMENT

Although there are many interesting therapeutic aspects to this case, most important for me was remaining patient and attending to my wish to find a discoverable key to this child's inner world. My initial diagnostic categorization of Jimmy's symptoms diminished my anxiety about treating him, but it may have delayed my discovery of the real meaning to Jimmy's art. Although medication might have reduced his anxiety and hastened the resolution of his symptom, play therapy enabled him to master his underlying fears. Our play also encouraged his use of another human being, his psychiatrist, to solve dilemmas and to experience shared moments of joy.

Why did this small boy so strongly identify with a Disney adolescent girl? I believe he shared a great deal in common with her. Human beings held great appeal for them both. Each was an outsider. Like a mermaid, or a "fish out of water," Jimmy could not easily navigate the social and vocal demands of the complex world outside his home.[118] *When I showed Jimmy that I understood and valued his metaphoric maiden of the sea, he immediately indicated that he would allow me to help.*

Unlike the pair of Little Mermaids who had endured a kidnapping and a rape inside a traumatized 4-year-old girl's mind, this Little Mermaid represented a kind of alter ego for a little boy who was awkward and lonely but untraumatized. It's clear that each particular mermaid fit one specific child. Once the proper fit was discovered by the psychiatrist, the proper solution could be given. The fit represented the child's inner mystery. The doctor's remark represented the solution.

As opposed to crime scene investigators, who conduct very precise and orderly routines, psychodetectives observe children in an unroutine manner, chatting with parents, playing or talking with kids, picking up outside information from doctors and teachers. In such "here and there" ways, I tried to understand why young Cammie Brooks had dreamed in horror all of her life about a dark, expanding opening. It was a terrifying dream, and she first told it to me when she was around 10 or 11. She told me that the dream had repeated for years. I had a huge stack of medical records, court reports, and depositions that Sandra and Tom had given me when they first brought Cammie. Many of these papers flowed from Cammie's exams at UCLA and Stanford and had to do with mental retardation or sex abuse. But others related to the story of her dead baby sister. Had Bethany been born at home? Could Cammie have witnessed the infant's birth?

From a sexually traumatized 1-year-old's perspective, that would have had to have been a horrendous experience. And it would have been literally repeated in a terrifying dream about an expanding opening.

The answer was no. I found a hospital chart indicating that Bethany had been born in a delivery room. But Cammie might have seen something first. I remembered how graphic Cammie had been when I first met her—"Sheep die, die sheep. Baby die, die baby." For years, I had been unable to determine what she had meant regarding the sheep, until Bonnie's cousin had solved the mystery. So this 1-year-old girl had been exposed to bloody killings of cats and sheep. And the death of her 3-week-old infant sister. Why not expose her to a woman's labor, as well? Or a sheep's. Or a cat's.

I decided to try out my solution to the nightmare problem, incomplete and guesswork that it was. I offered it to Cammie when she was 14 years old. The poor child was still complaining of that one, awful dream. Careful not to go too far, I talked about pregnancy and childbirth. How did advanced labor look from the doctor's perch at the foot of the bed? How did it feel to the woman experiencing it?

Cammie had drawn some pictures on a piece of paper when she was just 3 years old. Sandra, at my suggestion, had written down what Cammie had said about them. One drawing showed an adult woman stick-figure with huge "boobs" and red stuff painted between the stick-like legs. "What's that?" Sandra asked the toddler at the time. "Not talk bout dat," Cammie said. Sandra had taken word-for-word dictation. I kept a copy in my files. Now I took it out.

I showed Cammie my color copy. I told her I knew Bethany had been born in a hospital. Had Bonnie demonstrated something to Cammie first? I wondered aloud. Or perhaps it had been her aunt, who also had a young baby and lived nearby. Maybe it had been an animal in labor. I talked about the joys and distresses of childbirth. And then I guessed—telling her it was just a guess—that she might have watched a female in labor, or in childbirth, from the bottom of a bed or near an outdoor animal crib. Her parents had exposed her to a lot. Maybe she'd seen this, too.

Was I right? I feel like a second-rate Poirot even thinking about it. It was just a guess. But Cammie's dreams, frequent before, totally disappeared. She is 17 now, and there hasn't been another one for 3 years. Our discussion about animal and human labor—and the normal blood and vaginal stretching that it entails—helped young Cammie somehow. The dream remains a mystery, however. I could not determine exactly what exposure Cammie had actually had.

A therapist must be careful not to go too far with a hunch. All of us must work side by side with our little patients. But we must also be aware of an important role—as investigators and solvers of psychological puzzles. A child's memory, of course, must be guarded from the overly vigorous psychodetective.[119] But when there are internal confirmations in the patient's symptoms, we also have a mandate to relieve suffering.[120] Somehow, we must learn to strike a balance.

I've chosen not to call my dream interpretation Cammie's eighth moment. It is too controversial and still a little too puzzling.

Can parents solve psychological mysteries for their children? There are certain stories that circulate inside families, usually among cousins or siblings in the younger generation. They have to do with "Uncle Arthur's suicide," or "what great Grandpa Jones used to do when he was drunk," or even "Daddy's first marriage." These stories do not easily cross generational lines, and parents often seem offended or secretive when the histories of their families are brought to light by their children. By the time the family tales reach the parental generation, however, these child-perpetuated histories must be fully listened to. And then parents must answer. They don't need to answer all at once. They might decide, for instance, to tell the true story tomorrow, once they can determine together how they will present it. On the other hand, they might promise a child that they will tell the tale "once you're a teenager and can understand it better." Of course, they need to keep their promises.

What parents must *not* do is to lie. Family truths are usually known to more than one person. And these truths usually will come out. Without a good explanation—at the proper stage in a child's life—there will be lifelong misunderstandings and mistrusts, perhaps escalating from one generation to the others. Many an adult suffers from not having been leveled with by parents.

Families cannot possibly be perfect. Nor can their ancient reputations be preserved by lying to the younger generation. Parents, therefore, must be enabled by us professionals to present these true familial stories in as helpful a way as possible. This may be one of our important jobs as psychiatrists. We have intensely studied the stages of childhood. We are able to understand the origins of conditions that lead to suicides, substance abuse, alcohol deaths, dementias, and incest. We are knowledgeable about genetics. It is better to find ways to talk openly to children about such subjects. One doesn't necessarily have to "wear the facts on one's sleeve." But once a family mystery comes up with young people, it's best to solve it as soon as possible.

Family mysteries do not only reside in the facts about what actually happened to Aunt Irene or whether or not Grandma Smith was a kleptomaniac. Some of these issues are far more subtle, such as how mothers or fathers enact old behaviors from their childhoods toward their own children, how certain fears and attitudes come to roost on the next generation, how parents make the very same mistakes that were made upon them, and how they go so far to avoid those same mistakes that they create problems in the opposite direction.

Geri Fox, whose first vignette appeared in Chapter 11, describes here a mystery she solved within the family therapy framework. Interestingly, solving this particular mystery created a magical moment of change for the family's adolescent son. The doctor watched the boy turn around in the weeks after she surprised him with her solution to a family conundrum. The boy, in fact, had been the subject of his parent's concern—the designated "patient."

Crossed Wires

CONTRIBUTED BY GERI FOX, MD

Sixteen-year-old Allan was not performing up to his academic potential in a competitive high school. Because of Allan's Bs and Cs, his mother, Marion, was afraid she was failing as a parent. Marion was taking antidepressants and seeing an individual therapist. Allan's father, Bernard, habitually functioned as "family mediator." I decided to see the threesome together.

A key incident had occurred 2 years before we started. Fourteen-year-old Allan had asked for a cat. His mom countered that he would first need to demonstrate his responsibility by keeping his room neat. Allan did not measure up. When the cat never materialized, Allan verbally excoriated Marion, accusing her of purposely setting him up for failure—"You never really wanted me to have a pet!" Hurt to the core, Marion refused to speak to Allan for months. Bernard acted as go-between. After Marion and Allan finally resumed talking, the teenager developed an attitude of indifference.

In an early session with the family, I decided to inquire about Marion's life story. I requested that her husband and son listen carefully. When Marion was 14, she told us, her hardworking, distant mother divorced her easy-going alcoholic father. Marion believed the rift was entirely her own fault. Her dad's parting words—"Take good care of your mother"—didn't help. When Marion was 15, her mother attempted suicide. Again, Marion was riddled with guilt. Her mother remarried a year later, and Marion lurched prematurely into adulthood, completing high school in 3 years so she could escape home. When her father withdrew his child support halfway through college, Marion felt utterly devalued. She stopped speaking with her father.

At this juncture in Marion's story, I commented that Marion's decision not to talk to her father was exactly what she had done later to Allan. Bernard suddenly noted, almost in passing, that Allan was the living image of Marion's father. Allan looked intensely surprised at all of this. I then remarked to Marion, "Your emotional wires are crossed between Allan and your parents. You feel responsible for every single thing that happens to Allan, as you did long ago with your mom and dad. When Allan rejects your maternal efforts, it triggers the failure you felt when your mom attempted suicide, and the hurt you felt when your father stopped paying for college. Despite yourself, you react to Allan the way your mother treated you and your father." Allan silently listened, still looking taken aback by these new revelations.

Within the next few family sessions, Allan told us proudly that he had begun working on his own personal goals.

His grades were improving. Bernard could now stop acting as
a go-between. Marion became less sensitive to rejection. She
began to reach out to Allan, telling him she loved him. It was
what she had always yearned for from her own mother.

MEANING OF THE MOMENT

A probing psychotherapeutic inquiry is often aimed at linking
past with present. This can be a powerful technique in some-
what unusual places, such as family therapy.[121] *In this case,*
my inquiry and the interpretation that followed put together
the meaning of events in the mother's past with the meaning of
events in her boy's recent life. It was an unexpected gesture
from me, and it was done in just a few minutes. But it im-
proved the life of the entire family.

Geri Fox's case is a multigenerational mystery that was exposed
through a relatively complicated family interpretation from the doctor. Here was an apathetic boy who snapped out of his apathy almost
instantaneously, once he understood what had been going on between the generations of his family. First, young Allan needed to hear
a personal history from his mother. Mom laid out her story frankly
and without disguise. Then, Dad offered an important comment: His
son uncannily resembled Grandpa. The boy was ready for it. He listened. And then Geri solved the "mystery" of the family. The problems of one generation had been passed down to the next. Allan took
his psychiatrist's solution and ran with it.

I can't emphasize enough how little wishwork and guesswork actually
goes into solving most young people's mysteries. The majority of the
answers are straightforward, lying right before our eyes. The solutions depend upon picking up outside confirmations from sources
external to the child, as well as from observing the internal confirmations manifest in the young person's symptoms. Refusing to put the
obvious facts and observations together, however, may create such a
do-nothing therapeutic approach that the young patient eventually
drops out of treatment—worse off or at least unchanged. Not only
may the psychiatrist's refusal to "put two and two together" (into a

partial narrative) result in a failure of the child's psychotherapy, but it may also create a negative attitude in the patient about ever coming to treatment again, even as an adult or as the parent of a troubled kid.

One of the serious therapeutic problems, especially in "trauma" patients, generated by the fierce and very public "false memory debates" of the 1990s,[122] is shyness about working on solutions to the inner mysteries patients bring us. The debates and ensuing legal battles made some therapists feel that solving a young patient's mystery was almost akin to poisoning the child. Young people, however, sometimes need our help in making the tiny but necessary linkages between fragments of their narrative remembrances. When we are too afraid to consider possible psychological solutions, we leave our patients uncomfortably hanging in limbo.

Much of the work of memory retrieval can and should be done by the patient, not the doctor.[123] Yes, children can go back and ask their families of origin about a shard of remembrance. Older patients can look in their old hometown newspaper files. The adult or late-adolescent patient may be able to hire a private detective, or return for a visit to the house or the school where a number of old memories reside. Even a child may want to talk to an old friend, or with a parent, or take a look at an old medical file. In such instances, the young patient serves as the "investigator." The psychiatrist, like an experienced detective, is needed to solve the psychological mystery of the child and to figure out, wisely, where to go from there.

Having evaluated a number of memory returns in adults, I have concluded that, at any given time, a traumatized person may have five sorts of traumatic childhood memory: (1) true general memory of a trauma with true details; (2) true general memory with false details; (3) false general memory with true details; (4) false general memory with false details (these latter two categories may, at times, represent "implanted memories" or purposeful attempts to lie); or (5) no traumatic remembrance at all (through infantile amnesia or through a number of the defense mechanisms, such as denial, repression, suppression, displacement, and dissociation).

I include this to help contextualize what I did with Cammie Brooks's repeated nightmare of the expanding opening. In December, 2003, the *Journal of the American Academy of Child and Adolescent Psychiatry* published my 12-year case report of Cammie's ascent from "Wild Child" (the title of the paper) to civilized human being.[124] In the paper, I emphasized my treatment of Cammie's trauma through abreaction, context, and correction.

Because, at 13 months, the immaturity of Cammie's brain prevented her from fully processing "event memory," her tiny, but pungent, verbal impressions ("Baby die, sheep die") were unusual. But they were not absolutely unheard of. Especially considering how highly charged these events were, and how bright Cammie turned out to be, these "declarative" memories were not impossibilities.

I wanted my paper on Cammie to present my ideas about how to treat childhood trauma. In no way was it a lesson, or a treatise, on infantile memory. It was a report on psychotherapy. I did not consider the materials I offered Cammie during the latency stage of her childhood— the story of the baby's killing, the story of Cammie's examinations in the Central Valley E.R. or at Stanford, and at UCSF under anesthesia, or the time I told her the "facts of life"—to be suggestive. They were, instead, pieces of proven information. They were meant to make Cammie comfortable with the idea of having a life narrative, no matter how painful that narrative might be.

A couple of "false memory movement" supporters, however, read my paper and wrote to the *Journal.*[125] How could a 13-month-old girl remember anything? She must have been told—I might have suggested something to her in an early interview, or she must have overheard talk at home, they argued.

Sandra and Tom Brooks have always assured me that the events of Cammie's infancy were not discussed inside their house. They were afraid for Cammie to know. But for argument's sake, let's say that the Brookses were unaware of talking, or of others talking, or that they were lying to me. In that case, Cammie could have picked up "Baby die" somehow. She could have heard other detrimental things about Bonnie—although I doubt that "got boobies" and "trow away" would have been how Sandra and Tom described her!

But how could Cammie have known about dying sheep? At age 2, she told me, "Sheep die." She screamed at my toy sheep. She was afraid.

None of us knew the solution to this mystery until Bonnie's cousin turned up when Cammie was 8. For 6 years, no one could have suggested to Cammie her horrible memories of sheep being slaughtered. No one could have helped her with it, either, because we simply didn't know. Once Sandra and I understood the explanation for Cammie's mysterious memories of sheep, we had no compunctions about offering her the solution. It was now documented, as were all of her other memories that we had talked about in therapy. These were corroborated by outside observations, doctors' reports, coroners' reports, trial records, and even Bonnie's own behaviors and comments.

I did, however, make that one very speculative group of comments about Cammie's nightmare. I offered it as a tentative, and in no way final, solution. I described childbirth and wondered if Cammie had ever been exposed to it. We talked about it scientifically—from a doctor's point of view. And we talked about it—woman to woman—as a future and very normal process for any girl who eventually might want a baby of her own. I showed her the drawing she had made at 3. I didn't really know the answer, I said, but the solution to her repeated nightmare might lie somewhere in the realm of having watched a labor and delivery.

You seldom receive a confirmation from a young patient that your solution to her mystery has taken hold and is proving itself helpful. And you hardly ever get that confirmation as a birthday present! But here's a short follow-up to that horrible repeated nightmare: On March 27, 2004, Cammie turned 15 (I'll refrain from telling you the age I turned). For my birthday, she handmade me a pillowcase. It was constructed of blue cotton with white clouds all over it. The sewing was very carefully done. "Sleep in peace, Dr. Terr," Cammie wrote on her card. "You have taken away my bad dreams."[126]

CHAPTER THIRTEEN

Indulging in a Dramatic Moment or Two

We are racing toward Thanksgiving, my next-to-favorite holiday. It's totally American, and I like that. It's full of good flavors, especially the all-American turkey, stuffing, cranberries, pumpkins, and yams. The Pilgrim-Indian past, beyond that happy, first Thanksgiving Day, is checkered, to say the least. That said, the "familyness" of the holiday makes it special. Everyone who can seeks comfort on this day in their family—with parents, children, siblings, cousins, and the occasional friend with nowhere to go. I remember Gray Patton, an eminent San Francisco pediatrician, talking a while ago about a little girl from a very fancy private school.[127] He had seen her just before Thanksgiving Day. "Where are you going this year?" Gray asked her. "To our ranch," she said. "And are you bringing a friend?" he inquired. "No, no, silly," she answered. "At Thanksgiving, everybody goes to their *own* ranch!" That small-unit sequestering, as opposed to the explosion of American togetherness on July 4th, is the reason that Thanksgiving takes my second place and Independence Day gets my first prize.

We brought armfuls of pots and pans up north to our country place this weekend so that our family could dine on American bounty while watching the wild turkeys run around outdoors. It's not exactly a "ranch," but it's 6½ acres of beautiful California land. We're so lucky, I can't believe it. And that, of course, is what Thanksgiving is all about.

Is the holiday dramatic? The weather sometimes is. I remember a huge Thanksgiving snowstorm when I was a child in Cleveland. It took a week to dig out. There's many a Thanksgiving rainstorm in California. But in all my years of living through Thanksgivings, no costumed Pilgrim has ever entered my house on the great American holiday, no decorations other than flowers, gourds, or pumpkins have adorned the place, and no Indians have come to call. The presentation of the turkey can be dramatic—as in that famous Norman Rockwell poster. But in general, orange, brown, and cranberry red aren't particularly drama-filled colors. Nor are the dark, dark greens we place on our plates to try to stay "healthy" as we overeat.

I guess I'd have to say that there are far more small "dramas" played out in our child-psychiatric offices than one ordinarily sees at Thanksgiving time—except, perhaps, for those wild after-Thanksgiving sales at the malls. As I've noted before, those who deal with children do not shrink from dramatics, either in adopting personas and setting atmospheres or in finding something special to intone. Many times, these moments arrive on the doctor's impulse. Other times they come with careful calculation. The drama is usually served up by the doctor, not by the little patient. But one key thing about the young "audience" is that they know intuitively how to respond to a moment of high tension, ceremony, declaration, poetry, or dance. They join right in. And sometimes—just sometimes—they turn completely around as they participate. One wants to shout "Hallelujah!" when it happens. But instead, one thanks the Lord on days like Thanksgiving for the pleasure of watching, and sometimes getting to engineer, a childhood change.

Cammie Brooks experienced a moment of high drama near the time when she graduated from middle school. She was 15. Her dad was about to retire from his law practice, and the family planned to move to the Stockton region, where Marla, the oldest girl in the Brooks clan, had settled. Marla was married and raising a couple of very cute boys while continuing her nursing career near the University of the Pacific. We looked forward to Cammie's learning to be a comfortable, reliable babysitter for her two little nephews. With Sandra's backup help, it would serve as a powerful correction, we felt, to the murderous attacks Cammie witnessed and experienced as a baby.

In the process of saying goodbye to the San Joaquin Valley and everything she had known outside of her immediate family from 13 months on, Cammie received a remarkable invitation. The state organization of special-education teachers wanted Cammie to appear at their annual spring meeting as an invited speaker. Why? Because they knew she had gradually advanced herself from an I.Q. in the mentally retarded range to California's officially "gifted" status. And they wanted to hear directly from this child how she did it.

The "wild child" modestly spoke of the years of extra tutoring she had had—and was continuing to have. She praised the patience and expertise of her teachers. She was both humorous and corrective. "Don't talk about us kids [with learning and attention disorders] too loud when we're not on task," she said. "I don't exactly lie awake at night and say, 'Please, Lord, let me be off task today, so I can make the teacher mad at me in front of my friends and classmates.' " (We don't have to wonder where these comments came from. It's not every day that a child gets slapped in front of an entire third-grade class.) Cammie produced a list of "Ten Don'ts" for the special ed teachers—all strictly from a child's point of view—and then she concluded.

The teachers loved Cammie's talk. They presented her with a plaque. But the real drama happened afterward, informally. A teacher approached the podium to speak with her. "If my next baby is a girl," she said, "do you mind if I name her 'Cammie' after you?" Cammie nodded solemnly. She was visibly moved. Those are the kinds of things you give your thanks for on Thanksgiving.

Drama happens all year long in child and adolescent psychiatry. And these episodes are the easiest ones to remember. They are the peaks among the day-to-day plains we all live in. These little dramas underscore what our psychotherapies were always meant to say. They cement the meaning of the treatment more effectively than mere words.

The first vignette in this chapter illustrates the kinds of therapeutic "shows" that doctors put on for their patients. It comes from a nation that quietly, almost silently, celebrates its Thanksgiving in October. Although inhabited by all sorts of Native Americans, Canada did not house any Pilgrims to speak of. And although we don't usually think of Canadian behavior as particularly dramatic, there is no question that a few of my colleagues "north of the border" are capable of putting on quite a performance. Klaus Minde, is a well-respected infant researcher from Montreal. For years, he has conducted studies of mothers and babies that have made significant contributions to our knowledge about this all-important dyad. But Dr. Minde also treats young patients. One hot summer day—quite the opposite of the Canadian Thanksgiving season—an English-speaking family arrived back home in Montreal from one of the beautiful neighboring lakes. They were bringing in a childhood emergency. Use your mental eye to "see" this scene in McGill University Hospital's E.R. Use your inner ear to "listen." If your imagination works well, you may find yourself participating as the audience to a zany, but very effective, musical comedy.

Fly in the Poo

CONTRIBUTED BY KLAUS MINDE, MD

On a hot summer evening, I was asked to see 4-year-old Joan in the E.R. The preschooler was sure she had caused another child to drown. She was agitated and preoccupied with death. She had not eaten or slept in 48 hours. The whole family, including Joan's 30-month-old sister, Stacy, had been at a nearby lake 2 days before, when a public announcement instructed the lifeguards to assemble their rowboats and "practice a rescue." A woman within Joan's hearing commented, "I hope there is no real body to rescue." Joan immediately began to cry. She said, "I have killed someone," pointing to a ripple at the lake's edge. The child's agony persisted, despite her parents' attempts to console her. Joan began claiming that if she ate anything, she might accidentally swallow a fly and, thus, kill yet another living being.

When I entered the examining room, I found Joan sitting on her mother's lap, her face buried in her mother's breasts. Little Stacey was looking at a book. Both parents presented Joan's history, including her fear of swallowing a fly. The mother had a 10-year history of panic attacks, which she had overcome with medication and daily jogs. Joan unbuttoned her mother's blouse and snuggled even closer, as if increased bodily contact might provide a sense of security.

I had no idea how to help. Pure instinct and my cognitive-behavioral therapy experience, however, led me to say to little Joan, "What's the worse thing that would happen if you did swallow a fly?" Everybody stared at me in silence. So I answered my own question. "The fly might come out in your poo!" When Joan's little sister heard this, she shrieked in delight. The toddler chanted, "Fly in the poo! Ha, ha, ha!" laughing with giddy abandon. I picked up on it. Crouching on the floor, I began hopping around the room, singing, "Fly in the poo! Ha, ha, ha!" Within a minute, the mother and then the father, joined me in song. "Fly in the poo, fly in the poo, ha, ha, ha!" Joan looked at us in utter amazement. She descended from her mother's lap and came over to watch. The family left for home that evening with their "old Joan" in tow. She was symptom-free.

Joan had a slight relapse 3 days later, but she was talked out of it by her parents. Four years afterward, she developed more generalized anxiety symptoms, but when her pediatrician spoke with her about getting some psychiatric help, she said, "I don't need to be scared of flies in the poo!" She has been entirely well now for almost 4 years.

MEANING OF THE MOMENT

I see our moment in therapy as a stroke of good luck, triggered by a toddler's delighted response to my impulsively playful attempt to educate and soothe. By watching us sing and dance to her fears, Joan experienced an acute cognitive shift, escaping her "brain lock."[128] The catch word—"fly in the poo"—helped Joan later, as well. She could still remember our positive twist in music and in language that had allowed her to control her inherited propensity toward panic and anxiety. Realizing that her worries were "silly" enabled Joan to go on and think more reasonable thoughts.

When Joan's pediatrician told Klaus Minde, 4 years afterward, that his E.R. moment had held all that time, the revelation was almost as dramatic as the original moment of change. An 8-year-old child's statement,

"I don't need to be scared of flies in the poo," indicated that young Joan had remembered the events of the E.R. almost as a password. The original high drama that pointed this little girl toward health had functioned not only once, but also for a second time. Like Jerry Dodson's letters to and from Wes Craven, the song and dance "scene" in the E.R. could be pulled out again and again from the child's mental bank of memories. It would serve as an open sesame to the little girl's well-being.

Dr. Minde did absolutely nothing to preplan a musical comedy, using a chorus line of four family participants. He just picked up on a 2-year-old's glee, and then impulsively exaggerated that glee into a performance. But there are also calculated and preplanned ways that psychiatrists encourage this same combination of joy and madness in their offices. Giddy looseness, in fact, has the potential to create positive change in kids—some of it quick and momentous (magical), and some of it slow and just as complete. One preplanned technique I have already illustrated is the use of special languages. When you say the words out loud in "CDB" language, for instance, they come out with a ridiculous accent. Kids laugh raucously at the silliness of it all. Pig-latin, of course, is another way to communicate dramatically with children. Rap, with its rhyming couplets and heavy background beat (even when done with just a metronome), may accomplish this very same purpose. The idea is to talk so dramatically with a youngster that the child *really* talks to you.

No psychotherapist can plan for an operatic opportunity that would rival Klaus Minde's moment in Montreal. But one can plan to keep a number of storytelling techniques at hand. Winnicot's "Squiggle Game," for instance, is a way for the doctor to start—and the child to finish—a doodlelike drawing that eventually tells a story.[129] Usually this story is a good indication of the child's inner workings. Making a mutually designed cassette recording, a talk-radio show, even a TV presentation (if you keep a videocam in your office), turns the spotlight onto the child. Most children seem to relish participating in such a drama. In hiding behind the pretend and playfulness of such a conjoint enterprise, the youngster doesn't seem to realize that the "real" him or her is showing.

I've already referred to the technique of beginning a story in order to have a child end it. Sandra Brooks and I applied this technique to Cammie when she was just over 2 years old. Her "Sally stories" were for home use only. When Cammie was 15 and newly moved to a Stockton suburb—chosen, in part, for its very good public high school—she floored me by casually saying that her latest Sally stories were about the politics of getting along in her new school.

"Are you still telling those Sally stories?" I asked incredulously.

"Of course," Cammie smiled. "Mom and I never stopped. We've got a girl named Cammie in it now," she added. She had not realized, until I told her right there and then, that the character Sally had always been Cammie herself. Now she had two Cammies! How dramatic can you get?! She and Sandra continued their stories, however. It pleased them both to go right on with a ritual that had always worked.

Not all child psychiatric drama is employed to produce glee and madness. Some promotes empathy. In this respect, I will offer you a couple more examples from our contributors. The first comes from Mike Deeney, my shy Oregon colleague who used to drive that sporty old Jag. His dramatic moment was one of true, unmitigated reality. Mike's lifelong anaphylactic allergy to egg was the culprit. His adolescent patient, Philip, uncomprehending and naïve, served as the key actor. As it turned out, the doctor inadvertently created, produced, and directed their two-person "play." In addition to acting a part, Dr. Deeney revealed a crucial reality about himself to his young patient. Then they shared a true, life-threatening moment together. It was intensely dramatic. And the teenager in this performance seized the moment to dramatically change. In fact, his change has held for years.

The Egg and I

CONTRIBUTED BY JOHN M. (MIKE) DEENEY, MD

Philip (never "Phil") was 15, depressed, and somewhat anxious. He had recently moved with his divorced mother from a comfortable Midwestern college town to an affluent Portland neighborhood where he knew no one in his new high school. His mother was preoccupied with her challenging new job, and he heard little from his father, who had been angry about the mother's move with Philip. Already somewhat rebellious against his conservative parents, Philip had begun to wear black leather and chains and had a Mohawk-style haircut. He smoked cigarettes but used no drugs, and he had kept himself out of any real delinquency beyond skipping school. Philip's mother brought him for treatment both because of his unhappiness and because of her inability to deal with his angry complaining.

Early in his treatment, Philip appeared one day with his hair dyed and dramatically stiffened into tall vertical spikes. He seemed vaguely pleased with his new appearance but complained that classmates thought he looked "weird." As he sat beside my desk playing with his hair in my air-conditioned office, I began to become very short of breath. I am highly allergic to bird feathers, eggs, and some pollens, but I could not connect my current symptoms to anything in the room. Then, as Philip described how he had spiked his hair with egg whites, I suddenly realized he was dislodging bits of dried egg into the circulating air and I was then inhaling it. I had to excuse myself abruptly to take some medication for acute allergic reactions. On my return a bit later, I sat farther away from a puzzled Philip and turned off the ventilation, explaining my situation as honestly and objectively as possible. He immediately felt responsible and apologetic, and he attempted to find further ways to be helpful, including offering to leave early. He also suddenly became more friendly, more caring, and more open about his own feelings and needs. He seemed more invested and involved in his treatment, and the changes persisted into subsequent appointments.

MEANING OF THE MOMENT

Was the intensity of Philip's anger with his parents validated by the effectiveness of his rebellious appearance in influencing my behavior? Did I give him an opportunity to identify with me as another individual with problems? Did I permit him to become for the moment the solicitous parent to me that neither of his parents seemed able to do for him at the time? Perhaps all

of these things operated unconsciously to some extent. [130] *Some,*
in fact, were later discussed. More important, however, seemed
to be the unique opportunity presented for both Philip and me
to relate openly and honestly to each other as "real people," to-
gether addressing an immediate-reality problem. The appeal
to the healthier parts of Philip's personality appeared to help
him bridge the adolescent-adult relationship gap more quickly,
fostering early trust and facilitating more productive commu-
nication in his treatment.

The secret to Mike Deeney's extremely dramatic encounter with young
Philip was how "real" the doctor allowed himself to be perceived by
his mid-adolescent patient. Immediately, the boy handled himself in a
more caring, friendly, and open manner. The change, Dr. Deeney says,
has lasted. Coincidentally—or perhaps not—Philip now serves in one
of the helping professions. And, according to Mike, he serves people
well. It's another reason to give our thanks.

A nationally respected psychological researcher on child development—I'll call "Melanie"—attended the same Berkeley dinner party
I did a few weeks ago, and we were delighted to see each other again.
For years, we've been friendly. That night, I told her about my writing, and she recounted a small "magical moment" story of her own,
which in its drama and horrible reality reminded me of Dr. Deeney's
tale. Again, it represented a truly dramatic incident of danger to the
therapist. But it also became an incident of instantaneous change in
an extremely sick adolescent boy.

Melanie was in training when the incident occurred. She had been
treating a latency-age boy, Brian, for 2 or 3 years as an outpatient at
the Yale Child Study Center. The boy, who had a psychotic father, was
strange and awkward, partly as a result of being extraordinarily afraid
of wild animals. He was so phobic, in fact, that he could hardly leave
home. But Brian was also a basically giving, loving kind of person, and
Melanie empathized with him deeply. They quit treatment after he
vastly improved, and several years ensued. Then, one day, the doc-
toral candidate learned that 17-year-old Brian had suffered a "schizophrenic" breakdown and had been hospitalized at a notorious,

now-closed, New England state hospital.[131] She quickly set out to visit him. She needed to see how he was and whether there was anything she could do.

A staff person let young Melanie onto the locked "acute men's ward." But once the door was opened, the attendant left, locking the door behind him. Melanie looked around. There were no nurses or orderlies in sight. Gradually, she found herself surrounded by male patients. They were closing in. Slowly, they moved into a circle. She realized she was in danger. She watched, but did nothing.

Suddenly a strong, well-muscled young man, about 17, pushed himself through. He placed his body in front of Melanie's, turning about and staring down each of the psychotic individuals who was standing in the circle. It was silent. The crowd began to disband. A nurse finally came in. The "scene" was over.

The young psychologist expressed her heartfelt thanks to Brian, and told him of her distress that he had recently become ill. She sincerely wished him a quick recovery and left, but not without thanking him again.

She learned that Brian was discharged from the hospital within 3 days. The "schizophrenic" episode had apparently cured itself. Brian, a true rescuer, had paid his treating psychologist back for the loving help she had given him all those years before. The payback moment amounted to an almost operatic scene. And the occasion turned this late-adolescent boy completely around. Rather than identify with a psychotic parent any longer, Brian could now identify with all the great heroes of the world. He could be a man. As a dramatic and very real helper, he had "beat" the helpessness of psychosis. He certainly had also defeated the wild beasts he used to fear as a boy.

One way parents can dramatically help their own troubled kids is to advocate for them. Representing kids, making sure they get all the services they need, attending conferences, and "sticking up" for them are highly appreciated parental actions. Sometimes we need to advise mothers, fathers, or both about what their children will require and how to go about getting these services. Sometimes parents must set their attention to *how* the services will be delivered. Sometimes, in fact, they must hire school-savvy lawyers to make sure that the "program" they are hoping for goes into effect.

I don't mean that parents need to get into playground or Little League fights on behalf of their kids. Or take the neighbors to task, or threaten the authorities. No. Most parental advocacy is quiet, diplomatic, tactful, and polite. But children know when advocacy is occurring, and they appreciate it greatly.

Of course, children should learn to manage their own wars as well. But some occurrences, even with other kids, are insurmountable. Children occasionally need their parents to intervene—as Sandra Brooks did with little Andy's mother. Again, these interventions need not be overly aggressive or dramatic. And we can help the most by offering our suggestions and guidance.

Sometimes the psychiatrist must act the part of the child's advocate. This kind of advocacy may suddenly take on the intensity of a confrontation, even if the psychiatrist doesn't intend it. What should ordinarily be a quietly politic maneuver may—in an instant—become a moment of pure psychotherapeutic drama. A San Francisco teaching colleague of mine at UCSF, Lynn Ponton, found herself caught in such a situation when, right in front of her, a father brought himself into position to strike his adolescent daughter. Lynn reacted without pausing to think. Once again, "faster than you can say Jack Robinson," a psychiatrist found herself deeply enmeshed in a highly dramatic "scene."

Stand Up

CONTRIBUTED BY LYNN PONTON, MD

Sixteen-year-old Nathalie, who had struggled in vain for 2 years with treatment-resistant anorexia nervosa—four hospitalizations, seven therapists, and a current weight of 80 pounds—was sitting with her mother, brother, and me in my office, waiting for her father to arrive. He was 20 minutes late. This was Nathalie's and my third session together, and I had requested that the entire family attend. On this day, the usual entrance to my office was obstructed by a large mud-filled construction ditch. Nathalie was complaining that her father was never on time, when his head suddenly became visible through the glass door at the rear of the office, opening onto a muddy pit. I opened the door and her father, who had failed to notice the large signs indicating the alternative entrance, hoisted himself in, muddy shoes and all. We were at a loss for words. Then, Nathalie laughed and began poking fun at her father. He hadn't seen the signs. What a joke!

His face turned red, his mouth twisted, and he walked in Nathalie's direction, raising a hand to hit her. I was still reeling from his unexpected and extremely dirty entry into my office. But I swiftly stood up. I faced him and declared, "Not in my office, you don't!"

He slumped over and sat down. Nathalie shouted a profanity at him and ran out. Her father began to talk, holding back sobs about how hopeless he believed his daughter's situation was. He then apologized for getting ready to strike. When I questioned them further, Nathalie's parents told me he had hit her a couple of times years ago. As they said this, I looked over and spotted Nathalie's younger bother smashing his hand into a chair. Then, minutes later, a crying Nathalie knocked at my other door. All five of us spent the last minutes of the session discussing the very obvious problems that the family was struggling with.

MEANING OF THE MOMENT

In the next session, Nathalie thanked me for "standing up" for her and speaking out when her father got ready to strike. I responded that I would work with her family to try to make sure it would not happen again. I had already referred her father to an anger-management class. She and I talked about the fact that her father had missed all the signs indicating an alternative entrance, just as he had missed all the early signs of her anorexia. But I also noted that he had expended considerable energy to climb through the mud pit and hoist himself into my office. Recalling the moment, she giggled, "I guess he stood up, too."

Nathalie, her family, and I continued to work together for almost 3 years, during which time she graduated from high school, started college, and slowly recovered. Many times, she and her family referred back to our moment, calling it the "Day of the Mud." It became part of family mythology about how they all had changed.

Dr. Ponton's bravery and seriousness in the midst of what, up to then, had looked like something out of *Laurel and Hardy*, impressed an entire family. Much like "fly in the poo," "Day of the Mud" became a kind of motto among them. The anorexic girl, Lynn Ponton says, took a number of years to fully recover from her terrible eating problems. But the family, including the young patient, began coping far more normally with one another immediately following this remarkable incident.

I often bring an adult family member into my office—with the child's permission and presence—to advocate for a certain position I think the family ought to take vis-à-vis their youngster. Other times, however, we must talk it out alone. I might meet with parents on the phone, or set up a separate parental appointment. Or, if there are no parents, I will, at times, work out a meeting with the child's guardians or social workers. These meetings are hardly ever dramatic. But once in a while, our differences become passionately stated. Hopefully the agreements we eventually forge help kids to better manage their long arduous journeys toward normalcy.

Almost every time they occur, the child "subject" must know about such meetings. He or she must also receive the doctor's feedback afterward. Kids don't like being talked about. On the other hand, they like it even less when they have no one looking out for their interests. Our position as child advocates, therefore, is one of our very important functions. Hopefully, it does not frequently become a moment of high drama.

Probably the most ultimately dramatic and, in a sense, most unsatisfactory of our advocacy positions occurs when our obligation to the child, and to the state, crosses purposes with our obligation to families. In child abuse situations, even if only on suspicion, we must report the case to the authorities. There are no "ifs, ands, or buts" about it. We *must* report. Unfortunately, governmental agencies often mess up these cases. They don't tend to listen to us, the professionals who know the most about the particular individuals involved. We often lose the patient, too, because the parents are so upset at us about the reporting we did. We can only hope the child will subsequently be sent to a good therapist.

The area of child abuse is currently the place where child advocacy most seriously backfires. Counties and states have not been willing to spend enough money to hire the best-trained professionals, not only for their investigations, but also for the treatment phase. It also seems difficult for the public to "take up arms" on behalf of the children who are the victims of their own families. Sometimes, there was considerable love there, even though terrible mistakes were made. If we could ever get in the position of helping some of these more "attached" families remain intact, while supervising and treating them vigorously enough to engineer a change in their function (and also while treating the child victims for their traumas), we would make real headway. For this, I would forever give my thanks.

After her "thank-you session" with the special-education teachers and her graduation from middle school, Cammie moved to Stockton. She continued seeing me once a month. Sandra found her an excellent local tutoring service, and Cammie began having extra drills in reading, spelling, and math. She needed to cope in advance with her "scary" new high school. Sandra contacted the high school counselor and introduced her to Cammie's story. Everybody was getting ready, including the "wild child."

What we didn't know in advance, however, was that an entirely different story was evolving far to the north of Stockton. And that story was about to impinge—with terror, horror, and suspense—on young Cammie's life.

In the meantime, the maturing "wild child" thought long and hard about high school. Would people like her? How was she going to present herself? Would her Hispanic heritage show up as a disadvantage in her new, more affluent, more Caucasian surroundings? In the heat of the California summer, the "wild child," like all normal adolescents before her, worried about her identity.

At the children's library, or sometimes in a children's book shop, one finds a great teller of stories. The children's book is read like a dramatic script, sometimes an entirely memorized script, in fact. The great storyteller mesmerizes the young audience and then sends each child home, sated from a marvelous meal through the ears.

Child and adolescent psychiatrists are great storytellers, too.[132] The knack is to put together a terrific beginning, middle, and end—with dramatic buildup and some added punchy bits of dialogue to accentuate the whole process. It takes practice. It is, I think, part of dramatic tradition of our field.

The late Richard Gardner, of New York and New Jersey, used to produce wonderful stories, based on particular childhood diagnoses. He would offer, at the end, his own corrective conclusions, a "way out," a release from the particular problem. One fallen giant in our field, Bruno Bettelheim, collected college students' favorite fairytales and then—with insight and enthusiasm—analyzed what these stories might mean to the developing child. Others in our field have developed more generalized means of delivering stories in therapy—such as having a preset beginning that you can utilize any number of times, asking the child to eventually participate in making the story his or her own by inventing a middle and an end.

If the psychiatrist is a consummate actor and an impresario, as well, he or she may spontaneously create his or her own story. Such a tale may be so dramatic and so especially tailored to the child that it leads to a moment of change. This was the case with Ken Robson, of Hartford, Connecticut, who was asked to consult at a hospital that was trying to help a violent little girl get to sleep. Dr. Robson has a soft, buttery voice. At the medical meetings where I've heard him speak, it almost sounds like an old recording from "the velvet fog" himself, Mel Tormé. So Ken went to the hospital, on request, to treat an aggressive, sleepless little person. He decided to tell her a story. He called it a "soliloquy for two." He improvised all the way. Of course, the angry young girl had determined she wouldn't say a word. But, like the best of jazz musicians, Ken Robson eventually picked up enough from the child to "riff" on her tune. It was a tune that the little girl composed from her own chaotic life.

Sleepy Time Gal

CONTRIBUTED BY KENNETH S. ROBSON, MD

Maria, a plump, loud, unruly 6-year-old with hair askew, was referred to me by her hospital inpatient service for a one-time consultation. Their diagnosis was ODD. She had been put on the unit after threatening her infant brother with a kitchen knife. Brutal, impulsive violence was the lullaby of her early childhood: Her mother had been beaten regularly by a succession of drunken boyfriends whose eruptions Maria hated, feared, and regularly witnessed. In the hospital, Maria permitted only female staff to touch or approach her, watchfully avoiding all men. Her nights were full of screams, agitation, vigilance, and startle responses to noise of any kind. She did not sleep.

I could approach Maria only if she sat on the lap of a particular nurse who had befriended her. She assured me, nonverbally with blazing eyes, that she would not talk to me, pursing her lips into a hard, straight, bloodless line of defiance. In such situations, I have learned to deliver a monologue that is, in fact, a dialogue: a soliloquy for two.

I looked away and began describing a child I knew who was perpetually worried—a girl just her age who was always frightened by the loud noises of fights in her house. Maria glanced at me furtively. "Was the girl named Carmen?" she asked. I went right on. "Carmen was very angry that her mommy did not protect her from scary stuff." Maria nodded with grim seriousness. And, I added, there were many times that Carmen wanted to run away and find a mother who really loved her. Maria turned to her nurse and whispered, "I run away a lot." She sank further into the soft, ample cushion of her caregiver's lap. I continued to tell the "Carmen" story to Maria, avoiding her transfixed gaze. "Carmen needed to know," I said, "that she was safe, and that her mommy was safe, and that even 6-year-old kids can learn to dial 911 when they need cops or medics to help them." With this apparently novel advice, Maria yawned. The police, I reminded her, were waiting at the 911 telephone number, ready to protect little girls and to carry off noisy, dangerous men. "And do you know any lady police?" I kept talking as she barely

nodded, eyelids drooping. "They are just as strong as men."
The little girl's head fell forward as her little body fully relaxed.
I hoped she was dreaming of a career in law enforcement; it's
never too early to implant the seeds of purpose, competence, and
self-respect into a child. They may grow into a viable future,
even in the depleted soil of early trauma.

MEANING OF THE MOMENT

When I launched my monologue, I facilitated immediate con-
tact with a wary, resistant girl. By talking about another child
(just like my patient), I opened to scrutiny my patient's own
psychological problems and vulnerabilities. I have found that
untrusting children like Maria can accept confrontations and
corrections when they seem indirect. For Maria, my monologue
established enough sense of safety for her to be able to soothe
herself (as D. W. Winnicott so brilliantly explained in 1958)[133]
and to allow herself to separate—in the act of sleep—from her
frightening, yet loved, primary objects of attachment. Sleep
itself, thus, became a tiny therapeutic goal and a small thera-
peutic triumph.

Going to sleep is an extremely important function. And getting along in society is equally important. Ken Robson encouraged a dramatic shift of both of these functions in this deeply disturbed 6-year-old child by improvising a nighttime lullaby in prose. It was dramatic. It was personal. It was simply perfect.

Any child specialist can indulge in this kind of storytelling. Any parent can do it, too. It's such a marvelous way to offer contexts and corrections to a child that I sometimes wonder why we all don't spin out tales of childhood much more often. Then, too, look at what storytelling can do for relationships! I can just picture a distraught 6-year-old girl snuggling deeper and deeper into her newly cherished nurse's lap. I can hear Dr. Robson's smooth, foggy voice. With these dark November days, I'm about ready to fall asleep just thinking about it.

On a brilliant California Sunday late in June, the same year Cammie Brooks turned 15, an Oregon family man—along with his young, live-in girlfriend, and their children—went shopping at a large, busy, Central Valley California flea market. Browsing for a while, they suddenly sent up an alarm. The woman's 4-year-old daughter from a previous relationship was missing! Everybody at the market flew into emergency mode. News crews arrived. All day, people fruitlessly searched. By early evening I saw the story on the news. The girl's mother, a pretty, but obese, Hispanic-American woman was shown tearfully begging the public for her child's speedy, safe release.

By nightfall, and with the television cameras put to bed, the woman confessed. Her story evolved this way: Her little daughter had spent most of her young life with her grandmother in southern California. A month before the flea market episode, the girl had come to live in Oregon to be with her birth mother, her mother's boyfriend, and their two younger children, a 4-month-old girl and an 18-month-old boy. Since arriving in Oregon, the preschooler's behavior had been deemed unacceptable, largely by the boyfriend but also by the mother. (Apparently, complaints had been coming into the southern Oregon child protective services agency, not only about the little girl during that monthlong period, but also before, on behalf of the two tiny children. The agency had attempted to strike a "voluntary agreement" with the 34-year-old man and his young girlfriend. Whatever agreement had been made, however, had apparently not held.)

The Thursday before the flea market, the little girl misbehaved once again. This caused the boyfriend and the mother to hit her. She sustained wounds to her abdomen and head. Her skin was scalded. The boyfriend then got the brilliant idea of having this "bad child" stand in a corner all night long. He enforced it. Upon morning, he let her go to bed. There, she died. (Was it due to pooling of blood and fluids in her legs after already experiencing internal hemorrhaging? Or were the head or abdominal injuries enough to have killed her outright? Was it irreversible shock?) No responsible adult ever obtained help for this poor child. No matter what else, there was horrible neglect here.

The following day was a busy one for the remaining family. The four of them went to their local Wal-Mart, where they were videotaped buying garbage bags and a shovel. Then they drove to a nearby national forest to bury "big sister." By Sunday, they had driven hundreds of miles to the stepdad's old stomping grounds. There, they claimed, the poor unfortunate preschooler had wandered off, or had been abducted.

On Monday, the young mother showed the Oregon authorities her daughter's shallow grave. Quickly, she turned "state's evidence" against her boyfriend. She, herself, was charged with murder. Depending upon the evidence she gave in the future, a deal on her behalf might be struck. The woman's two younger children were taken away, and as far as I know, they have been adopted by a well-qualified family. The boyfriend, however, faces "murder one" charges, and "aggravated murder" at that. In Oregon, a conviction of "aggravated murder" can bring with it the death penalty.

Of course, you already know this particular "boyfriend." You probably recognized him from his animalistic disregard for the youngest, most helpless people among us. It was Nick! Cammie's birth father had apparently left Bonnie and their very young son to take up with a much younger woman (who could have been, for all their resemblance, Bonnie's little sister). Moving hundreds of miles north to start his life all over again, Nick had continued, instead, right where he left off. Harming and torturing young children was Nick's *modus operandi*. If he could get away with a killing, he would. And if he could get his current "woman" to help him accomplish his unbelievable acts of cruelty, he'd do that, too.

There was no way to hide this despicable story from Cammie. First, it was national news when it first came out, and it would become national news again, once Nick's death-penalty trial came up. Second, Sandra, Tom, and I offered the evidence we had collected on the old California case to the Oregon authorities. We held copies of a number of materials about Bethany that the California authorities had somehow "lost." The Oregon investigators wanted to keep checking in, especially with the Brookses (and they did). Third, we had the imperative of keeping Cammie safe, not only from Nick and his "representatives," but also from Bonnie and her large and scary clan.

We decided to tell Cammie at once. She needed to know this story for her own safety. And she needed to hear it first from us.

Poor Cammie received just one horrible message from the entire affair. "I'm doomed," she told me on the phone that first week after the killing. "I have terrible genes."

"People can overcome their genes," I said, and I meant it.

Cammie didn't tell me for a couple of weeks, but she had misheard me. When I said "can," she had heard the word *can't*.

I straightened out our misunderstanding by the time Cammie's July appointment came along. But Cammie's 15-year-old summer continued to be gloomy, largely because of the atrocities Nick had committed. Despite a remarkably helpful tenure with the younger kids at Heart Camp, Cammie started her new high school discouraged, lonely, and sad. That horrible sense of genetic disaster had not left her.

One of the saddest sides to the trend in recent years to "remedicalize" psychiatry is the sense of "doom" it imparts to doctors and patients alike. Yes, we have to be realistic about genetically carried psychiatric conditions like schizophrenia, bipolar disorder, and chronic, barely remitting depressions. On the other hand, however, we must hold onto our optimism and use everything at our disposal—including good, intelligently administered psychotherapy—to help our patients with these dark diagnoses. Just hearing a diagnosis affixed to a certain person shouldn't take away from that person's—and our—hope. Look at the young man who saved Melanie. Brian had had a horrible "label" put to him, schizophrenia. His father, chronically psychotic, had earned the label for him, as well as for himself. But the genetics didn't mean that Brian couldn't protect a person he cared about. And the genetics, in the long run, didn't mean that Brian had to be compelled to behave in an out-of-control fashion. If he wanted to, he could become a hero. And he did. In fact, Brian's turnaround fought his genetics, as well as the established labels that come with those oh-so-formidable genes. From Brian's defiance of the worst flows a learning and relearning experience—and a renewal of optimism—for us all.

Because of the extreme drama of the next vignette, and because of the terrible prognosis that the boy, Cedric, carried, I have saved this story as the last in this chapter, and, thus, in this book. Cedric's tale is one of the most miraculous moments I know of. The boy seemed doomed by his diagnoses as well as by his own behaviors. (He might have been doomed a bit, too, by his race and poverty level.) Cedric was institutionalized in a special facility in Arkansas because he hadn't been able to be handled, even by the local state hospital where he had been involuntarily confined. He carried two gloomy diagnoses—mental retardation and schizophrenia.

At his new institution, Cedric met up with a counterforce to all that doom. Richard Livingston, a gifted child/adolescent psychiatrist with both optimism and drama inside his soul, watched Cedric watching his peers. Dr. Livingston noticed something puzzling: How could a mentally retarded, psychotic boy understand chess? And how could such a boy think four or five moves ahead of the others? Richard knew he was dealing with a difficult and dangerous young man. So he muttered a statement just above the boy's ability to hear. It was extremely nervy. And it was extremely dramatic. It was just the kind of move, in fact, that a magician, conjurer, or illusionist might have made. Watch carefully. Listen. Here are child psychiatry dramatics at their best!

Cedric's Secret

CONTRIBUTED BY RICHARD LIVINGSTON, MD

Staff at the holding facility where I consult described Cedric as the "3M Kid." That meant he was "Mentally retarded, Mentally ill, and Mean as hell." At 15, Cedric stood 6'3" and weighed in at 280, so it was no great surprise that he was put into maximum security as soon as he arrived at the juvenile justice center. We knew he arrived heavily medicated, so it was also no shock that he was unable to suppress the tremors and restlessness induced by massive doses of depot haloperidol (Haldol, an antipsychotic drug with a number of neurological and neuromuscular side effects). Cedric was already legendary. At the state hospital where he had been before, he beat up staff, broke another kid's nose, and yelled obscenities at the walls and windows.

Cedric's hospital records revealed that he did not voluntarily accept oral meds. "Too paranoid," a previous evaluator had concluded. His diagnosis was schizophrenia. Aside from hollering at the unseen, however, he had not shown a positive sign. He refused to talk to me the day we first met. I offered him medication to reduce the side effects from his injected drugs, but he shook his head "no." I wrote a propranolol order (a beta-blocker that helps with Haldol's side effects), and urged our talented and grandmotherly nurse-manager to offer it to Cedric every day. She, like the boy and about half of our staff, was African-American. (My ancestors are Cherokee and Dutch, but I look more Dutch.) Cedric repeatedly declined the medication.

Cedric had been raised by a pleasant, but sickly, grandmother. As a toddler, he lost his mother to a drug overdose. He had been a quiet and unobtrusive child, despite his size. Sitting in resource classes because of learning difficulties, he had always had one or two close friends. He was sent to the state hospital after he beat an older boy senseless because he had teased one of Cedric's pals.

In the day room one morning, I noticed that Cedric was surreptitiously watching a couple of white boys play chess. He murmured, "dumb ass" and moved away. After a few minutes, I approached Cedric apart from the crowd. "What was that kid doing wrong in the chess game?" He stared at me a minute and then responded, "He brought the queen out too quick and he's fixin' to lose her." He was absolutely right. Impulsively, I almost whispered, "Your secret is safe with me." And I walked off.

The next day, Cedric sought me out. "What secret did you mean?"

"I know you're not retarded, and I'm beginning to suspect you aren't crazy either," I said.

"Go on," he permitted me to say what I thought.

"Here you are, in kid jail. You're heavily medicated. Adults and kids are all scared around you. They underestimate your brains. What makes it worth it?"

"Two things," he replied softly. "First, nobody messes with me. Other thing, if a black kid acts smart, what do the brothers call him? 'Oreo.' Then I'd have to hurt somebody to show they were wrong." ("Oreo" is an insult that means, like the cookie brand, you're black on the outside but white on the inside. The Cherokee version is "Apple.")[134]

Again, I repeated myself to Cedric. "Your secret is safe with me."

For the next 2 months, Cedric refused to let me talk over his secret with selected staff. Finally, he allowed me to arrange psychological testing, with privacy insured. I also made a deal with him—no medicines, oral or depot, as long as he stopped short of physical aggression. As a result, Cedric ceased looking like a zombie. His verbal I.Q. turned out well within normal limits and his reading comprehension, far better than that. I asked Cedric about college. "Good dream, man." But in an amazing display of interagency cooperation, arrangements were made, grant money found, and Cedric's high school graduation equivalency exam (GED) completed. Finally, I obtained his permission to tell the staff his secret, but only as he was being discharged. His grandmother's most recent report said that Cedric has completed two semesters of junior college with Cs. He has had no trouble with the law. Grandma is very proud.

MEANING OF THE MOMENT

Cedric's secret—that he was neither mentally retarded nor psychotic—was not an easy one for me to keep. I was criticized at our institution for keeping it. People felt betrayed, saying, for instance, that I had let them remain unnecessarily fearful. But eyeball to eyeball with Cedric, I knew I was doing the right thing. We had always shared an implicit understanding that his secret would eventually have to come out. But my temporary complicity gave Cedric enough time and freedom to try out his new self-image. It gave him someone to trust. For him, it was a world-altering paradigm shift.

Sometimes a truly creative move on behalf of a child is misunderstood by others. The institutional staff who had housed Cedric were not at all happy with Dr. Livingston's secrecy about this dangerous boy. But Richard had to stick with his secrecy because a promise had been made to his young patient. Was it in the child's best interests? Yes. Did it conform to the community's medical standards? Yes. The promise in no way endangered anyone else. All it did was buttress the staff's actual security, while failing to relieve their anxiety about their imagined lack of security. And when you think of it that way, there was no harm done.

Why was Dr. Livingston's move with Cedric so incredibly effective? It was counterintuitive, unexpected, and unlike anything anybody else had done in this boy's lifetime. The recipient—a jaded, almost hopeless boy—heard a stranger's six-word assurance and experienced a moment of mutuality with him. Everything Cedric had heard in schools, institutions, even mental hospitals, sounded different from this. This one statement—"your secret is safe with me"—forged a connection. "You and me, we're in this together" was what Richard Livingston meant from his heart. And he followed through on what he said. It was "Richard and Cedric, Cedric and Richard." Even when the hospital staff criticized him, the psychiatrist stuck to his guns. He had made Cedric a promise and he would keep it. In return, Cedric fulfilled his own life promise.

Here, then, was a modern-day peacepipe, shared by an older part-Cherokee and a younger black man. This particular covenant would, indeed, hold. In fact, this kind of meeting of the minds is the greatest gift we psychiatrists hope for—sometimes against all hope. When it happens, the doctor is repaid a hundred times over for his or her efforts. With this blessing, we practitioners can celebrate our own personal Thanksgivings, even when the holiday is long out of sight.

For Cammie Brooks, the first year of high school was no holiday. Nor was there much to give thanks for. The more demanding classes were a shock. The necessity of taking "No Child Left Behind" exit exams was a shock as well.[135] The teachers' demands of no talking, no whispering, and no undelivered homework assignments shocked Cammie, too. Beyond that, her gut acted up fiercely. It looked as if parts of her large intestine had failed to be enervated. She might need surgery. That, too, was shocking. But the worst of it all was Nick. News kept arriving about him. A very effective, anti-death sentence defense attorney had been hired. It was questionable if Bethany's killing could come into the Oregon case at all. Much of the official California material had been irretrievably discarded. The Oregon D.A.'s office was struggling to find more California evidence. Cammie's sense of doom overrode her usual good spirits. Toward spring, I thought of some-thing—actually a dramatic, "tried and true" technique. "Why don't you write a letter to the judge?" I suggested.[136] Eight months had elapsed since Nick's arrest. Lots of babysitting. Lots of dog-minding. But very little lifting of Cammie's spirits.

Cammie loved the idea of a letter to Nick's judge. She talked and I took dictation. The first letter, a short one, sounded as if it was written to God, not a jurist. It had to do with Cammie's wish that Nick would "burn forever in hell." There was absolutely nothing redeeming about him, she said in her missive. But the following month, Cammie dictated a longer, more sensible letter, still arguing for Nick to get the death sentence. Would the judge, for instance, consider the health problems that Nick had visited upon her? Would he consider her worries about her upcoming adult life—sex, childbirth, and taking care of children, for instance? This group of problems, too, had largely come from Nick, although her birth mother had contributed quite a bit as well. Did the judge realize that nobody had ever punished Nick on Cammie's be-half? Would the judge—in addition to the murdered Oregon girl—think of her? She, Cammie, had had to witness a baby's murder at her father's hands. In fact, some of her first words had been "Baby die. Die baby." Indeed, it was a miracle that Cammie, with all her physical and mental injuries, had survived at all.

We typed up the letter on plain white paper. It took up only a page. It looked beautiful, official. It was worded in adolescent words, but careful and well-considered ones. Then we put the letter into Cammie's file. I would keep it for her until Nick's sentencing procedure came up. Then, if she wanted, she could sign it and send it to Oregon.

There were a number of instances in which Cammie and I looked at one another as she gave me her dictation. But it wasn't so much the eye contact that accounted for Cammie's eighth moment of change—it was the power of her own words. She realized that in choosing well-deliberated, cautious language for an official in power, she herself could exert her own power. She recognized that in expressing her injuries and her sense of outrage to a judge, she might actually have a voice in what happened in the world. Then, too, she might not. But she might as well try.

As of today, as I tell this story, Nick's sentencing procedure has not yet come up, and the letter still sits in Cammie's files. However, regardless of whether she ever ultimately sends it to Oregon, the letter was a dramatic and effective effort. It has restored her sense of autonomy. It has made her feel that she might be able to control her own young life. In fact, the letter has proved to Cammie that how you live outweighs what you've inherited.

Let's look one more time at the seven highly dramatic moments in this chapter. Three of these moments stemmed from inadvertent emergencies, and the doctors responded by being intensely "real." Dr. Deeney, for instance, certainly wasn't looking for an anaphylactic episode, nor was Melanie wanting to be locked up and surrounded by psychotic males. If Dr. Ponton had been "given her druthers," she certainly wouldn't have wished to go into battle, head to head, with a furious, full-grown man. What happened with these three therapists was that they took advantage—on behalf of their patients—of an inadvertent and dramatically difficult situation. This created a stunning change in the child.

Conversely, the other four dramatic moments began and ended under the doctor's own control. After about 8 months of Cammie's slogging along in "genetic doom," I came up with the suggestion that she write a letter to an Oregon judge. The old, tried-and-true remedy in dealing with trauma occurred to me suddenly. Why then? I think it was my unconscious speaking. When Dr. Robson made up his bedtime tale, his unconscious was working overtime, too. He was "plugged into" a 6-year-old's mind, and he "got" her completely. When Dr. Livingston murmured his six-word pithy phrase after watching a chess game, the particular phrase streamed from his unconscious as well. Yes, I think our subliminal mental processes serve us well. Dr. Livingston's statement came so quickly and reflected such a wise condensation of chess knowledge, psychiatric knowledge, cultural/racial knowledge, and boy knowledge that it probably bubbled up from his very depths. Finally, when a professor decided to sing and dance in his own distinguished university's emergency room, where do we assume that behavior came from? The unconscious. Believe me, if Dr. Minde had paused to think, no musical comedy would have ever come about. To start with, he knew a lot about CBT. He knew all about toddlers and preschoolers, too. The silent side of his brain made a miraculously quick connection. And he got down on the E.R. floor and danced.

So what does it take to help create magical moments of change for children? It takes the best training one can find. It takes experience. It takes only one commandment: "Do no harm."[137] It takes a lifelong commitment to keep reading, keep thinking, and keep trying. And it takes a big, big dose of playfulness.

Yes, a psychotherapist can—and should—occasionally act on impulse. Yes, it's okay to be counterintuitive. Yes, surprise wakens the weary child. Yes, drama works.

And yes, I believe in magic.

Looking Back,
Looking Forward

"You need a history and you need a theory, then you must forget them
both and let each hour stand for itself."

— Erik Erikson*

When I was in training in Ann Arbor, the chairman of the psychiatry department at the university, Raymond Waggoner, told us residents a story I never forgot. Dr. Waggoner had started treating a woman patient (he did not tell us her diagnosis), whose psychotherapy was so fascinating that he decided to take session-by-session notes. What the well-respected doctor didn't know, however, was that the woman, herself, had been doing the very same thing. Then, the woman died. In her will, she left Dr. Waggoner her notes.

He sat down and compared each hour—his impressions, her impressions. They did not coincide. Each participant thought something interesting had taken place at the various junctures of treatment. But each produced a different impression of what had happened.

One moment, however, stood out in the patient's mind. Dr. Waggoner had helped her on with her coat! She saw it as her most important instant of change. He had taken no note of it. For him, the act carried no particular significance. But for her, clearly, the doctor had made a "gesture."[138]

*As quoted by M. Gerald Fromm in the *Austin Riggs Review*, 19: 4–9, 2007.

I believe that doctors' "gestures" happen with children and adolescents much more frequently than we think. A special meeting of the minds, an instant of mutual understanding, a loan (of a toy, for instance), or a silly new riddle may make a sizable difference to a certain child. Although many of the change moments recounted in this book have been strikingly dramatic, we must equally value the subtler, yet still meaningful, moves a doctor frequently makes. Experiences as simple as a psychiatrist nodding and understanding a little boy's position in his family as the "monkey in the middle" (Victor Fornari), or as minimal as a doctor quietly listening with interest, but no tears, to a preschooler talk about her own impending death (Ron Benson), make a considerable difference. Years ago, Dr. Waggoner's lesson about his adult patient taught me the importance of these subtler kinds of gestures. I hope that, as we study turning points further into the future, we will better be able to capture the smaller, but highly important, moves that we make—almost without thought—on behalf of children.

Looking back at the 3-year process of gathering treatment vignettes for this book—and at my own reflections on my young patients, who allowed me to look carefully at their own moments of transformation—I see the entire project as a gigantic "clinical case report." This kind of consolidation of cases often represents the first step in the process of scientific discovery. You ask yourself a question, as we did: "Can we learn anything about psychotherapy by considering childhood moments of change?" And then you gather as much information as you can from the various people working directly in the field. And then you say, "What does all this show me?" and "What does it mean?"

Later, and with a new research design, you test, as scientifically and rigorously as you can, "what the first study showed." So that's for the future. And I'm optimistic that it will happen. But let's step back for a moment and look at what this "clinical case report" demonstrated to our writers, to me, and hopefully to you.

The first overarching point is how playful, creative, and elastic good child/adolescent psychotherapy is. A number of the early- and mid-20th-century pioneers in our field showed us this kind of playfulness in their writings, speeches, and case examples. What caught me breathless, however, were the newer-fangled variations on the old adages to play. Stewart Teal's chalkboard (and his subsequent eraser fights), Rita Rogers's ragdoll for a mute Iranian boy, Ken Robson's "soliloquy for two," George Stewart's scooter—each of these were stunning, and new. They are inspiring examples of where we can go today with the idea of play. The idea of offering play to a mid-adolescent child is not entirely new, yet it was used so cleverly (by Henry Massie) to defuse a horribly negative atmosphere that I wanted to exclaim "Aha!" at the revelation. We can take play even farther. We must think about play wherever we go.

In thinking about play, I cannot help but leap to a related and impressive finding in this large clinical case study—and that is how playfully and well-crafted the various doctors' remarks to their patients turned out to be. Wordsmithing is not a craft that is much emphasized in our field, yet look at how inventive some of these doctors' phrases were: "Your secret is safe with me" (Richard Livingston); "That's a great one!" (George Stewart); "You'll have to go UUUUUH-HHH, if you want things to happen" (Jack McDermott). Not only are doctors' comments filled with considerable punch these days, but psychiatrists are using words as tools in the act of play itself. Child-friendly languages, like CDB, limericks, and stories; like the terrifying tale of a mother and baby bird (Stewart Teal); like letters to Wes Craven (Jerry Dodson) or to an unknown Oregon judge (Cammie); like songs and dances such as "Fly in the Poo" and "Dance Lady, Dance," are crafted on behalf of specific children. They are set up to elicit change. And they serve to enlist a young patient's cooperation and enthusiasm.

Then, too, the metaphors that the psychiatrists in our group created, and the communication codes they shared with young children, struck me as special. Mental pictures—like a bald doctor with "purple hair" (Victor Fornari), an apathetic boy becoming "Julius Caesar" (me), a family resolving a long-standing mystery because they finally realize that "Allan looks just like Grandpa" (Geri Fox)—served to engage young people in change. Among the wonderful examples of using language to engage and entertain were the inventive uses of children's pop culture, which sprang up among our doctors and patients.

Work with Little Mermaids, Potato Heads, Harry Potter, and Freddy Krueger proved, indeed, as encouraging examples of helping children to change through using the children's vernacular itself. Here, the language instantly became one of shared experience.

In considering how psychiatrists use play, metaphor, and even test taking to point things out to disordered children, an interesting historical argument appeared to resolve itself among our clinical cases. Doctors' commentaries and actions, both inside and outside the microcosm of the child's fantasy world, are effective. Both work! Some children respond better to a remark made inside of a creative effort or a test. Others want to hear the psychiatrist's language more directly applied to themselves. Some kids, in fact, prefer resolutions applied in actions and not in words at all. The doctor probably has to try out each of these approaches with any particular child in therapy. The approach does not seem to hinge on the stage of development or the condition of the child. Thus, we must make ourselves comfortable with all of these ways of dealing with youngsters, just as we must make ourselves comfortable with our own realities as people—and the kinds of personae we wish to adopt with the kids we treat.

A related and very large point that comes from this study is how important the doctor-patient relationship is to the achievement of childhood turnabouts. Yes, big moments gather around shifts of the child's feelings concerning the psychiatrist. When both doctor and patient share the same sense of being flawed, as in Aubrey Metcalf's case, or when the psychiatrist confronts a little girl with her concerns about not being powerful or male enough (Nancy Winters), the child may decide—on the basis of the relationship—to become different. Some of these changes reflect transference. But many others reflect real-and-true, here-and-now relationships.

This brings me to the "real," which is such a huge part of what our group learned from our conjoint efforts. "Realities" about life and about both the child and the doctor are big enough, important enough, to turn young people around. A doctor's truthful remark, "I can't beat that," in reference to a new, red Corvette (Peter Blos, Jr.) might influence the young patient to turn himself around a couple of years after it is spoken. A doctor's very real egg allergy (Mike Deeney) might create so much empathy for the first time in an apathetic adolescent's life that it lasts a lifetime. Training a boy to "poop" (Jack McDermott), defending an anorexic girl from a slap in the face (Lynn Ponton), showing a boy how to act in a household run by two gay men (Ken Braslow), demonstrating how people run on artificial legs (me)—all of these psychiatric endeavors do not deal with imaginings, the usual objects of classic psychoanalytic interpretation to children. Instead, they help children to cope with the realities they need to overcome. And in contemporary child psychotherapy, realities quickly become every bit as important as fantasies.

This brings me to a couple of particularly interesting new findings that evolved from putting all of these clinical cases together—the fact that the psychiatrist's instantaneous actions and statements, and the psychiatrist's counterintuitive moves, appeared to make such a difference to troubled children. The "surprises" that sprang up among our 48 vignette cases truly surprised me! How something blurted out, done on impulse, said on a lark, affixed into a play scenario, or muttered in the middle of a "scene" or a tantrum could mean so much to a disordered kid—that is really an astonishing finding. One thinks and thinks about children. One plans and plans to help them unlock their own self-imposed prisons. One studies all about their conditions. And then, without thinking, something emerges. And it works! That's mind-blowing for me. I found it fascinating to see so many examples of inspirational flashes in this collection.

Thanks to the *Washington Post* psychology writer, Malcolm Gladwell, many of us can see today how creative, interesting ideas do indeed come in a "blink."[139] One of my favorite supervisors during my training years, Herbert Schmale, used to talk of heeding this very same kind of phenomenon in conducting psychotherapy with relatively healthy adults. But at the time Dr. Schmale was admonishing me to listen to my instincts, I had few instinctive moments. I needed to know more, see more, and understand more before a brilliant thought could emerge "sideways." The instinctive comment, gesture, or play move comes from thinking a lot, not a little, about a case. After thinking, reading, planning, and observing, something may just fly into mind, or out of the mouth, or even into the hands or feet. That something, in fact, could very well turn out to be an inspiration.

Along these same lines, the success of child/adolescent psychiatrists' counterintuitive approaches also surprised me. Refusing to take a stand on how much psychotherapy a troubled girl needs (James Powers), or complimenting a boy on his erection when most people might have ignored it or criticized the child's choice of time and place (George Stewart), or feeding ice cream to a greedy, grabby little girl (Saul Wasserman)—these were so different from what one expects from a clinician that it gives one pause. Child and adolescent patients, when they receive these kinds of the counterintuitive gestures, must indeed feel surprised. When you see so many and so varied counterintuitive moves, you realize that our professional impulses and decisions to walk a different path from the ordinary actually create—at times—special moments for children.

Finally, I am struck by the occasional instance where a doctor's psychological understanding of a case far outweighs the medical terms affixed to it. Certainly, both diagnosis and formulation must exist in each and every clinical situation with children. But sometimes, one must make the decision, as Louis Fine did, to treat a child's postoperative depression entirely psychologically—or to treat an unhappy adolescent, as Mike Deeney did, with ongoing conversation about an old Jaguar—rather than immediately opting for medication. Certainly the deaf and disfigured little girl Mike Brody saw suffered from a "school phobic" disorder. But she needed to play with Mr. Potato Head before she could undergo the standard behavioral regimen for kindergarten or preschool phobias (being gradually separated from Mom). Formulation in child and adolescent psychiatry counts. It enhances our diagnoses. At times, it dominates our plans.

We should take note here once again that what we have done up to now represents just a beginning. Since Daniel Stern's book was published in 2004,[140] his Boston group of adult analysts has continued studying and discussing "change moments" in their older patients. One colleague of mine recently suggested that we begin studying "moments of *failure*" in our work with kids.[141] Another suggested studying "moments of change in families." Hopefully, both of these psychiatrists will take it upon themselves to get their own researches started. Hopefully, others in the various mental health disciplines will consider embarking on such studies, too. A person like me heartily enjoys seeing a good idea take fire in a number of places and among a number of different people. I am hoping that, in the long run, there will be more formalized studies and better proof of how youngsters change in psychotherapy. It appears to be a rich new area for exploration.

How does my case of the "wild child," Cammie Brooks, fit into this scheme? Well, I give Cammie credit for starting the gigantic "clinical case report" you have just read. I began working with Cammie in 1992. She sparked my interest as I observed her abrupt transitions toward normalcy. Other patients of mine showed me their moments, too. I watched them all in passing, however. I hadn't paid full attention—yet. By the time, early in 2004, when Jack McDermott asked me to think of a way that a group of us former Michigan trainees could memorialize Saul Harrison, Cammie had just turned 15. She had already undergone six of her eight turnarounds. The idea of looking at several other people's moments with kids didn't hit me, in fact, until Jack asked me his question.

Suddenly I said, in response, "Let's all write up case reports illustrating positive turning points in kids' therapy!" I was hardly thinking—it came in a "blink." Jack liked the idea. We were off and running. We had no idea where we would end up, or what, if any, conclusions we might glean. But we knew it would be interesting—and fun.

As for Cammie, I could then look back at her long-term treatment and spot her "moments" as if they were plastered on billboards. Eight turning points eventually emerged as this spitting, vomiting, hissing, biting, grabbing, and growling little monster slowly, slowly changed into a composed, lively, intelligent young woman. The first moment came when I shared my birthday with 2-year-old Cammie. With me, at that time, and only with me, she chose to employ human behavior as opposed to her usual animalistic stuff. Our second moment evolved over 2 years of taking "tea" together. By age 4, Cammie chose civilized behavior within society over her large variety of animalistic acts. The third moment occurred when Cammie, at 6, realized that her admired Wolf was "weird." She immediately chose "normal" behaviors, at home and in society, over the bizarre. Her fourth moment, when she was 8, was related to her learning the story from me of her first year of life and her subsequent visit to her baby sister's grave. From that time on, she chose being "good" over being "bad." Cammie's fifth moment was her temper tantrum at age 10, in the third grade. It led her to prefer being "attached" to others, rather than being a "loner." Her sixth moment occurred, also when she was 10, when she learned the "facts of life" from me and subsequently turned down her kindergarten-age pursuer. This time, she selected mature sexuality and love over polymorphous perversity. Her seventh moment happened at 14, when Cammie tentatively joined the "Goths." I interpreted her "comfort" with this outlying group as a return to the "comfort" of her first year of life. In changing herself this time, Cammie chose conscious reasoning over blind unconsciousness. Cammie's eighth moment did not occur until our vignette project was well underway. Months after her father was discovered to have killed a child in Oregon, Cammie, at age 16, wrote a letter—at my suggestion—to her father's criminal judge. In so doing, she gave up believing she was a prisoner of her genetics and chose, instead, her environment and her "will" as the most important factors in her future. This put a new, positive direction to Cammie's quest for identity.

Cammie will be turning 18 in the spring. Somehow, I'm glad I'll be able to finish this writing before she becomes an adult. It's hard to think of a "wild child" eligible to vote, capable of signing up for the Armed Forces, allowed—on her own—to marry, expected to sign herself in and out of surgery—or school. Yet the amazing thing is that Cammie will be fully capable and competent to take on any of these actions if she wishes.

Why did she do so well, when other "feral children" have fared so poorly? First, as opposed to poor "Genie" and "Victor," Cammie was granted almost the entire period of her childhood to be "cured" (Genie and Victor were adolescents when they were discovered). Second, it was always clear that I would be the only professional in charge of her case (in Genie's situation, "too many cooks spoiled the broth").

Third, I've never seen better foster, and then adoptive, parents than Sandra and Tom Brooks; any of us would have benefited from their parental skills, had they taken us on as kids. And fourth, "trauma," Cammie's problem, is my research, my interest, my life—if somebody could have helped Cammie, I was certainly one of those "somebodies."

But the true wonder of Cammie's movement from wildness to profound human consciousness lies, of course, in Cammie Brooks herself. How such marvelous clay emerged from the slag heap that bore her is a miracle well beyond my own understanding.

Cammie is now a high school junior. She briefly planned to have sex with one of those blond boys—I think his name was Trent—but she must have thought the better of it and left a gigantic clue for Sandra, who "stopped the whole thing cold." Today Cammie is a "virgin," at least in terms of willing sexual contact. She has replaced Trent with a boyfriend from camp, of whom her family approves. The only problem, however, is that she spent $200 last month on cell phone calls, so she's lost her phone privileges for a good long time. Oh well, this is "only" the second time it's happened.

In other words, her current life is mostly quite normal. She's furious at a close girlfriend who appears about to launch into a sexual relationship with Trent, regardless of what the girlfriend sees as a very "old and unimportant" situation between him and Cammie. She is about to become a counselor-in-training at the UCLA Heart Camp this summer, which will entail a bit of fun-filled counselor education at Disneyland and Universal Studios. Will her boyfriend be there? The one with the "Good Housekeeping seal" of family approval? And how will Cammie handle it? She says she wants to be a nurse, but she is open to other ideas. She thinks she'll start with junior college first. All that feels "right" to Cammie, and it's an overall good plan, I think.

But there are two notable exceptions to Cammie's "normal" problems these days. First, there's Nick. His trial date keeps getting delayed. The district attorney's inspectors say that Nick's lawyer is "real, real good." So we have no way of predicting how that story will end. This, of course, leaves Cammie afraid for her safety and afraid that Nick will be unleashed, once again, upon humanity. She remains sanguine, for the most part, however, about the chances that Nick will be convicted. And her letter remains in its clean, unsent state, awaiting use, if Cammie wishes, for Nick's official sentencing.[142]

The second exception is the California state exit examination in math. Last year Cammie and I went into our birthday week in March recognizing that she had taken both the English and math portions of the exit exam, and had probably made it only in English. She phoned me on her 17th birthday (and my big day, of course, as well) and we sang "Happy Birthday" simultaneously over the phone. Cammie had failed math by just a few points, and she will have to take the test all over again. Yes, she'll get two more tries, if she needs them. But it's a huge worry all the same. Shaken babies don't necessarily see their numerical concepts the same way that the government hopes everybody will.

In the meantime, Sandra has three different tutors working on implanting those fraction and percentage concepts into poor little Cammie's head. Altogether, 46,000 unfortunate kids flunked California's high school exit tests last March. However, Cammie is working like mad to make sure she is one of the ones who will make it this time. With an optimism that has always been a wonder to me in such a brutalized baby, Cammie tells me, "Don't worry this time, Dr. Terr, about whether or not I'm going to get through my math exam. I'll ace it!"

And—you know—she is usually right.

CONTRIBUTORS

A. REESE ABRIGHT, MD   Dr. Abright is Chief of Child and Adolescent Psychiatry and the Director of the child psychiatry fellows' residency training program at St. Vincent's Hospital in New York. He is also Professor of Clinical Psychiatry at New York Medical College. He has served as president of the New York Council on Child and Adolescent Psychiatry, and has received awards from the American Psychiatric Association for excellence in medical student education and from the New York Council on Child and Adolescent Psychiatry for his contributions to the field. In the aftermath of 9/11, Dr. Abright did yeoman's work in setting up treatment programs and research protocols for the young people of New York City.

JOSEPH BEITCHMAN, MD   Dr. Beitchman is Professor and TD Financial Group Chair in Child and Adolescent Psychiatry at the University of Toronto, Ontario. Since 1985, he has headed the child psychiatry program at the Centre for Addiction and Mental Health (formerly the Clarke Institute of Psychiatry) in Toronto. He served as Psychiatrist-in-Chief at the Hospital for Sick Children from 1998–2004. Dr. Beitchman's major research activities have focused on exploring (1) the interface between childhood speech/language impairment and psychiatric disorders, and (2) the genetic factors associated with aggressive behavior in children.

RONALD M. BENSON, MD   Dr. Benson is a training and supervising analyst at the Michigan Psychoanalytic Institute and is Adjunct Clinical

Associate Professor at Wayne State University. He is also the immediate
past chairman of the Board on Professional Standards of the American
Psychoanalytic Association and a trustee of the Accreditation Council for
Psychoanalytic Education. He has a special research interest in the
"imaginary companions" of childhood.

PETER BLOS JR., MD   For more than 40 years, Dr. Blos has practiced
child, adolescent, and adult psychoanalysis and psychotherapy. He has
published 25 professional papers, and teaches and lectures both nationally and abroad. He is Past President (1992–1994) of the Association for
Child Psychoanalysis, and chaired the Committee on Child and Adolescent Psychoanalysis of the International Psychoanalytic Association,
where he now serves on the governing board.

KENNETH BRASLOW, MD   Dr. Braslow serves as Chief of Pediatric
Mental Health at Spangdahlem Air Force Base in Germany. He received
his fellowship training in child and adolescent psychiatry at the University of California San Francisco (UCSF). Dr. Braslow has published in the
*Journal of the American Academy of Child and Adolescent Psychia-
try, Academic Psychiatry,* and *Psychosomatics,* and has also written
pieces for the *Los Angeles Times.*

MICHAEL BRODY, MD   Dr. Brody, currently in private practice in Maryland, was the creator and CEO of Psychiatric Center, the largest provider
of mental health services in the District of Columbia. He is Chair of the
Television and Media Committee of the American Academy of Child and
Adolescent Psychiatry, and served as Professor of American Studies at
the University of Maryland. His latest publication was a chapter in the
edited book, *Using Superheroes in Counseling and Play Therapy.*

JOHN M. (MIKE) DEENEY, MD   Since 1968, Dr. Deeney has been a
child psychiatrist in Portland, Oregon. Over the years, he has served as a
consultant to a number of treatment and social service agencies, school
and hospital programs, and other services for children and families. He
supervises and teaches psychiatric residents and child psychiatry fellows
at the Oregon Health and Sciences University in Portland.

JERRY W. DODSON, MD   Dr. Dodson began his career as an Army psychiatrist, and he is currently in practice in San Angelo, Texas. He has

spent most of his professional career serving children and adolescents who live in relatively sparsely populated areas in the Western United States.

SUSAN DONNER, MD   Dr. Donner is Assistant Clinical Professor of Psychiatry at the UCLA David Geffen School of Medicine, where she teaches medical students and supervises residents and child psychiatry fellows. Practicing in Woodland Hills, California, she has found many opportunities to help engineer magical moments of change. Drawing on her undergraduate experience as an art history major at Harvard University, she focuses on art and play as they relate to childhood healing and well-being.

MARTIN DRELL, MD   Dr. Drell is currently the Carl P. Adatto, MD Professor of Community Psychiatry at Louisiana State University. He serves as Professor of Clinical Psychiatry and Vice Chair for Child Psychiatry at the Health Sciences Center of New Orleans. He works at the LSU Health Sciences Center and the New Orleans Adolescent Hospital and Community System of Care. In the aftermath of hurricanes Katrina and Rita, Dr. Drell became intensely involved in rebuilding and adding professional services to meet the mental health needs of greater New Orleans. This work continues.

SPENCER ETH, MD   Dr. Eth serves as Professor and Vice Chairman of the Department of Psychiatry and Behavioral Sciences at New York Medical College. He is also Senior Vice President and Medical Director of Behavioral Health Services at the Saint Vincent Catholic Medical Centers. He is a graduate of New York University and UCLA Medical School, and as a Rhodes Scholar attended graduate school at Oxford. He received his psychiatric training at Payne Whitney (New York Hospital–Cornell) and his child psychiatry training at Cedars-Sinai Medical Center in Los Angeles. Dr. Eth is the author or co-author of 88 journal articles and 49 book chapters, and has edited or co-edited four books. His specialty is childhood trauma, and after 9/11 he was a prime planner, organizer, and treater of children in New York.

LOUIS L. FINE, MD   Dr. Fine is both a board certified psychiatrist and a pediatrician. For years, he served as Director of Psychiatric Consultation Services at the Denver Children's Hospital. Now he is in private practice in Centennial, Colorado. He is the author of numerous published papers as well as the book, *After All We've Done for Them . . . Understanding Adolescent Behavior.*

BARBARA FISH, MD   A native New Yorker initially in private practice, Dr. Fish eventually became Professor and Director of Child Psychiatry at Bellevue Hospital–NYU Medical School. She was later named the Della Martin Professor of Psychiatry in the child division of the Neuropsychiatric Institute at UCLA. Her research, begun in 1952, was the first prospective longitudinal study of the neuropsychological antecedents of schizophrenia. In 1987, she received the Agnes Purcell McGavin Award from the American Psychiatric Association "for outstanding contributions to the prevention of mental disorders in children."

VICTOR FORNARI, MD   Dr. Fornari serves as Director of the Divisions of Child and Adolescent Psychiatry at both North Shore University Hospital and Long Island Jewish Hospital in New York, and is Professor of Psychiatry at NYU School of Medicine. Dr. Fornari has been actively involved in the training of residents in both general psychiatry and child/adolescent psychiatry. In addition, he maintains a clinical practice with children and adolescents, focusing on traumatized youth and adolescents with eating disorders.

GERI FOX, MD   Dr. Fox is Professor of Clinical Psychiatry at the University of Illinois, where she has dedicated her career to serving as a clinician-educator. She is Director of Undergraduate Medical Education in Psychiatry and Director of Graduate Medical Education Programming. She also serves as Special Assistant to the Associate Dean for Educational Affairs. Previously, she functioned as Director of Child and Adolescent Psychiatry Training. In addition to teaching child development, she also enjoys treating patients of all ages, as well as their families, in her clinical practice.

THEODORE J. GAENSBAUER, MD   Dr. Gaensbauer is in full-time private practice in Denver, Colorado and serves as Clinical Professor of Psychiatry at the University of Colorado Health Sciences Center. His clinical and research interests are in the development of emotional regulation and attachment relationships in infancy and early childhood, and the impact of trauma on young children. In 2006, he won the Norbert and Charlotte Reiger Psychodynamic Psychotherapy Award from the American Academy of Child and Adolescent Psychiatry.

AJIT JETMALANI, MD Dr. Jetmalani was trained in adult psychiatry at the University of California San Francisco (UCSF) and in child and adolescent psychiatry at the Yale Child Study Center. He returned to Portland, Oregon to pursue private practice in 1988. Dr. Jetmalani teaches child psychiatry fellows at Oregon Health and Science University, and works in community mental health at various agencies in the Portland area.

RICHARD LIVINGSTON, MD Dr. Livingston is the author of *Impulse: A Handbook for the Moral and Spiritual Challenges of ADHD,* as well as many textbook chapters and journal research articles. He practices child and adolescent psychiatry in central and western Arkansas, and teaches at the Medical School of the University of Arkansas, Little Rock.

HENRY MASSIE, MD Dr. Massie practices child, adolescent, and adult psychiatry in Berkeley, California. He is a former clinical faculty member of the Department of Psychiatry at the University of California San Francisco (UCSF), and conducts research on the longitudinal effects of developmental problems and autism. His publications include *Lives Across Time/Growing Up: Paths to Emotional Health and Emotional Illness from Birth to 30 in 76 People* (with Nathan Szajnberg), *Childhood Psychosis in the First Four Years of Life* (with Judith Rosenthal), and *The Massie-Campbell Scale of Mother–Infant Attachment Indicators During Stress (ADS Scale;* with B. Kay Campbell).

JOHN (JACK) F. McDERMOTT, MD Dr. McDermott is Emeritus Professor and Chair of Psychiatry at the University of Hawaii School of Medicine, and has been a visiting professor at both Oxford and Cambridge Universities in England. He has edited and written many scientific books and articles covering all aspects of child and adolescent psychiatry, and for 10 years served as Editor of the *Journal of the American Academy of Child and Adolescent Psychiatry.* Currently, Dr. McDermott teaches a psychotherapy seminar for the child psychiatry and triple board (psychiatry and pediatric) residents in Honolulu.

AUBREY METCALF, MD Dr. Metcalf recently retired from private practice but continues as Clinical Professor of Psychiatry in the Division of Child and Adolescent Psychiatry at the University of California San Francisco (UCSF). His research interests include autism, infant attachment, and the psychotherapy of children and adolescents, along with their parents.

KLAUS MINDE, MD, FRCP(C) Dr. Minde is Professor of Psychiatry and Pediatrics at McGill University in Montreal. He also serves as Director of the Anxiety and Infant Mental Health Clinic at the Montreal Children's Hospital. From 1989–2001, he was Chairman of the Division of Child and Adolescent Psychiatry at McGill. After training in pediatrics and psychiatry, Dr. Minde also obtained a graduate degree in developmental psychology and was certified as a psychoanalyst. He has published some 180 articles and chapters on issues pertaining to infant mental health, parent-child attachment, problems of immigrants and refugee children, and the impact of chronic medical illness on family functioning and child behavior. He is presently studying the impact of postnatal environment on the developmental outcomes of infants who originally suffered adversities in utero.

MARIA PEASE, MD Dr. Pease is Assistant Clinical Professor at the University of California San Francisco (UCSF). In private practice, she sees children, adolescents, and adults, and her subspecialties include parent-infant psychiatry and sports psychiatry. An avid surfer and a former Olympic Trials swimming competitor in 1976 and 1980, she was also a member of Stanford's 1980 Division I AIAW National Championship Swimming Team, and served as an assistant coach to Stanford's 1983 NCAA National Championship Women's Swimming Team. She was recently a contributor and advisor for Brook de Lench's *Home Team Advantage: The Critical Role of Mothers in Youth Sports.*

LYNN PONTON, MD Dr. Ponton grew up in Wisconsin and after college worked at the Pasteur Institute in Paris. She then returned to the University of Wisconsin Medical School and completed her fellowship in child and adolescent psychiatry at the University of California San Francisco (UCSF). She was trained as a psychoanalyst and eventually joined the faculty at UCSF. In addition to her current work there as

Professor of Psychiatry, she conducts a clinical practice, writes in a number of scholarly journals and textbooks, and has been interviewed by numerous television and radio shows, magazines, and newspapers. She is the author of *The Romance of Risk: Why Teenagers Do the Things They Do* and *The Sex Lives of Teenagers: Revealing the Secret World of Adolescent Boys and Girls*.

JAMES POWERS, MD   Dr. Powers is a private practitioner of child and adolescent psychiatry in Portland, Oregon. He also consults at the Christie School, a residential treatment program. He originally trained at the University of California San Francisco (UCSF).

KENNETH ROBSON, MD   Dr. Robson was born in Chicago and now lives and works in West Hartford, Connecticut, where he practices child and adolescent psychiatry. For many years, he trained residents and fellows at Tufts University Medical School in Boston.

RITA ROGERS, MD   Dr. Rogers is Distinguished Clinical Professor of Psychiatry at the University of California Los Angeles (UCLA). She is the founder of the Division of Child Psychiatry at UCLA and served as its chief for many years. She was awarded the Humanist of the Decade Gold Medal by the International League of Humanists on May 24, 1998 in Sarajevo, and in 1990 was given the Gold Medal of the World Association of Dynamic Psychiatry. A survivor of the Holocaust, Dr. Rogers is the author of 98 publications, most of them dealing with cultural and international understanding. Her autobiography, *The Alchemy of Survival*, was written with John Mack, MD.

WILLIAM SACK, MD   Dr. Sack is Emeritus Professor of Psychiatry at the Oregon Health and Science University in Portland, Oregon, where for 22 years he directed the Division of Child and Adolescent Psychiatry. He currently consults at the MacLaren Center for Boys in Woodland, Oregon, a correctional facility.

GEORGE H. STEWART, MD   Dr. Stewart is a psychoanalyst and child, adolescent, and adult psychiatrist in Berkeley, California. Half of his professional time is devoted to consulting at a locked, intensive, long-term residential treatment facility for adolescents. He is Associate Clinical

Professor in the Department of Psychology at the University of California Berkeley, and he serves as a faculty member of the San Francisco Psychoanalytic Institute.

STEWART TEAL, MD   For 35 years, Dr. Teal has conducted private practice of child and adolescent psychiatry in the Sacramento area. He serves as Clinical Professor of Psychiatry at the University of California Davis. His professional interests include psychiatric assessments and supervision of psychiatrists' treatment of young people.

SAUL WASSERMAN, MD   For 20 years, Dr. Wasserman was the director of a child and adolescent psychiatric inpatient unit in San Jose, California. He also served on the clinical faculty of Stanford University Medical School. With Drs. Alvin Rosenfeld and Bruno Bettleheim, he created a set of new strategies for treating abused and neglected children, which was presented in *Healing the Heart*.

NANCY WINTERS, MD   Dr. Winters is Associate Professor of Psychiatry and Pediatrics and Director of the Child and Adolescent Psychiatry Residency Program at Oregon Health and Science University in Portland. She has written a number of articles on children's mental health services and co-edited *Handbook of Child and Adolescent Systems of Care: The New Community Psychiatry*. Her other interests include childhood eating disorders, psychoanalysis, and telepsychiatry.

JOEL P. ZRULL, MD   Dr. Zrull is Professor Emeritus of Psychiatry at the University of Toledo College of Medicine (previously Medical College of Ohio), where he was Professor and Chairman of the Department of Psychiatry from 1975–1997. He completed his psychiatry residency and child psychiatry fellowship at the University of Michigan Medical Center, where he remained a faculty member until 1973. In May 2003, he received the Agnes Purcell McGavin Award from the American Psychiatric Association for distinguished career achievement in child and adolescent psychiatry.

NOTES

Introduction

1. Itard, J. M. (1801). *Memoire sur les premier developpments de Victor de L'Averyron.* Paris: Goujon. Itard, J. M. (1806). *Rapport sur les nouveaux developpments de Victor de L'Aveyron.* Paris: de L'imprimerie Imperiale. For a review of this work in English, see Humphrey, G., & Humphrey, M. (1932). *The wild boy of Aveyron.* New York: Appleton-Century-Crofts.

2. Truffaut's film puts a positive spin on Victor's initial outcome, so it tends to give the movie-goer false encouragement regarding the ease of treating such children. The hero, Dr. Itard, who was indeed a hero for trying such an experiment, was played by Francois Truffaut.

3. Curtiss, S. (1977). *Genie: A psycholinguistic study of a modern-day wild child.* San Diego, CA: Academic Press. Rymer, R. (1993). *Genie: A scientific tragedy.* New York: Harper Collins.

4. Terr, L. C., McDermott, J. F., Benson, R. M., Blos, P., Jr., Deeney, J. M., Rogers, R. R., & Zrull, J. P. (2005). Moments in psychotherapy. *Journal of the American Academy of Child and Adolescent Psychiatry, 44,* 191–197.

5. The first is cited in endnote number 4. The other three are: Terr, L. C., Deeney, J. M., Drell, M., Dodson, J. W., Gaensbauer, T. J., Massie, H., Minde, K., Stewart, G., Teal, S., & Winters, N. (2006). Playful "moments" in psychotherapy. *Journal of the American Academy of Child and Adolescent Psychiatry, 45,* 604–613. Terr, L. C., Beitchman, J. H., Braslow, K., Fox, G., Metcalf, A., Pease, M., Ponton, L., Sack, W., & Wasserman, S. (2006). Children's turn-arounds in psychotherapy: The doctor's gesture. *Psychoanalytic Study of the Child, 61,* 56–81. Terr, L. C., Abright, A. R., Brody, M., Donner, S., Eth, S., Fine, L., Fornari, V., Jetmalani, A., Livingston, R., Powers, J. H., & Robson, K. (2006).

When formulation outweighs diagnosis: 13 "moments" in psychotherapy. *Journal of the American Academy of Child and Adolescent Psychiatry, 45,* 1252–1263.

6. For a 12-year summary of Cammie's psychotherapy, see Terr, L. C. (2003). Wild child: How three principles of healing organized 12 years of psychotherapy. *Journal of the American Academy of Child and Adolescent Psychiatry, 42,* 1401–1409.

7. Person, E. S. (2000). Change moments in therapy. In J. Sandler (Ed.), *Changing ideas in a changing world* (pp. 149–154). London: Karnac.

8. Stern, D. (2004). The present moment in psychotherapy and everyday life. New York: Norton.

Chapter One

9. Grant, M., & Hazel, J. (1967). *Gods and mortals in classic mythology.* Springfield, MA: G&C Merriam.

10. Bettleheim, B. (1990). Feral children and autistic children. In *Freud's Vienna and other essays* (pp. 166–188). New York: Knopf.

11. Frith, U. (1989). *Autism: Explaining the enigma.* Oxford, England: Basil Blackwell.

12. Rutter, M., Anderson-Wood, L., Beckett, C., Bredenkamp, D., Castle, J., Groothues, C., Keaveney, L., Lord, C., & O'Connor, T. G. (1999). Quasi-autistic patterns following severe early global privation. *Child Psychology and Psychiatry, 40,* 537–549.

13. The social workers phoned Sandra Brooks while she was at a beauty parlor and pleaded with her for 10 minutes to take on the difficult foster-care situation. Sandra then contacted Tom to discuss it. It didn't take more than a few minutes for the couple to agree.

14. See Terr, L. C. (1990). *Too scared to cry.* New York: Harper & Row. See also Terr, L. C. (1991). Childhood traumas: An outline and overview. *American Journal of Psychiatry, 148,* 10–19.

15. Sandra informed me about three separate interviews in which Bonnie spoke of Nick's growling and his devil worship. A series of films depicting children embodying or possessed by Satan were popular in the late 1960s and early '70s. *The Exorcist* (1973), directed by William Friedkin, includes "devil-inspired" vocal effects by Mercedes McCambridge. These sounds are put into the child character's mouth.

16. Rymer, R. (1993). *Genie: A scientific tragedy.* New York: Harper Collins.

17. Terr, L. & Watson, A. (1968). The battered child rebrutalized: 10 cases of medical/legal confusion. *American Journal of Psychiatry, 124,* 126–133.

18. Bugental, J. (1964). The person who is the psychotherapist. *Journal of Consulting Psychology, 11,* 272–277. For a twentieth-century review of the mental

treatments of children, see Group for the Advancement of Psychiatry (GAP) Committee on Child Psychiatry. (1982). *The process of child therapy*. New York: Brunner/Mazel.

19. Tumulty, P. A. (1970). What is a clinician and what does he do? *New England Journal of Medicine, 283*, 20–24.

20. For a history of psychiatry, see: Zilboorg, G., & Henry, G. W. (1941). *A history of medical psychology*. New York: Norton. Howells, J. G. (Ed.). (1974). *World history of psychiatry*. New York: Brunner/Mazel. For a biography of Freud, see Jones, E. (1953–57). *The life and work of Sigmund Freud* (3 volumes). New York: Basic.

21. Colby, K. M. (1951). *A Primer for psychotherapists*. New York: Ronald Press. Tarachow, S. (1963). *An introduction to psychotherapy*. New York: International Universities Press. Wolberg, L. R. (1977). *The technique of psychotherapy* (2 vols., 3rd ed.). New York: Grune & Stratton.

22. Sulloway, F. J. (1979). *Freud: Biologist of the mind*. New York: Basic.

23. Masson, J. M. (1984). *Assault on truth: Freud's suppression of the seduction theory*. New York: Farrar, Straus & Giroux. Masson, J. M. (Trans. and Ed.). (1985). *The complete letters of Sigmund Freud to Wilhelm Fleiss 1887–1904*. Cambridge, MA: Belknap, Harvard.

24. The cure rate for childhood leukemia has miraculously improved over the past 30 years. It represents a striking example of "cure by committee"—groups of pediatricians at various medical centers followed strict medication protocols until they figured out empirically what worked, in what doses, and with what side effects.

25. Levy, S. T., & Inderbitzin, L. B. (1992). Neutrality, interpretation, and therapeutic intent. *Journal of the American Psychoanalytic Association, 40*, 989–1011.

26. Rosenfeld, A. R., & Wasserman, S. (1990). *Healing the heart: A therapeutic approach to disturbed children in group care*. Washington, DC: Child Welfare League of America.

27. For a Ghandiesque twist on positiveness, see Omer, H. (2004). *Nonviolent resistance: A new approach to violent and self-destructive children* (S. London-Sapir, Trans.). Cambridge, UK: Cambridge University Press.

28. Winnicott, D. W. (1958). Clinical varieties of transference. In *Collected papers: through pediatrics to psychoanalysis* (pp. 295–299). New York: Basic.

Chapter Two

29. Bemporad, J. R., & Hallowell, E. (1987). Advances in the treatment of disorders of elimination. In J. D. Noshpitz, J. D. Call, R. I. Cohen, S. I. Harrison, I. N. Berlin, & L. A. Stone (Eds.), *Basic handbook of child psychiatry 5* (pp. 479–483). New York: Basic.

30. The first group of similarly traumatized children studied following a single trau-
    matic event were the 26 Chowchilla bus-kidnapping victims of July 15, 1976.
    Much of what we know today about childhood PTSD comes from these children,
    and from the comparison group to them, from McFarland and Porterville, Cali-
    fornia. The three most important papers about this group are: Terr, L. (1979).
    Children of Chowchilla: A study of psychic trauma. *Psychoanalytic Study of
    the Child, 34,* 547–623. Terr, L. (1983). Chowchilla revisited: The effects of psy-
    chic trauma four years after a schoolbus kidnapping. *American Journal of Psy-
    chiatry, 140,* 1543–1550. Terr, L. (1983). Life attitudes, dreams, and psychic
    trauma in a group of "normal" children. *Journal of the American Academy of
    Child and Adolescent Psychiatry, 22,* 221–230.

31. I have been writing on treatments for traumatized children since the early
    1980s. The best summary of "abreaction, context, and correction" is in Terr, L.
    (2003). "Wild child": How three principles of healing organized 12 years of psy-
    chotherapy. *Journal the American Academy of Child and Adolescent Psy-
    chiatry, 41,* 1401–1409. For a more general account, away from the story of
    Cammie, see Terr, L. (2001). Childhood posttraumatic stress disorder. In G. O.
    Gabbard (Ed.), *Treatment of psychiatric disorders* (3rd ed., pp. 293–306).
    Washington, DC: American Psychiatric Press. For a discussion of play therapy in
    childhood PTSD, see Terr, L. (1983). Play therapy and psychic trauma: A prelim-
    inary report. In C. Schaefer & K. O'Conner (Eds.), *Handbook of play therapy*
    (pp. 308–319). New York: John Wiley & Sons.

32. Betsy's story is told in the publication on play therapy cited in endnote num-
    ber 31, and in *Too Scared to Cry*, cited in endnote number 14. "Ed's" name
    was "Frank" in *Too Scared to Cry*. The wording is different in the three publi-
    cations. My newer ideas on therapy are voiced in the book you are currently
    reading.

33. Weisz, J. R. (2004). *Psychotherapy for children and adolescents: Evidence-
    based treatments and case examples.* New York: Cambridge University Press.

34. Pavlov, I. P. (1927). *Conditioned reflexes: An investigation of the physiolog-
    ical activities of the cerebral cortex.* London: Oxford University Press. Skinner,
    B. F. (1938). *The behavior of organisms.* New York: Appleton-Century-Crofts.
    Skinner, B. F. (1953). *Science and human behavior.* New York: Free Press.
    Watson, J. B. (1913). Psychology as the behaviorist views it. *Psychological Re-
    view, 20,* 158–177. Watson, J. B., & Rayner, R. (1920). Conditioned emotional
    reactions. *Journal of Experimental Psychology, 3,* 1–14. Wolpe, J. (1958).
    Psychotherapy by reciprocal inhibition. Stanford, CA: Stanford University
    Press. Wolpe, J., & Lazarus, A. A. (1966). *Behavior therapy techniques: A
    guide to the treatment of neurosis.* New York: Pergamon.

35. See: Weisz, J. R. (2004). *Psychotherapy for children and adolescents: Evi-
    dence-based treatments and case examples.* New York: Cambridge University
    Press. Kazdin, A. E., & Weisz, J. R. (Eds.). (2003). *Evidence-based psychother-
    apies for children and adolescents.* New York: Guilford.

36. I refer here to Salvatore Minuchin, a well-known American family therapist. Consider: Minuchin, S., & Fishman, C. (1981). *Family therapy techniques*. Cambridge, MA: Harvard University Press. Minuchin, S. (1974). *Families and family therapy*. Cambridge, MA: Harvard University Press. As for Anna Freud, her complete works can be found in one place: Freud, A. (1968–74). *The writings of Anna Freud* (Vols. 1–5). New York: International Universities Press.

37. Furman, E. (1957). Treatment of under-fives by way of parents. *Psychoanalytic Study of the Child, 12*, 250–262. Furman, E. (1979). Filial therapy. In J. Noshpitz, (Ed.), *Basic handbook of child psychiatry, Volume 3* (pp. 149–158). New York: Basic.

38. Freud, S. (1953–74). Analysis of a phobia in a five-year-old boy. In J. Strachey (Ed. and Trans.), *The standard edition of the complete psychological works of Sigmund Freud* (Vol. 10, pp. 3–147). London: Hogarth. (Original work published 1909)

39. The idea of finding corrective endings for early traumas in children's post-traumatic play and stories has come to me over the years. One can find the idea in several chapters and articles I have written. See, for instance: Terr, L. (1983). Play therapy and psychic trauma: A preliminary report. In C. Schaefer, & K. O'Conner (Eds.), *Handbook of play therapy* (pp. 308–319). New York: John Wiley & Sons. Terr, L. (1987). The treatment of psychic trauma in children. In J. Noshpitz, J. D. Call, R. L. Cohen, S. I. Harrison, I. N. Berlin, & L. A. Stone (Eds.), *Basic handbook of child psychiatry, Volume 5* (pp. 414–421). New York: Basic. Terr, L. (2001). Childhood posttraumatic stress disorder. In G. O. Gabbard (Ed.), *Treatment of psychiatric disorders* (3rd ed., pp. 293–306). Washington, DC: American Psychiatric Press.

    The idea of mutual storytelling for all sorts of disorders originates, as far as I can tell, with Richard Gardner. In his technique, the child starts the story and the doctor finishes it. See Gardner, R. (1971). *Therapeutic communication with children: The mutual storytelling technique*. New York: Science House.

    My current idea of "correction" includes one important addition. Therapeutic suggestions may be made and clues given by the psychiatrist, but in the end a child should try to conceptualize the corrective solutions himself. See Terr, L., Bloch, D., Michel, B., Shi, H., Reinhardt, J., & Metayer, S. (1997). Children's thinking in the wake of Challenger. *American Journal of Psychiatry, 154*, 744–751.

40. Piaget's psychology is well summarized in Flavell, J. H. (1973). *The developmental psychology of Jean Piaget*. Florence, KY: Van Nostrand Reinhold.

Chapter Three

41. Two very important early observers and describers of child's play, in terms of psychoanalysis, are: Waelder, R. (1932). The psychoanalytic theory of play. *Psychoanalytic Quarterly, 2*, 208–224. Klein, M. (1932). *The psychoanalysis of children*, Strachey, A. (Trans.) New York: Dell (1975). In more recent times,

play has been observed and analyzed in all sorts of interesting ways, such as: Looking at group trends among children, Sutton-Smith, B. (1982). *A history of children's play: The New Zealand playground 1840–1950*. Philadelphia: University of Pennsylvania Press. Animal play behaviors, Fagan, R. (1981). *Animal play behavior*. New York: Oxford University Press. The anthropology of play, Schwartzman, H. (1978). *Transformations: The anthropology of children's play*. New York: Plenum. Gender differences, Thorne, B. (1994). *Gender play: Girls and boys in school*. New Brunswick, NJ: Rutgers University Press.

42. The textbooks of child and adolescent psychiatry are excellent sources for the hows, whys, and whens of assessment. I'd suggest: Noshpitz, J. (Ed.). (1979–87). *Basic handbook of child psychiatry* (Vols. 1–5). New York: Basic. Noshpitz, J. (Ed.). (1995). *Handbook of child and adolescent psychiatry* (Vols. 1–7). New York: John Wiley & Sons. Lewis, M. (Ed.). (1991 & 1996). *Child and adolescent psychiatry: A comprehensive textbook*. Baltimore, MD: Williams & Wilkins (its most recent edition was published in 2002 by Lippencott Williams & Wilkins in Philadelphia). Weiner, J. M., & Dulcan, M. K. (Eds.). (2004). *The American psychiatric publishing textbook of child and adolescent psychiatry*. Washington, DC: American Psychiatric Press (a new edition is about to be published).

43. Jellinek, M. S., & McDermott, J. F. (2004). Formulation: Putting the diagnosis into a therapeutic context and treatment plan. *Journal of the American Academy of Child and Adolescent Psychiatry, 43*, 913–916. See also Shapiro, T. (1989). The psychodynamic formulation in child and adolescent psychiatry. *Journal of the American Academy of Child and Adolescent Psychiatry, 28*, 675–680.

44. McDonald, M. (1965). The psychiatric evaluation of children. *Journal of the American Academy of Child Psychiatry, 4*, 569–612.

45. These ideas are expressed in my writings about how to handle patients' returning traumatic memories. See: Terr, L. (1994). *Unchained memories*. New York: Basic. Terr, L. (1996). True memories of childhood trauma: Flaws, absences, and returns. In K. Pezdek & W. P. Banks (Eds.), *The recovered memory/false memory debate* (pp. 69–80). San Diego, CA: Academic Press.

46. This idea has been tackled by a few different writers. One of the earliest is Garfield, P. (1984). *Your child's dreams*. New York: Ballantine.

47. Terr, L. (1990). *Too scared to cry*. New York: Basic. Also see Terr, L. (1990). Childhood trauma and society: The pebble and the pool. In J. Hammer (Ed.), *The 1990 distinguished visiting professorship lectures* (pp. 71–91). Memphis, TN: University of Tennessee.

48. Freud, A. (1965). *Normality and pathology in childhood*. New York: International Universities Press.

49. Terr, L. (1991). Childhood traumas: An outline and overview. *American Journal of Psychiatry, 148*, 10–20.

Chapter Four

50. My cousin died in late October, 2006, from complications of her anticancer treatment.

51. I previously wrote about "Laura" in the context of her mother, whom I had seen when she was a returning parentally kidnapped child, Terr, L. (2006). Double snapshot: A single trauma captured twice in life. *San Francisco Medicine, 79,* 17, 21.

52. This use of the therapist's positive, supportive attitudes and basic optimism was emphasized by an American pioneer of child psychiatry, Fred Allen. Allen, F. L. (1962). *Positive aspects of child psychiatry.* New York: Basic. Allen, F. (1942). *Psychotherapy with children.* New York: Norton.

53. The doctor's gesture might have been termed a "corrective emotional experience" for his patient. See Allen, F. L. (1962), cited in endnote number 52. See also Group for the Advancement of Psychiatry, Committee on Child Psychiatry. (1982). *The process of child therapy.* New York: Brunner/Mazel.

54. Tsiantis, J., Sandler, A. -M., Anastaopoulos, D., & Martindale, B. (1996). *Countertransference in psychoanalytic psychotherapy with children and adolescents.* London: Karnac.

55. Johnson, A. (1949). Sanctions for superego lacunae of adolescents. In K. Eissler (Ed.), *Searchlights on delinquency* (pp. 225–254). Oxford, UK: International Universities Press.

56. Gladwell, M. (2005). *Blink: The power of thinking without thinking.* New York: Little, Brown.

57. Stern, D. L. (2004). The present moment in psychotherapy and everyday life. New York: Norton.

58. Weiner, M. F., & King, J. W. (1977). Self disclosure by the therapist to the adolescent patient. In S. Feinstein & P. Giovacchini (Eds.), *Adolescent psychiatry, Volume V* (pp. 449–459). New York: Jason Aronson.

Chapter Five

59. There is a developmental sequence regarding what defenses a child is able to use at what time in childhood. For the "classic" on the childhood defenses, see Freud, A. (1937). *The ego and the mechanisms of defense.* New York: International Universities Press. For an interesting paper on the developmental use of defenses in infancy, see Fraiberg, S. (1987). Pathological defenses in infancy. In L. Fraiberg (Ed.), *The selected writings of Selma Fraiberg* (pp. 183–202). Columbus, OH: Ohio State University Press. In terms of what defenses adults use, George Vaillant of Harvard is the expert. See Valliant, G. (Ed.). (1992). *Ego mechanisms of defense: A guide for clinicians and researchers.* Washington, DC: American Psychiatric Press. Valliant, G. (1977). *Adaptation to life.* Boston: Little, Brown.

60. Winnicott, D. W. (1971). *Playing and reality*. New York: Basic.

61. You have already read Peter Blos, Jr.'s, vignette about the red Corvette. His father was a well-respected analyst with a career focus on adolescence. He wrote about uneven teenage development in Blos, P. (1962). *On adolescence*. Glencoe, IL: Free Press.

62. There is an interesting series of books, edited and partly written by Nancy Boyd Webb of Fordham University, on using play therapy with traumatized or severely stressed children. Webb, N. B. (Ed.). (1991, 1999, 2007). *Play therapy with children in crisis* (eds. 1–3). New York: Guilford.

63. Here one can put the two definitions of *play* together: (1) an activity done strictly for the fun of it, and (2) a production performed in a theater for an audience. Through miniaturization, both put the world into a new perspective. I am interested in the development and uses of adult play as well as the play behavior of children. Terr, L. (1999). *Beyond love and work: Why adults need to play*. New York: Scribner (Touchstone, paperback). Note that in this book, Cammie was called "Janie." My apologies for the mix up. In all other places I know of, Cammie is "Cammie."

64. From the next generations of child analysts following the "founding mothers" (Freud and Klein), a number of interesting takes on play came forward. See, for instance, Erik Erikson's Homburger, E. (1937). Configurations in play. *Psychoanalytic Quarterly, 6*, 139–214. Fraiberg, S. (1977). *Insights from the blind*. New York: Basic. Levy, D. (1939). Release therapy. *American Journal of Orthopsychiatry, 9*, 713–736. Erikson, E. (1950). *Childhood and society*. New York: Norton. Winnicott, D. W. (1971). *Playing and reality*. New York: Basic.

65. Many child and adolescent programs in the mid-20th century taught residents to accompany patients on walks. Who originated this, I do not know. It is one of the staples of doing educational and supportive therapy with highly disordered children. We see walk taking again in Chapter 7, in Joel Zrull's vignette, "Elevator Going Up."

66. Terr, L. (1981). "Forbidden Games": Post-traumatic child's play. *Journal of the American Academy of Child Psychiatry, 20*, 741–760.

Chapter Six

67. See Whitaker, C. (1975). The symptomatic adolescent: An AWOL family member. In M. Sugar (Ed.), *The adolescent in group and family therapy* (pp. 205–215). New York: Brunner/Mazel.

68. For a discussion of attachment to the therapist see: Wilkenson, M. (2006). *Coming into mind*. London: Routledge.

69. I never got to hear the great psychologist, Gregory Bateson, talk about families. But the idea of putting off punishments until parents determine exactly the right time apparently comes from him. I cannot find this reference—I don't even know if Dr. Bateson wrote it down—but here are two Bateson references for the

interested reader: Bateson, G. (1956). The message 'this is play.' In B. Schaffner (Ed.), *Group processes: Transactions of the second conference* (pp. 145–246). New York: Josiah Macy Foundation. Bateson, G. (1972). *Steps to an ecology of the mind*. New York: Ballantine.

70. Henry Massie, recently published a book describing the personal journeys of 76 individuals toward emotional health. Massie, H., & Sjanberg, N. (2005). *Lives across time/growing up*. Philadelphia: X Libris.

71. By midcentury, a great divide had been set up between "uncovering" (interpretive, occasionally confrontational, minimally educational treatments) and "supportive" therapies (largely educational, real, explanatory, minimally transferential). The New York psychoanalyst Heinz Hartmann helped break down this division, showing that with children, considerable clarification is necessary, even when one is probing deeply. Hartmann, H. (1965). Notes on the reality principle. *Psychoanalytic Study of the Child*, *2*, 31–53.

Chapter Seven

72. For transitional objects, see Winnicott, D. W. (1949). Transitional objects and transitional phenomena. *International Journal of Psychoanalysis*, *30*, 89–97.

73. Having one family member who *is* psychotic and another who picks up the member's symptoms and behaves psychotically is known as *folie à deux* (psychosis for two). In child and adolescent psychiatry, one other syndrome in which the child is actually more normal than he looks is Munchausen by Proxy. Here, a parent sets the child up to appear as if he has a serious illness. See Schreier, H. (1993). *Hurting for love: Munchausen by Proxy syndrome*. New York: Guilford.

74. Many years ago, Joel Zrull wrote this particular case up in a different fashion. Zrull, J. (1967). The psychotherapy of a pair of psychotic identical twins in a residential setting. *Journal of the American Academy of Child Psychiatry*, *6*, 116–130.

75. This occurred in the San Francisco Bay Area, and afterward, I heard an audio recording made by the early adolescent children. I do not remember the particular traumatic circumstances, but I remember the enthusiasm, energy, and expressive language of the group.

76. Some games, especially post-traumatic ones like "Ring Around the Rosie," spread around the world and through many subsequent generations. See Terr, L. (1990). *Too scared to cry*. New York: Harper & Row. "Smear the Queer," however, does not apparently have that kind of contagious power.

77. Fraiberg, S., Adelson, E., & Shapiro, V. (1975). Ghosts in the nursery. *Journal of the American Academy of Child Psychiatry*, *14*, 387–421.

78. Piaget, J. (1926). *The language and thought of the child*. New York: Harcourt Brace.

79. Steig, W. (1968). *CDB!* New York: Aladdin. Steig, W. (1984). *CDC?* New York: Farrar, Straus, Giroux.

80. After the war, the poet was incarcerated at St. Elizabeth's Hospital for allegedly traitorous activity against the United States. His correspondence was censored during his confinement. It was decoded by a psychiatric colleague of mine. Occasionally, too, one finds these same kinds of letter-codes in *New York Times* crosswords.

Chapter Eight

81. Yates, A., & Terr, L. (1988). Anatomically correct dolls: Should they be used as the basis for expert testimony? *Journal of the American Academy of Child and Adolescent Psychiatry, 27,* 254–257, 387–388.

82. Freud, S. (1953–74). Beyond the pleasure principle. In J. Strachey (Ed. and Trans.), *The standard edition of the complete psychological works of Sigmund Freud* (Vol. 18, pp. 3–64). London: Hogarth. (Original work published 1920)

83. Erikson, E. (1950). *Childhood and society.* New York: Norton.

84. Winnicott, D. W. (1971). *Playing and reality.* New York: Basic.

85. For "regression," see Freud, S. (1953–74). Beyond the pleasure principle. In J. Strachey (Ed. and Trans.), *The standard edition of the complete psychological works of Sigmund Freud* (Vol. 18, pp. 3–64). London: Hogarth. (Original work published 1920)

86. For the origins of displacement, see Freud, S. (1953–74). The interpretation of dreams. In J. Strachey (Ed. and Trans.), *The Standard Edition of the complete psychological works of Sigmund Freud* (Vol. 4–5, pp. 1–621). London: Hogarth. (Original work published 1900). See also Sulloway, F. J. (1979). *Freud: Biologist of the mind.* New York: Basic.

87. Freud, A., & Burlingham, D. (1943). *War and children.* New York: Medical War Books. An expanded version of the Anna Freud group's war reports is titled *Infants Without Families* and appears as volume 3 of *The Writings of Anna Freud.* Dr. Eth is an important contributor to the childhood trauma field. See, for instance, Pynoos, R. S., & Eth, S. (1984). The child as witness to homicide. In G. S. Goodman (Ed.), The child witness. *Journal of Social Issues, 40,* 87–108. Eth, S. (Ed.). (2001). *PTSD in children and adolescents.* Washington DC: American Psychiatric Press.

88. Coppolillo, H. (2002). Use of play in psychodynamic psychotherapy. In M. Lewis (Ed.), *Child and adolescent psychiatry: A comprehensive textbook* (pp. 992–998). Philadelphia: Lippincott Williams & Wilkins.

89. Marshall, R. (1979). Countertransference in the psychotherapy of children and adolescents. *Contemporary Psychoanalysis, 15,* 599–629.

90. Although adolescence is the classic time for consolidating "identity," even in kindergarten, a child's identity may represent a challenge. For an important book on the subject of teenage identity formation, see Erikson, E. (1958). *Identity: Youth and crisis.* New York: Norton.

Chapter Nine

91. Bowen, C. D. (1950). *John Adams and the American Revolution.* Boston: Little, Brown. This is a wonderful, history-based, but partly fictional, story of the second U.S. president's young life.

92. Ellis, J. (2004). *His excellency: George Washington.* New York: Knopf.

93. Silberschatz, G. (2005). The control mastery theory. In G. Silberschatz (Ed.), *Transformative relationships* (pp. 3–24). New York: Routledge.

94. It's well worth the energy to reread Anna Freud's (1936). "The Ego and Mechanisms of Defense" in volume 2 of *The Writings of Anna Freud* (1966), published by International Universities Press in New York.

95. Pregnant women using stimulant drugs, especially in high doses and over a period of time, may experience sudden losses of blood supply to the uterus, causing abrupt cessations of blood flow in the fetus and infarcts of certain fetal tissues. Also, such maternal drug use can simply cause development distortions and deviations in the fetus. The fetal problem depends upon maternal dose (of street drugs) and intensity (of drug use). This explanation was given to me by John Mendelson, Senior Scientist at the California Pacific Medical Center Research Institute in San Francisco, CA. Cammie's problems with nerve conduction—brain (seizures), heart (rhythm problems), and colon (propelling difficulties)—have been analogously replicated in rats, where high doses of amphetamines are known to be neurotoxic (also according to Dr. Mendelson).

96. A highly readable book for both parents and professionals on the psychological development of youngsters up to age 6 is Fraiberg, S. (1959). *The magic years.* New York: Scribner.

97. The person who taught me to sit through children's shenanigans and take it was Stuart Finch. See my memorial to him: Terr, L. (1991). Stuart Finch (1919–1991). *Journal of the American Academy of Child and Adolescent Psychiatry, 30,* 859.

Chapter Ten

98. The animated Disney movie, very loosely based on the Hans Christian Andersen tale, was directed by John Musker in 1989.

99. *Star Wars* (1977) was the first of three films in the original series. Three more "prequels" were produced two decades later.

100. Dr. Gaensbauer wrote about "Mark" in a previous publication: Gaensbauer, T. J. (2000). Psychotherapeutic treatment of traumatized infants and toddlers: A case report. *Clinical Child Psychology and Psychiatry, 5,* 373–385. He has also written on infantile memory. See Gaensbauer, T. J. (2004). Telling their stories: Representation and reenactment of traumatic experiences occurring in the first year of life. *Journal of Zero to Three, National Center for Infants, Toddlers, and Families, 24,* 25–31.

101. Hannibal led the Cathaginian troops over the Alps in the Second Punic War (218 B.C.) and then harassed Rome on the Italian peninsula for almost 15 years. Hannibal was defeated in 202 B.C. at the battle of Zama, near the capital of Carthage. Julius Caesar lived more than a century later and was assassinated on March 15, 44 B.C. He, too, had been a general, as well as a Roman political ruler, and he exemplified the leadership qualities I was trying to impart to Edison. See Hadas, M. (1965). *Imperial Rome*. New York: Time Life.

102. The noted adolescent researcher Daniel Offer sees the three sequential tasks of adolescence as acceptance of one's own body (ages 12–14), separation from the world of family (ages 14–16), and achievement of sexual and vocational identity (ages 16–19). For a summary, see Offer, D., Schonert-Reichl, K. A., & Boxer, A. M. (1996). Normal adolescent development: Empirical research findings. In M. Lewis (Ed.), *Child and adolescent psychiatry: A comprehensive textbook* (pp. 278–290). Baltimore, MD: Williams and Wilkens.

103. The Harry Potter book series and movie sequences are among the most popular ever in the world of kids. The books are written by J. K. Rowling of the U.K. and have been published in the U.S. by Scholastic, in New York, beginning in 1998.

Chapter Eleven

104. See Schulman, J. L., Delas Fuente, M. E., & Suran, B. G. (1977). An indication for brief psychotherapy: The fork in the road phenomenon. *Bulletin of the Menninger Clinic, 41,* 553–562.

105. For a classic example from a "classic" writer on adolescence, see Erikson, E. (1958). *Young man Luther*. New York: Norton.

106. I discovered the importance of "futurelessness" in the traumatized children of Chowchilla, and in a comparative study at McFarland and Porterville, CA. This led me to strongly suggest that all of us pay special attention to children's ideas and attitudes about the future. See Terr, L. (1983). Chowchilla revisited: The effects of psychic trauma four years after a schoolbus kidnapping. *American Journal of Psychiatry, 140,* 1543–1550. Terr, L. (1983). Life attitudes, dreams, and psychic trauma in a group of "normal" children. *Journal of the American Academy of Child Psychiatry, 22,* 221–230.

107. Beitchman, J. (1978). Confrontation in psychotherapy with children. *Psychiatric Journal of the University of Ottawa, 3,* 5–11.

108. The concept of "flow" comes from University of Chicago psychologist Mihaly Csikszenmihalyi. His best-known work on the subject is Csikszenmihalyi, M. (1991). *Flow: The psychology of optimal experience*. New York: Harper Perennial.

109. This is the technique first evident in Freud, S. (1953–74). Analysis of a phobia in a five-year-old boy. In J. Strachey (Ed. and Trans.), *The standard edition of the complete psychological works of Sigmund Freud* (Vol. 10, pp. 3–147). London: Hogarth.(Original work published 1909)

110. For channeling early emotions into therapeutic play, see: Settlage, C. F. (1989). The interplay of therapeutic and developmental process in the treatment of children. *Psychoanalytic Inquiry, 9,* 375–396. Tyson, R. L. (1986). The roots of psychopathology and our theories of development. *Journal of the American Academy of Child and Adolescent Psychiatry, 25,* 30–39.

111. I wrote about what happens to "time" concepts after children have been traumatized in Terr, L. (1984). Time and trauma. *Psychoanalytic Study of the Child, 39,* 633–666.

112. The idea of "modeling" comes from behavioral-modification therapy. See: Bandura, A. (1969). *Principles of behavior modification.* New York: Holt. Bandura, A. (1986). *Social foundations of thought and action.* Englewood Cliffs, NJ: Prentice-Hall. Modeling is not only used for parents, but can apply to children as well, especially youngsters needing training in social skills. See Lord, C. (1995). Facilitating social inclusion: Examples from peer intervention programs. In E. Schopler & G. B. Mesibor (Eds.), *Learning and cognition in autism* (pp. 221–240). New York: Plenum.

113. *The World of Henry Orient* (1964) directed by George Roy Hill. *The Parent Trap* (1961) directed by David Swift. *The Princess Diaries* (2001) directed by Garry Marshall. *Finding Forrester* (2000) directed by Gus Van Sant.

114. Steig, W. (1968). *CDB!* New York: Aladdin.

115. Sandra does not know if or when the authorities ever checked on the status of Bonnie and Nick's son.

116. See Terr, L. (1988). What happens to the early memories of trauma? *Journal of the American Academy of Child and Adolescent Psychiatry, 27,* 96–104. For different terminology and an interesting perspective on early memory, see Siegel, D. J. (1999). *The developing mind.* New York: Guilford.

Chapter Twelve

117. A few references on this huge, important field include: Fritz, G. K. (1990). Consultation-liaison in child psychiatry and the evolution of pediatric psychiatry. *Psychosomatics, 31,* 85–90. Lewis, M., & King, R. (Eds.). (1994). *Consultation-liaison in pediatrics (Child and Adolescent Psychiatric Clinics of North America).* Philadelphia: Saunders. Jellinek, M. S. (1982). The present status of child-psychiatry in pediatrics. *New England Journal of Medicine, 306,* 1227–1230. Children's conceptions about their illnesses are fascinating, and some of these appear in: Perrin, E., Sayer, A., & Willett, J. (1991). Sticks and stones may break my bones: Reasoning about illness causality and body functioning in children who have chronic illness. *Pediatrics, 88,* 608–619. Wilkinson, S. (1987). Germs: Nursery school children's views on the causality of illness. *Clinical Pediatrics, 26,* 465–469.

118. Here, Dr. Jetmalani refers to his little patient, Jimmy, as though the doctor still considers the boy to be suffering from a very mild form of Asperger's disorder.

See: Volkmar, F. R., & Cohen, D. J. (1988). Diagnosis of pervasive developmental disorders. In B. Lahey & A. Kazdin (Eds.), *Advances in clinical child psychology, Volume* 2 (pp. 249–284). New York: Plenum. Frith, U. (1989). *Autism: Explaining the enigma*. Oxford, UK: Basil Blackwell.

119. Cues given to children may lead to false details of memory or entirely false memories. For experimental evidence, see: White, T. L., Leichtman, M. D., & Ceci, S. J. (1997). The good, the bad, and the ugly: Accuracy, inaccuracy, and elaboration in preschoolers' reports. *Journal of Applied Cognitive Psychology, 11,* 537–554. Saywitz, K. J., Goodman, G. S., Nicholas, E., & Moans, S. (1991). Children's memories of physical examinations involving genital touch. *Journal of Consulting and Clinical Psychology, 59,* 682–691.

120. Terr, L. (1994). *Unchained memories*. New York: Basic. Also, see: Terr, L. (1990). Who's afraid in Virginia Woolf? Clues to early sex abuse in literature. *Psychoanalytic Study of the Child, 45,* 533–546. Terr, L. (1991). Childhood trauma: An outline and overview. *American Journal of Psychiatry, 148,* 10–20.

121. Ackerman, N. (1958). The psychodynamics of family life: Diagnosis and treatment of family relationships. New York: Basic. Ackerman, N. (1966). Treating the troubled family. New York: Basic.

122. For a relatively fair-minded collection of writings, done during this period of hot controversy, see: Pezdek, K. & Banks, W. P. (Eds.). (1996). *The recovered memory/false memory debate*. San Diego, CA: Academic Press. Cicchetti, D., & Toth, S. (Eds.). (1998). Risk, trauma, and memory [special issue] *Development and Psychopathology, 10*(4).

123. This point is made in Terr, L. (1994). *Unchained memories*. New York: Basic. It is also demonstrated in an interesting study done 7 years earlier: Herman, J., & Schatzow, E. (1987). Recovery and verification of memories of childhood sexual trauma. *Psychoanalytic Psychology, 4,* 1–14. For those readers further interested in Judith Herman's books, see Herman, J. (1992). *Trauma and recovery*. New York: Basic.

124. Terr, L. (2003). "Wild child": How three principles of healing organized 12 years of psychotherapy. *Journal of the American Academy of Child and Adolescent Psychiatry, 41,* 1401–1409.

125. The letters were written by Sjöberg, R. L. (2004), and French, A. P. (2005). *Journal of the American Academy of Child and Adolescent Psychiatry, 43,* 647–648, and *44,* 1.

126. This statement still holds today, late January, 2007.

Chapter Thirteen

127. Years ago, Dr. Patton wrote a book on a phenomenon that has intrigued me since my internship in pediatrics—the fact that a few traumatized, neglected, or abused children fail to grow. See Patton, R. G., & Gardiner, L. I. (1963). *Growth failure in maternal deprivation*. Springfield, IL: Charles C. Thomas.

128. Schwartz, M. (1996). *Brain lock*. New York: Regan.

129. Winnicott, D. W. (1971). *Therapeutic consultations in child psychiatry*. New York: Basic. See also Shapiro, T. (1983). The unconscious still occupies us. *The Psychoanalytic Study of the Child, 38,* 547–567. Dr. Shapiro's paper tells of a two-session cure of a little girl named "Emily," age 5, who played an uninterpreted "Squiggle Game" only one time. This art and play session completely cleared up the little girl's sleeplessness. This, indeed, represents an interesting magical moment of childhood change.

130. Mishne, J. M. (1986). The treatment relationship: Alliance, transference, countertransference, and the real relationship. In J. Marks (Ed.), *Clinical work with adolescents* (pp. 325–341). New York: Free Press.

131. With the state hospital closings of the 1980s, a number of bad hospitals shut down, along with some very good ones. Afterward, we no longer had enough suitable public facilities for the long-term care of chronically disordered children (see J. Zrull's vignette in Chapter 7).

132. Gardner, R. (1971). *Therapeutic communication with children: The mutual storytelling technique*. New York: Science House. Bettleheim, B. (1976). *The uses of enchantment*. New York: Knopf.

133. Winnicott, D. W. (1960). The capacity to be alone. In D. W. Winnicott (Ed.), *The maturational process and the facilitating environment* (pp. 29–36). New York: International Universities Press.

134. "Apple" is a new one on me. It shows, once again, the power of metaphor. It also demonstrates that Native Americans don't necessarily mind using the idea of being "red skinned" among themselves—they mind outsiders' use of this kind of metaphor to demean or set them apart.

135. The "No Child Left Behind" bill, signed by a bipartisan Congress, provides for testing at several points during children's schooling. Its purpose was to put public schools on notice to provide better educations. Since the exit tests have come into operation, however, it has become clear that many American children with different learning styles or with learning disorders are having problems taking these examinations. This puts hard-working kids, not just the schools, on notice.

136. Much as I would like to cite the original source for this kind of therapeutic gesture, I do not know where the technique comes from. As early as the late 1930s, a teenaged Judy Garland, on film, began such an imaginary letter to a distant "Mister Gable" (Clark Gable) at the opening to *You Made Me Love You (I Didn't Want To Do It)* (*Broadway Melody of 1938*, directed by Roy Del Ruth). The idea has entered pop culture in other ways, as well—see Marshall, E. & Hample, S. (Eds.). (1966). *Children's letters to God*. New York: Pocket Books. Certainly, letters to Santa have long been a childhood tradition.

137. This is a paraphrase (actually stated by Florence Nightingale) of the Hippocratic Oath, which many medical schools still use as their keystone to professional ethics.

Epilogue

138. I asked Raymond Waggoner, Jr., a child/adolescent psychiatrist in Columbus, Ohio, if his father had ever written up this case. Ray, too, remembered the case. However, he could not come up with a written reference.

139. Gladwell, M. (2005). *Blink: The power of thinking without thinking*. New York: Little, Brown.

140. Stern, D. (2004). The present moment in psychotherapy and everyday life. New York: Norton.

141. Stuart Copans, of Brattleboro, Vermont, chaired an interesting seminar on "moments of failure" at the Academy of Child and Adolescent Psychiatry Annual Meetings, San Diego, October 2006. His group considered medication failures, parental failures, and a number of other factors, in addition to the problems in psychotherapy with children.

142. This is the coda to the story: Nick was supposed to come to trial on "murder one, special circumstances" charges in January, 2007, just before this book went to press. At the very last minute, he plea-bargained a manslaughter conviction, carrying a sentence of 25 years in state prison. The D.A. accepted this plea bargain because his investigators and lawyers were not sure that they could meet the requirements for an airtight "murder one" presentation.

    Nick's girlfriend had turned out to be a very weak witness against Nick. In fact, she seemed almost "crazy" or "retarded," the investigators said. Then, too, the county where Nick was tried in California had lost much of their official documentation regarding the earlier killing. As for Cammie's situation, the statute of limitation had probably run out—and the Oregon officials did not want to endanger or upset this poor child any more than she already had been.

    Sandra and Cammie drove up to southern Oregon one weekend in January to hear the prosecution's "take" on their case after it was concluded. The D.A. himself came to meet them, along with his chief investigator, who had put off retirement until he could finish Nick's prosecution. Cammie was treated "like a celebrity." In fact, the D.A. and his investigator couldn't say enough nice things to Cammie about how they thought she had turned out. (What a contrast she was to her horrible father!) They graciously thanked Cammie and Sandra for their help. And they repeatedly and emphatically assured the Brooks family that Nick would serve every day of his quarter-century sentence.

    So Cammie, like so many others of us, never got to deliver her letter.

INDEX